TO PROTECT
AND TO SERVE
A HISTORY OF POLICE IN AMERICA

ROBERT C. WADMAN

WILLIAM THOMAS ALLISON

PEARSON

Prentice
Hall

Upper Saddle River, New Jersey 07458

Library of Congress Cataloging-in-Publication Data

Wadman, Robert C.
  To protect and serve : a history of police in America / Robert C. Wadman,
William Thomas Allison.
    p. cm.
Includes bibliographical references and index.
  ISBN 0-13-112064-6
  1. Police—United States—History.   2. Law enforcement—United States—
History. I. Allison, William Thomas.   II. Title.
  HV8138.A583 2004
  363.2'0973—dc21

                                              2003013366

Editor-in-Chief: Stephen Helba
Director of Production and
    Manufacturing: Bruce Johnson
Executive Editor: Frank Mortimer, Jr.
Assistant Editor: Korrine Dorsey
Editorial Assistant: Barbara Rosenberg
Marketing Manager: Tim Peyton
Managing Editor—Production:
    Mary Carnis
Manufacturing Buyer: Cathleen
    Petersen
Production Liaison: Denise Brown

Full Service Production: Karen Ettinger,
    The GTS Companies/York, PA Campus
Page Composition: The GTS
    Companies/York, PA Campus
Design Director: Cheryl Asherman
Design Coordinator: Miguel Ortiz
Cover Image: ©PEMCO-Webster &
    Stevens Collection; Museum of
    History and Industry, Seattle/Corbis
Cover Printer: Phoenix Color
Printer/Binder: R. R. Donnelley &
    Sons, Harrisonburg

Credits and acknowledgements borrowed from other sources and reproduced, with
permission, in this textbook appear on appropriate page within text.

Pearson Education LTD.
Pearson Education Singapore, Pte. Ltd
Pearson Education, Canada, Ltd
Pearson Education—Japan

Pearson Education Australia PTY, Limited
Pearson Education North Asia Ltd
Pearson Educación de Mexico, S.A. de C.V.
Pearson Education Malaysia, Pte. Ltd

10 9 8 7 6 5 4 3 2 1
ISBN 0-13-112064-6

For Bev & Jen

CONTENTS

ACKNOWLEDGMENTS

We conceived the idea of a history of police to fill what we saw as a glaring void in introductory criminal justice courses. It was not until well into the research for the book that we began to see that a history of police in America would not only serve the needs of criminal justice. Perhaps it would more so address a failing that only a small handful of historians had attempted to address in history. This book is a work of history, social history to be specific, and points to the need to expand scholarly research into the area of police history. What we hope to present in the following pages is a cohesive, comprehensive look at the history of American policing, designed to provide undergraduates in criminal justice and history a solid examination of the history and important issues that make this such an intriguing American story.

We are indebted to many. Shaun Paddock successfully sold our idea to Prentice Hall, which brought us into the able arms of Kim Davies, Frank Mortimer, Korrine Dorsey, and Marjorie Ballentine. Their guidance, advice, and enthusiasm for the project made our relationship with Prentice Hall a wonderful experience. Colleagues in the Department of History and Department of Criminal Justice at Weber State University have been wonderfully supportive and helpful, especially Professors L. Kay Gillespie, Michelle Heward, Paul Johnson, Susan J. Matt, Scott Senjo, and Gene A. Sessions.

We would have been nowhere without the efficient diligence of Deborah Stevenson and the Interlibrary Loan Office at the Stewart Library on the Weber State campus and that of Edith Williams and her interlibrary loan staff at the Air University Library at Maxwell Air Force Base. What they found, and how quickly they found it, amazes us still. A special thank you goes to Eileen Kennedy Morales and Anne Guernsey of the Museum of the City of New York and the staff at the photo-duplication service of the Library of Congress for their wonderful assistance. Of course, there are many that we are thankful to for letting us wittingly or unwittingly pick their brains in informal conversations about the project. We would also like to thank the many police officers and departments around the United States that responded to our requests for information amidst so many other pressing matters that they contend with on a daily basis, especially Philadelphia Police Officer

Phil Bowdren, Dallas Police Sergeant Andrew H. Davis, Phoenix Police Commander Lyle H. Rodabough, Sergeant Michael J. Holland of the Berkeley Police Department, and the staff of the Montana Law Enforcement Museum. On the scholarly end, we thank blind reviewers for their frank and constructive critique, all of which made this a better book. Finally, where would we be without the love and support of our understanding and patient partners in life, Jennifer Allison and Beverly Wadman?

In the end, this book reflects our views and interpretations, and any faults or errors found within are our responsibility, good or bad. It was, at times, a trying process, but we are happy to report that our friendship has survived.

ROBERT C. WADMAN
WILLIAM THOMAS ALLISON
Ogden, Utah
January 27, 2003

INTRODUCTION

From the creation of night watches in colonial settlements and the development of early police departments in New York, Boston, and Philadelphia to the near mythical exploits of sheriffs and marshals in the frontier West and the advent of crime-fighting technologies in the twentieth century, the very concept of policing in America has an interesting and storied past that begs examination. The history of police in America often mirrors the social and political development of the United States and has much to say about race, power, and authority in a democratic nation of people who value civil liberties and look upon centralized authority with some misgivings. Policing in America is unique and fascinating and provides an excellent lens through which we can both examine American history and help students of law enforcement better understand the heritage they will inherit and the role they will play in American society.

The history of police in America touches so many areas of criminal justice and historical study, including social, cultural, political, legal, and policy history, as well as urban studies, criminology, and institutional studies. The primary objectives of this book are to share this history and place the development of police in the broader historical context of American history, so that students, scholars, citizens, and the law enforcement community can better appreciate this rich heritage.

The history of law enforcement is often misconstrued in American myth and culture. It is certainly picturesque but equally disheartening that popular culture has made such infamous outlaws and criminals as the Younger Gang, Al Capone, and Baby Face Nelson well known. Contemporary criminals like Gary Gilmore, Ted Bundy, and Timothy McVeigh have also achieved notoriety. Even the Mafia and the Medellin Cartel are legendary. Unfortunately, police, detectives, and other law enforcement officials who pursued and apprehended these felons remain little known. Popular fiction has tended to romanticize the erstwhile detective and beat patrolman, whereas Hollywood and television have drastically influenced the way police are seen in American society through shows such as *Cops, Law and Order,* and *NYPD Blue.* The terrorist attacks of September 11, 2001, of course, have had an amazing impact on police and fire departments and on the way the American public views them.

Police have always been and always will be real people (*Robocop* notwithstanding) in an organizational structure who undertake an arduous but necessary job. Take, for example, the work of an alert Oklahoma highway patrolman who, armed with limited information, pulled over a beat-up 1977 Grand Marquis for not having a proper license plate. Patrolman Charlie Hanger quickly noted the person driving the car fit the description of a man connected with the bombing of the Murrah Federal Building in Oklahoma City, Timothy McVeigh, and made the historic arrest that led to McVeigh's conviction and execution. Consider as well that although many recognize Theodore Roosevelt as the boisterous charger up San Juan Hill and bullish president of the United States, few recall that as police commissioner of New York he led a major progressive reform of the very corrupt New York City Police Department. This text will recognize not just those law enforcement officers who fought crime but also those officers and citizens who contributed to the evolution of policing in America.

There is a curious thinness to the limited history of police in America. Little attention has been given to explaining the practical and theoretical development of policing from a national, even regional, viewpoint. There are, however, some outstanding scholarly works. The most comprehensive works are David R. Johnson's *American Law Enforcement: A History* (1981), which briefly covers local, state, and federal law enforcement; and Bryan Vila and Cynthia Morris's *The Role of Police in American Society: A Documentary History* (1999), which is a fine look at the development of local, state, and federal law enforcement agencies through primary documents. The best works on the development of police theory and reform are Samuel Walker's *A Critical History of Police Reform: The Emergence of Professionalization* (1977) and Robert M. Fogelson's *Big-City Police* (1977). Both offer insightful discussions of reform movements and police response to changing urban conditions in a historical context.[1]

Regional and local studies are also thinly represented. There are a few solid histories of law enforcement in the American West, notably Frank R. Prassell's *The Western Peace Officer: A Legacy of Law and Order in the American West* (1972), Roger McGrath's *Gunfighters, Highwaymen, and Vigilantes: Violence on the Frontier* (1984), and Larry D. Ball's *Desert Lawmen: The High Sheriffs of New Mexico and Arizona, 1846–1912* (1992). Police development in the antebellum South has finally received thorough attention from Sally E. Hadden's *Slave Patrols: Law and Violence in Virginia and the Carolinas* (2001), which examines the formation and function of slave patrols as police forces in the southern United States.[2]

Local studies have been a great help in understanding not only police history but also urban and social history. Major cities have been the subject of many of these works, including Roger Lane's *Policing the City: Boston, 1822–1885* (1967), Douglas Greenberg's *Crime and Law Enforcement in the Colony of New York, 1691–1776* (1974), and James F. Richardson's *The New York Police: Colonial Times to 1901* (1970), as well as Joseph Laythe's "'Trouble on the Outside, Trouble on the Inside': Growing Pains, Social Change, and Small Town Policing: The Eugene Police Department, 1862–1932" (*Police Quarterly*, 2002).[3] State police histories are few and far between, but Robert A. Harris's *Keeping the Peace: Police Reform in Montana, 1889–1918* (1994) and Charles M. Robinson's *The Men Who Wear the Star: The Story of the Texas Rangers* (2000) are representative of these useful studies.[4]

There are some classics in criminal justice that have deeply contributed to police history. Many of these come from police reformers themselves, including Raymond Fosdick's *American Police Systems* (1920), which details the reforms of the

Progressive Era; August Vollmer's *Police and Modern Society* (1936), which examines the history of police and promotes police professionalism; Bruce Smith's *Police Systems of the United States*, in which he applied his vast experience in public administration to examining police departments; O. W. Wilson's influential work, *Police Administration* (1950); and James Q. Wilson's *Varieties of Police Behavior*, the first substantive community study of police effectiveness (1968).[5] These are but a few of the many important works produced by professionals in the field of policing that utilize history to illustrate issues and suggest changes in police policy.

Textbooks from the criminal justice field surprisingly overlook the history of police in America. At most, these texts dedicate only a few pages or a brief chapter to discuss in the most general terms the development of organized police. This restricted history, forced into a few introductory pages, scarcely provides a foundation to identify problems in American policing.

For students of criminal justice and history, then, no up-to-date, thorough survey of police history is available. This book endeavors to fill this gap by bringing together the growing scholarship on police history with classic criminal justice works to create a chronological survey of American police history. Through this survey, the book hopes to provide wider coverage of organizational development, police theory, and regional evolution of policing in America.

The central themes of the book revolve around four interconnected ideas. First, policing in America has been for the most part reactive and influenced by several factors. Frequently, it has been reaction crisis that has forced change on American police departments. Although many criminal justice texts mention only Sir Robert Peel's Metropolitan Police Act (1829) as the principal foundation of the development of police in the United States, it is more complex and comes from a wider range of influences than just those of Peel.[6]

Second, reform has been a hallmark of American police history. Professionalization, urbanization, industrialization, and a whole myriad of trends and factors have spurred police reform, particularly since the mid-nineteenth century. The result of these reforms has been to build a professional police concept that values shared ideas and information, training and education, and a strict code of ethics. Of course, reform and practice were often two different things.

Third, theories of policing that have often grown from intellectual and ideological trends (such as the Calvinist protestant work ethic, republicanism, social Darwinism, and Max Weber's rational bureaucracy) have profoundly influenced the development and study of police. Theories and practices developed by such police innovators as Sir Robert Peel, George W. Hale, August Vollmer, O. W. Wilson, among others, have greatly influenced the art of policing. From the "watchman" style of policing in the mid to late 1800s to the "service" or "community policing" styles found in contemporary America, police organizations have attempted to maintain the status quo in a constantly changing society through theoretical innovations.

Fourth, readers familiar with the work of Thomas Kuhn will notice throughout the book that the development of American police is filled with paradigm shifts. Kuhn's work in explaining the nature of scientific revolutions applies equally to the nature of organizational evolution. The paradigm, or model, of an organization and how it behaves becomes ingrained and unquestioned until crisis does just that—question the paradigm.[7] The history of police in America is one of paradigm shifts and resistance to new ideas before accepting them in the face of crisis. The best known shifts are what James Q. Wilson identified as styles of policing: watchman, service, and community. But there are other, smaller shifts that deserve examination, such as the change in public perception of police as feeble-minded bullies to professional public servants, the impact of technology on patrolling, and the advent of community policing. George L. Kelling's "broken windows" model and Herman Goldstein's ideas on corruption and police in a free society come to mind. The idea of a paradigm shift is an important concept to understand. It points to the pendulum of police reform, swinging from the often corrupt but known neighborhood beat cop of the late nineteenth century to the nameless, bureaucratized patrolman of the twentieth century; and to the late-twentieth-century swing back toward the center, attempting a balance between the two extremes in the face of social unrest and tension.[8]

Throughout this book, it is important to recognize that the words "law enforcement" and "sustaining tradition" are synonymous. From the rules that control a tribe of aborigines to the laws of contemporary legislatures, in an attempt to live in an organized social environment, humans have developed guidelines by which they live. In striving for order, whether based on religious belief or on the support of a political, economic, and/or racial majority, society's traditions are sustained by a commitment to a given set of rules. Whether outlined in Exodus 20:15 ("Thou shalt not steal") or in a state penal code, the taking of a neighbor's personal property, for example, has long been viewed as inappropriate behavior and worthy of effort designed to prevent it from recurring. As a society's traditions develop, so too does the need to ensure a commitment to those emerging traditions. Rules, cultural norms, and laws become mechanisms within a society to sustain tradition. The American police system, in essence, is an organizational mechanism for sustaining traditions. The curse of a tribal witch doctor and the sentence of a district court judge have the same purpose—to sustain tradition.

Effective law enforcement is the art of sustaining tradition. As change in society emerges, whether it is by legitimate (e.g., legislative process) or by questionable means (e.g., civil unrest), the police organization is in the forefront of the process, attempting to maintain peace and order in a constantly changing society. The paradox of this historical effort is evaluating change in the very organization whose responsibility it is to sustain the current traditions of society.[9]

To say that the American police organization has been reactive to criminal behavior is simplistic. To understand the police, one must explore the development of the American police effort, both from a historical context and through an evaluation of the environment in which American police have evolved. This book is organized as a chronological survey to illustrate and examine these themes.

Chapter 1 begins the survey with an examination of early police practices in early America, looking at English traditions, pragmatic responses to frontier conditions, and ideological resistance to centralized police authority, as the English colonies transformed from isolated settlements to an independent nation based on republican ideals. Chapter 2 examines the advent of organized police departments in pre-Civil War America, focusing on Boston, New York, and Philadelphia as leaders in early organizational development. As watch systems proved inadequate to deal with expansive growth and subsequent public order issues, cities attempted to reorganize law enforcement for better and more efficient service and protection.

Chapter 3 looks at regional police development in the South during the nineteenth century. The environment in the Southern United States before and during the Civil War was uniquely different from that of other regions of the country.

The enforcement of slave codes, and evolution of slave patrols into police forces, and the impact of the Civil War and Reconstruction gave Southern police departments a different organizational evolution. Chapter 4 takes the story to the American West, where Spanish and English police traditions collided with frontier conditions to evolve into organized local law enforcement. Vigilantism, private security agencies, federal marshals, and little-known Native American police forces contribute to this exciting period in American history as the frontier West transformed into urban settlements. The tradition of home rule and decentralization played strong roles in the frontier West.

Chapter 5 discusses the impact of urbanization and industrialization on police and then examines the Progressive Era response to police problems, particularly the advent of professionalization through the birth of national police organizations, police training and education, and civil service oversight of police. By 1900, police departments across the nation had either organized or were in the process of organizing in a similar manner, showing a consensus on policing. By the 1920s, however, police departments had again reached a point of crisis and a need for additional reform.

Chapter 6 takes on the pre-World War II reform movement and how police departments reacted to change in crime, namely, organized crime and other acts associated with Prohibition and the Great Depression. World War II and the postwar years also forced police to adapt to change in American society, particularly as materialism and civil unrest spread selectively across the country.

Chapter 7 discusses the influence of technology since the Industrial Age, including the impact of the signal box, the automobile, fingerprinting, and other innovations in policing. Like most bureaucratic organizations, police departments resisted change, especially technological change, but gradually came to accept technology as a way to make police more effective. Chapter 8 looks at the careers of several policing leaders who strongly influenced the development of police in the twentieth century. Both before and after the historic work of England's Sir Robert Peel, Americans committed to professional policing were hard at work. Little has been written about these leaders of American police development. This chapter explores their respective contributions to modern policing.

Chapter 9 covers police history since World War II. Modern policing and the advent of community policing theory, organization management, and how police have responded to new threats are the critical developments during this period. Race-related civil unrest rocked America in the 1960s. In reaction to the nationwide impact of riots and increased crime, President Lyndon Johnson took steps to address the crisis. This national review of the criminal justice system, and in particular that of America's police, set the stage for the development of community policing and advanced technology. From the 1970s on, the idea of community policing held center stage, yet old problems continued to surface as police struggled with the inflexibility of professionalism and the vagaries of rebuilding police–community relations.

Throughout these chapters, a great effort has been made to place the evolution of police within a historical context. It is imperative that students of criminal justice and history alike appreciate the context in which these developments take place. Historical forces more often than not influenced policing. This book should give students in criminal justice and history a solid overview and provide historians and criminal justice scholars a springboard to broaden and deepen the scholarship on the history of police in America.

In the end, police are necessary to protect and serve the public good, uphold the rule of law, and deter crime. The development of police in a democratic society where civil liberties and republicanism are held most dear is an intriguing story, full of challenges and great moments, but littered with infringements on the delicate balance of the American system. These traditions are the foundation of the American republic. As these American traditions continue to mature, so too does the need to ensure a commitment to emerging traditions and an openness to change. Rules, cultural norms, and laws become mechanisms within a society to sustain these traditions. The American criminal justice system, in essence, is a mechanism designed to sustain American traditions and cultural values. Effective police work makes this possible. As changes in society emerge, whether by legitimate means or by crisis, police have been and remain at the forefront of the process, trying to maintain order in a constantly changing society. As students and citizens, it is imperative to understand and appreciate the history and role of police.

CHAPTER 1

POLICE IN EARLY AMERICA

INTRODUCTION

Over a period of two hundred years, law enforcement in early America evolved from pragmatic reactions to crime and public disorder to the beginnings of organized police departments. Several factors influenced this development, including the nature of crime, the growth of cities, political and economic conditions, and the ideological foundation of the nation itself. In the end, the English colonists who founded the United States borrowed from their own English law enforcement heritage to start the tradition of decentralized policing in the context of the new republican ideology. Individual liberty, fear of a standing army, and suspicion of centralized authority made people wary of establishing formalized police departments. As a consequence, citizens had to deal with ineffective law enforcement to handle widespread crime and disorder.[1]

ENGLISH TRADITION

According to the concept of cultural mimesis, a people that leave their homeland to settle in another place will bring their culture with them and, in fact, will replant it where they settle. This was certainly the case for the English colonization of the Atlantic seaboard of North America. From Georgia to the Chesapeake, even New England with its Puritan founding, English immigrants predominantly settled these regions, reestablishing English traditions, ideas, and culture. This included law enforcement.

The English sheriff system, a community-based police arrangement, made up the greater part of law enforcement tradition for most English colonists. Citizen involvement in law enforcement began in England as early as the tenth century. Later known as *posse comitatus* and "hue and cry," the concept of "kin police," in which neighbors were obligated to assist fellow neighbors in distress, usually from marauding bands of outlaws, predated the Norman conquest of 1066. The Normans transformed this model into the "frankpledge" system, where all male freeholders were obligated to participate in protective groups known as "tithings." Ten men usually made up a "tithing" and were responsible for protecting citizens in a designated area of their own community or neighborhood. Ten "tithings" made up a "hundred" under the leadership of a constable appointed by the local lord. Ten hundreds formed a "shire." A "shire" came under the command of a nobleman appointed by the king to enforce the king's law, called a "shire reeve" or sheriff.

Although the "shire" system worked well in rural settings and small villages and towns, it did not serve citizens well in more urban areas. Cities required a more regulated, organized system. By the 1600s, a night watch and day constabulary began patrolling larger cities in England such as London, Manchester, and York. Earlier versions of this more formalized system dated back to Norman times, and these patrols proved only superficially effective in even reacting to criminal incidents. In the 1660s, the new watchmen, called "Old Charlies" by citizens because they were instituted by King Charles II, faired no better because of Parliamentary restrictions and debate on the balance between civil rights and the power of authorities to maintain law and order. Still, the law enforcement tradition in England remained decentralized and local and centered on reacting to crime rather than on preventing it.

It was this debate between the power of police and civil liberties that came to characterize the very nature of a free society, which both England and its colonies considered themselves to be. As English immigrants flocked to "pursue their happiness" in the American colonies during the 1600s, they brought with them these concepts of law enforcement and the accompanying debate. Public virtue and personal accountability in society fed the notion that a civilized, enlightened people should police themselves rather than hand the job over to a centralized authority that might abuse its power. As the idea of republicanism took hold in the colonies, this debate intensified.[2]

THE NATURE OF CRIME IN COLONIAL AND REVOLUTIONARY AMERICA

On the surface, conditions in the colonies appeared ripe for crime. Economic uncertainty, danger from hostile attack, and the large number of convicts that participated in the migration made an atmosphere perfect for widespread criminal behavior. These very problems indeed forced colonists to adapt more formalized watches and constabularies over time, surpassing in some cases law enforcement organization in the mother country. The important question is not how much crime occurred in this colony or that; rather, what the nature of crime was and how effectively did law enforcement deal with crime in early America.[3]

The economic uncertainty of the colonial mercantile system brought many unsavory characters to the forefront in colonial society. Frequent disruptions in trade by war, storms, and economic downswings adversely affected the growing number of port towns and cities up and down the Atlantic seaboard. These conditions made for a fluid, transient population that shifted from port to port with the economic wind. These mobile colonists unsettled the more stable settlers, who on their own accord began to organize for the protection of their lives and property.[4]

Danger from hostile attack was a constant menace to the colonists. Threats included Indians, particularly in outlying, sparsely settled areas. Land-hungry colonists often clashed with natives, who quickly and efficiently adapted to the violent, deadly colonial style of warfare. Protection from Indian attack required diligent, constant watch. Pirates hounded coastal ports, especially in the southern colonies, and, of course, the threat from foreign enemies, namely, France, seemed continual. Numerous wars between colonists and Indians, colonists and the French, and colonists and both easily characterize the colonial experience in America from the 1620s through the 1750s.[5] A militia system based on the English model evolved in the colonies for defense against these threats, but it was also utilized for policing. To protect themselves from these threats, communities drafted small numbers of militia for security duty principally through watch patrols.[6]

Another factor influencing the development of police in early America came from the large numbers of convicts sent to the colonies from England. James I began the first formal transportation of convicts in 1615. English law for felonies was very clear: either death or acquittal. James I ordered that clemency be used in some cases and specifically ordered that these "reprieved" offenders be sent to "parts abroad where it shall be found fit to employ them," that is, in the colonies.[7] Serious offenses, such as murder, violent robbery, and the like were usually exempt from this policy; thus, offenders were seldom reprieved to the colonies. Petty thieves, arsonists, minor swindlers, and prostitutes, however, frequently found their way on to reprieve lists bound for Virginia and other colonies throughout the 1600s. These sorts of criminals, if they chose to continue their antisocial behavior, could easily thrive in the colonies.

The process varied over the course of the seventeenth century, be it reprieves from courts, royal pardons, or banishments (usually seven years). The numbers are not clear, probably only in the hundreds for the seventeenth century. By 1700, Virginia and Maryland had actually passed laws in their respective legislatures banning the importation of convicts, whereas other colonies continued to reluctantly accept them. It seems local citizens did not care for the extra flavor brought into their colonies by the convict transportation policy.[8]

The numbers increased dramatically in the eighteenth century. Parliament, in 1718, passed the Transportation Act, which instituted banishment as a preferred sentence for property crimes, which made up the majority of criminal cases at that time. London's Old Bailey, for example, sentenced to exile more than two-thirds of all felons from 1718 to 1775, many of whom were shipped to Maryland and Virginia and sold as servants, now that Parliament had superseded the colonial convict importation bans of those respective colonies. In all, at least thirty thousand felons were shipped to America from 1718 until the American Revolution abruptly halted the practice in 1775. Adding transportees from similar policies in Scotland, Ireland, and Wales brings the total estimate to fifty thousand.

Although this policy may have purged Great Britain of a large criminal segment of the population, the colonies, with their own law enforcement issues, found themselves flooded with unwelcome guests. Some of the strongest prerevolutionary protests from the colonies came against the transportation policy. Benjamin Franklin, finding the policy insulting, even suggested sending rattlesnakes to England in return. Several colonies attempted to levy import duties on convicts, some as much as £100 per convict, but these attempts came to naught as Parliament often overrode them. The idea of sending a country's outcasts to another civilized, settled region is heinous at best and shows how out of touch England's Parliament had become in relation to colonial affairs. The impact of these transportees is difficult to define, but some assuredly did engage in their previous occupations, adding to criminal behavior already present in the colonies.[9]

All of these issues influenced the nature of crime in early America, and crime most certainly was a problem of great concern for town and country alike. Apart from general works, much needs to be done in examining crime in the various colonies, but some intriguing studies have been completed which examine crime in Massachusetts, New York, and North Carolina. These provide a glimpse into both the criminal world and what citizens and nascent police forces faced in maintaining law and order.

Studies show that Massachusetts suffered a range of serious crimes from murder to violent theft, but citizens concerned themselves more with lesser crimes such as selling liquor without a license and "misbehavior on the Sabbath." Counterfeiting in particular drew the ire of Massachusetts citizens. Even into the early republic period, Massachusetts remained a rather homogeneous, native-born population, still deeply influenced by its Puritan founding. Some suggest that this homogeneity kept the level of serious crime low in Massachusetts compared to that in other colonies, such as New York.[10]

Additionally, historians also suggest that the out-migration from Massachusetts to neighboring colonies and later states contributed as well to lower crime levels. As the Puritan theocracy declined and population increases caused more competition for resources, younger people moved away from the formally tight-knit congregational structure of Massachusetts to pursue their happiness elsewhere. Often associated with deviant behavior, this out-migration perhaps helped keep crime levels low.[11]

Sexual crimes also occurred, apparently with uncomfortable regularity. William Bradford's early history of Plymouth Plantation lamented the frequency and nature of sexual offenses, including adultery, incest, sodomy, and molesting children. "Buggery," or bestiality, was a capital offense. One of the worst cases involved a teenage boy who "was detected of buggery and indicted for the same, with a cow, two goats, five sheep, two calves, and a turkey." In strict accordance to Leviticus 20:15, the animals in question were slaughtered in front of the boy, who was then hung.[12] In addition to "buggery," adultery and sodomy (homosexuality) were also capital offenses, based on Biblical law more so than on English common law. In Massachusetts, however, executions were rarely ordered for adultery and sodomy. Rape, like "buggery," however, did warrant frequent death sentences, as did inciting insurrection and, of course, witchcraft.

Executions, in the English tradition, were designed to be a deterrent; thus, the process could be extremely painful and drawn out. Even punishment for noncapital offenses could be severe. Slander, for example, was a serious offense in New England. A man found guilty of slanderous remarks against the governor of Massachusetts in 1624 suffered having his arms broken, his tongue "bored through with an awl," and then running a gauntlet of forty men who each "butted" the man as he passed. The man was then banished from the colony. This may seem excessive for slander, but considering the delicate, even fragile, construct of early settlement in North America, the need for firm respect for authority demanded such deterrents.[13]

Massachusetts, like most of America during the colonial and early republic periods, also had a problem with drunkenness. Salem, famous for its witchcraft episode, annually dealt with more cases of drunkenness in its local courts than any other offense. The reasons for this problem were many, including idleness, the stress of a hostile environment (at least early in the colonial period), economic anxiety, and political uncertainty. Drunkenness in New England flew in the face of the moral high ground held by most Puritans. Public intoxication was not tolerated and usually resulted in swift punishment. Drunks could expect to spend up to twelve hours in the stocks, and repeat offenders often found themselves humiliated in front of the congregation by the local minister. This shame-based method of social control was by many accounts effective and in keeping with the Puritan tradition of mixing church and justice.[14]

Crime in Massachusetts and New England was not a large problem relative to modern standards, but it was a problem as perceived by the citizens of the region. It certainly gave citizens pause when considering their public safety.

Unlike Puritan New England, New York was ethnically diverse, filled with lively political factions, and widely settled, perhaps making the colony more accepting of higher crime rates, thus less likely to be more active in organizing effective law enforcement. Originally settled by the Dutch (New Amsterdam) in 1625, New York became a royal colony in 1664, mixing Dutch and English law enforcement traditions.[15]

Crime in New Amsterdam became a problem almost as soon as the settlement was founded. The first *scout-fiscal*, the equivalent of a sheriff, took office in 1625. As a small trading post on the island of Manhattan, criminal behavior came in small doses, mainly drinking on the Sabbath and the occasional street brawl. With no jail, whipping served as the primary method of punishment. The first crime wave hit the colony in 1638. Growth had brought not only more Dutch colonists but also German, French, Irish, and English, in addition to many runaway indentured servants from surrounding colonies. Murder, drunkenness, and petty theft increased to the point that the colony's administrators had to pass more strict ordinances against such behavior. Nonetheless, crime and disorder continued to be a problem, giving New Amsterdam the reputation as the most "boisterous" settlement in North America.[16]

The establishment of British rule over New Amsterdam in 1664 did not lessen the crime problem. Like Massachusetts, breaking the Sabbath, drunkenness, carousing, theft, and contempt of authority were the primary violations of law and order. Widespread and frequent contempt for authority is, in particular, indicative of the weakness of law enforcement in the colonies. Resisting arrest was most frequent, including an incident in 1692 involving the arrest of Daniel Lawrence. Lawrence refused to come in with the constable of Newtown, New York, who claimed Lawrence yelled at him, "God damn their souls and blood, he would see them all damned in hell before he would undervalue himself for to come afore them and further that he would not be taken alive." One Thomas Willet threatened to slit the throat of Zachariah Mills, the Sheriff of Queens, when Mills attempted to arrest him in 1702. Contempt of authority did not stop at resisting arrest; it found its way into ignoring the authority of the courts and even into the destruction of law enforcement symbols. In 1702, a New York court issued a reward of sixty pieces of eight for the arrest of those responsible for cutting down the gallows.[17]

The most common crime in the colony of New York involved "acts of personal violence." From 1691 to 1776, roughly 21.5 percent of all accusations and the same percentage of all convictions came from assaults, rape, attempted murder, and other violent deeds. Those accused of physical assault came from all walks of society. Servants accused masters of "cruel usage" as well as neglect. Although masters rarely received punishment if convicted of assaulting a servant, servants received the full force of the law for assaulting their owners. The Court of General Sessions, for example, subjected the servant of one John Peck Taylor to thirty-one lashes for being "unruly." Rape and attempted rape also made up a large portion of assaults. In 1766, John Domine was indicted for assaulting with intent to rape an eight-year-old girl and sentenced to receive thirty-nine lashes for three days straight. Murder, the most serious offense, resulted from a variety of circumstances then as it does today. Court records show that accidental shootings, self-defense, and using insanity as a successful defense in court were not uncommon. Those convicted of murder faced swift and severe punishment. In 1708, for example, an "Indian Man Slave" and a Negro woman were found guilty of brutally killing the mother and father of five children. The court sentenced the man to be hung and the woman to be "burnt."[18]

A New York City watchman, 1693. (Print Archives, Museum of the City of New York. Gift of Mr. Harry DePauer)

Other problems of disorder included violations of public peace and keeping a disorderly house. Violations of public peace included rioting, destruction of property, and public drunkenness. These offenses had high conviction rates in New York courts, mainly because the offense normally was committed in public view; thus, numerous witnesses made certain that the act and the accused were accurately described, resulting in a sure conviction. Keeping a disorderly house referred to a public establishment accused of some criminal or moral wrong, including houses of prostitution, illegal taverns and "bawdy" houses, and places where stolen goods were found. Unlike violations of public peace, keeping a disorderly house was difficult to prosecute. Accusing an individual of keeping a disorderly house was often easier to do than to actually prove in court because of so much evidence based on hearsay.[19]

These crimes and acts of disorder were common through the early 1800s in New York. Crime, social heterogeneity, servitude, transient port cities, economic swings, contempt for public authority, and later the presence of British soldiers combined to make New York a diverse place in many ways.

Although Massachusetts and New York qualify as among the earliest settled places in early America, North Carolina was a comparative newcomer. Founded in 1663, North Carolina remained small in population through the 1750s (only around sixty thousand, including several thousand slaves). North Carolina did not have the moral influence of Puritan Massachusetts but did develop a powerful political elite from the planter class. Social control was indeed present, but in a more subtle way than that of the Puritans to the north.

Crime in North Carolina was similar to that in New England and New York. Sexual offenses represent the one distinct difference. Though laws against these acts were on the books, few seem to have been arrested for such violations. Capital offenses included felonies and treason. The most common crimes were assault, theft, moral crimes (drunkenness, adultery, swearing, etc.), murder, animal theft, and counterfeiting (which apparently drew the same ire as it did in Massachusetts).

Again, one of the most prosecuted offenses was contempt of authority. This involved such violations as resisting arrest, not responding to a court order, and harassing constables, tax collectors, and justices of the peace. Those found guilty of hindering a law officer in his duty could face fines or imprisonment. It is not exactly clear why this was such a problem in North Carolina. Speculation suggests that the nature of the colony, its rather "wild" atmosphere, and, simply, freedom running amok might explain this flaunting of authority. Violence was, after all, a cultural given, particularly in the southern colonies. To illustrate the seriousness with which the courts considered this particular crime, 43 percent of those individuals charged with contempt of authority from 1720 to 1740 were indicted, almost twice as often than any other criminal charge.

Theft of property represented a rather large portion of arrests. Just as wealthy landowners and merchants were more likely to commit crimes of violence, poor laborers, seamen, and street women were the likely culprits for stealing another's property. Women were more likely to be arrested and prosecuted for this crime than any other. Again, the economic uncertainty and unequal distribution of wealth that characterize the southern colonies certainly contributed to the high incidence of theft. Punishments for theft normally included receiving lashes, up to one hundred in some cases, but only occasionally included jail time.[20]

CITIZEN RESPONSE—CONSTABLES AND THE WATCH

Considering the political, social, and economic situation in early America, how then did citizens protect themselves and their communities from criminal activity and behavior? Beginning with their English traditions, citizens of early America adapted and adjusted to suit their perceived community security needs, although rarely with any efficiency. There was much trial and error as well as grumbling by those forced to participate in these premodern attempts to maintain order. Over time, however, these often ineffective, poorly organized attempts at policing evolved into the beginnings of effective, organized community police forces.

Criminal justice and law enforcement seldom worked together, and by 1830 many larger cities and some smaller towns and villages had reached a point of crisis, requiring major police reform. The beginnings, however, were quite modest in comparison. Major cities, such as Boston, New York, Philadelphia, Charleston, along with smaller towns and villages, all had to institute some variation of police soon after being settled.

Early settlements in the colonies had to have some form of security by necessity of the hostile environment around them. Problems arising from rapid growth because of increased immigration also contributed to the need for order. Watches, constabularies, and the use of militia as police during this early period were pragmatic responses to practical problems. Colonists relied upon their experience with law enforcement from their homeland in England. Later generations would adapt these concepts to meet their particular needs.

Most settlements in the colonies quickly established constabularies, although small and usually undermanned, within a few years of initial settlement. Duties of constables were numerous and onerous. The description of the duties of Massachusetts constables from 1646 is typical:

> Evry cunstable . . . hath, byt virtue of his office, full powr to make, signe, & put forth pursuits, or hues & cries, after mrthurers, manslayrs, peace breakrs, theeves, robbers, burgalrers, where no magistrate is at hand; also to aprrhen without warrant such as are ovr taken with drinke, swearing, breaking ye Saboth, lying, vagrant psons, night walkers, or any other yt shall break our lawes; . . . also to make search for all such psons . . . in all houses liccnsed to sell wither beare or wine, or in any othr suspected or disordered places, & those to apphend, & keep in safe custody. . . .[21]

The constable served as the chief law officer of the town and normally patrolled in daylight hours. The job was not a sought-after one, and many citizens did what they could to avoid being appointed. In 1653, Boston city leaders established a fine of £20 for refusing to serve in the constabulary, and by 1690, there is evidence that those who could afford it paid the fine rather than serve. In North Carolina, a man was fined £10 for refusing the court's appointment as constable. It is not surprising that many citizens who had the means accepted and paid the fines instead of serving a position that demanded so much yet was held in such low social esteem by the community.[22]

Indicative of the nature of crime in early America, constables often found their authority subject to ridicule and in some cases simply ignored. In Newport, in 1643, the local constable had a difficult time getting one Job Tyler to answer a summons by the local court. He reported that the man said "he car'd not a fart [or] turd for all their warrants." Tyler was arrested for refusing the summons and whipped "till his back bloody." A man, apparently of the planter class, attacked and beat a Raleigh constable who tried to arrest him in 1738. North Carolina constable John Simpson tried to arrest a Robert Atkins, who resisted violently, claiming the warrant was "good for nothing." Simpson returned a few days later with help, only to find Atkins pointing a gun at him and threatening to shoot him if he tried to arrest him again.[23]

Communities usually appointed one or two constables to serve for a year's term. Even large cities with populations of several thousands appointed small numbers of constables. Charlestown had only five in 1685; New York City appointed one in its six wards in 1686; Boston used eight in 1690; and Newport enjoyed the protective services of two in 1688. As populations grew and the colonial wars disrupted populations across New England and the middle colonies, more constables were needed. In 1704, Newport was divided into four wards with one constable appointed to each ward. Philadelphia, the same year, created ten wards, again with one constable assigned to each ward.

Despite these organizational reforms, city fathers discovered that finding willing citizens to serve as constables was very difficult, as many opted to pay the fine instead. Courts normally appointed constables from the lower ranks, because those with even a little money might not afford the £10 to £20 fines for refusing service. Constables could keep a portion of fees and fines they collected in the course of their duty, but they were not yet paid for their service. Keeping their own businesses running while doing daily constabulary duty for a year certainly hurt their income. Moreover, they received little thanks for their dangerous and tiresome work.[24]

In addition to unenthusiastic, reluctant citizens, other problems remained. Constables only walked the streets of their respective towns during daylight hours, not at night. Crime continued and in many cases increased. Even as cities grew and the frontier moved farther west, lessening the threat of hostile activity from natives or foreign enemies, ports grew busier, bringing in a more transient and criminal population. Constables could not be on duty twenty-four hours a day. (They even worked Sundays to make sure no one broke the Sabbath.) Thus, a night watch was instituted to complement the day patrol of the constabulary.

Night-watch duty was virtually the same all over the colonies. Most operated only during summer months, with only a bellman during winter. They kept a lookout for crime, made sure the city was quiet, and dealt with drunks and vagrants who might be out on city streets during the night. Some cities had curfews enforced by the night watch. Night watchmen made the familiar "all's well" regular time announcements and reported citizens' calls for help through the "hue and cry." Like the constabulary, though, night watchmen were poorly paid, if at all, had no training, and often came from the lower ranks. And like constable service, substitutes could be used and fines could be paid to avoid the unpopular duty.[25]

The best known of the early American night watches belonged to Boston. Established in April 1631, a year after the city was founded, the Boston watch was originally a military guard of one officer over six men. In 1636, this was changed to a community-based watch in which every able-bodied male was obligated to serve when called upon. The penalty for missing watch was ten shillings per night. The watch operated in Boston from one hour after sunset to around four o'clock in the morning, from late spring to early fall. A constable set the watch each night.

Beginning in 1654, the city of Boston employed two men at ten shillings per week to serve as bellmen during the winter months. The number of watchmen on duty each night increased to six in 1677 after a horrible fire broke out the previous year, and fire duty was added to the watch's list of obligations.[26]

Watch duty in Boston typified that of many other early American cities and towns: effectiveness depended for the most part on whether or not the watch received compensation and if public monies supported the watch. Beginning in 1732, Boston public coffers paid watchmen ten shillings per month, and by 1735, the city committed £1,200 per year for the watch. This was indeed an extraordinary amount to spend on a watch, even by colonial standards. In subsequent years, Boston reduced the number of watchmen to cut costs, but these savings were offset by commitments to support watches on the Long Wharf and the Boston Neck.[27]

War and then revolution strained the Boston watch system. As a staging area for British operations in the French and Indian War (1756–1763) and then as the center of anti-British protest in the 1760s and 1770s, Boston had its share of lawlessness and antigovernment riots, which challenged the watch's ability to maintain consistent order. The watch itself, seen as a symbol of established authority, was often attacked by angry mobs. In 1761, Boston increased the number of watchmen and raised wages to thirty shillings per month. That British troops were permanently stationed in the Boston area in 1768 caused more problems for the watch. Officers and troops alike showed disdain toward the colonial authorities. The situation grew so severe that selectmen requested the governor of Massachusetts, Thomas Hutchinson, to provide a military watch. Hutchinson did nothing, and citizens continued to fear not only the usual criminal element of the city but also the carousing soldiers disturbing the peace on a near nightly basis. Boston spent a sizable sum each year on its watch, only to see British troops berate and terrorize their own citizens and efforts to police the city in troubled times. No wonder colonials came to fear a "standing army."[28]

New York City had a similar watch arrangement to that of its northerly neighbor. Beginning in 1658 when New Amsterdam burgomasters instituted an eight-man rattle watch, New York City's watch dealt primarily with drunkenness (which was rampant in the city from the 1650s through the early 1700s) and looking out for fire. Rattle watches were distinguished by the unique handle-held rattle mechanisms that enabled watchmen to instantly raise an alarm. Night watchmen who caught any thief or troublemaker would detain the suspect and then turn him over to the *schout*, later called the constable, in the morning. Similar watches kept the peace at night in the surrounding counties of Brooklyn, Queens, and the Bronx.[29]

Like Boston, New York City relied upon a paid watch. Low salaries, however, made reliable recruits hard to find. Moreover, citizens found the additional taxes to pay for the watch hard to stomach, particularly in tough economic times. Crisis, however, often overcame economic hesitancy to employ a watch. Indian scares and threatened slave uprisings kept a watch in service throughout the 1670s and 1680s. Sometimes the watch was supported by a detachment of militia during heightened danger. During this time, New York City had as many as forty-five paid watchmen and constables on duty, making it one of the better policed cities in the colonies *and* England.[30]

Occasionally, as with the constabulary, citizens themselves would patrol at night when city coffers could not provide a paid watch. As usual, the poorer citizenry got stuck with the duty, whereas wealthier citizens paid for replacements and avoided the unpopular service. Substitutes proved ineffective and unreliable, characterized by one local newspaper as a "parcel of idle, drinking, vigilant Snorers, who never quelled any nocturnal Tumult in their Lives."[31] Because of these organizational and budgetary problems, the number of watchmen on duty failed to keep pace with the rapidly increasing population of the city, which in turn contributed to the rise in crime.[32]

Thus, despite the watch, by 1749, crime had become a severe problem in New York City. Few dared to walk the streets at night alone for fear of attack, and most who did go out at night did so in groups of three or four and were well armed.[33] This did not change until the 1830s, when meaningful police reform brought organized law enforcement to New York City. From all accounts, the problems suffered by the constabulary and night watch of New York City characterized the law enforcement experience of the rest of the colony. Sheriffs, constables, and watchmen alike were poorly paid and their offices garnered little respect among their fellow citizens. Insufficient numbers, poor quality, and corruption hampered law enforcement efforts in New York throughout the early American period.[34]

Charleston, South Carolina, was the largest, busiest port south of Philadelphia, and as such required diligent law enforcement like its neighbors to the north. Founded in 1670, much later than the northern settlements, Charleston's isolated location made security a major concern for citizens and administrators alike. And like Boston and New York, threats from Native Americans and foreign attack (primarily from Spain) combined with crime typical of an early American port city to make a watch system necessary in Charleston.

City authorities began a constable's watch in 1685, consisting of one constable and six watchmen who made nightly rounds of the city. The city was divided into four precincts for effective enlistment of citizens. Each able-bodied male was liable for service, but those serving their turn at watch were not compensated. Problems plagued the Charleston watch. Many fell asleep while on duty, ignored disorders committed on their watch, or simply refused to serve.

In 1696, city authorities attempted to redress these problems by implementing tax-supported paid watch of one captain and five men. This arrangement lasted but two years, as the paid watch proved just as unreliable as the older citizens' watch. After returning to the old system in 1698, Charleston attempted to improve watch duty for those on watch by building sentry boxes and a watch house to temporarily hold wrongdoers and to make the watch more effective by instituting fines for sleeping on duty and other infractions.

Frequent colonial wars interrupted the citizen-based system. During times of threatened danger, Charleston replaced the citizen watch with a military patrol to maintain order and safety in the city. In 1703, the military watch consisted of an officer and twelve guards at a cost of £550 per year. The Yamassee War of 1715 threatened Charleston enough to increase the size of the military watch to twenty-two guards, with eight patrolling the city each night.

Despite these efforts to form an effective citizen and military watch, Charleston authorities failed to properly oversee the watch. Although Boston and New York had their share of problems with watchmen and citizens evading service, Charleston seemed to have unusually bad luck with its watch. Lack of oversight by authorities and less than adequate candidates made the watch a mockery. Similar to its northern counterparts, the Charleston watch suffered a lack of respect from its own citizens as well as from the itinerant sailors from the port. The problem became so bad that brawling sailors began to purposefully target the watchmen on their rounds, sometimes beating them severely.[35]

War with France and then revolution did not improve matters for the Charleston watch. The war for independence in particular affected South Carolina as guerilla warfare spread across the state. Charleston suffered from an increase in refugees from rural areas, a disrupted economy, and an overall neglect of city services during these hard times. Distracted with other more pressing matters, the governor often appointed men of low character as constables to oversee the watch. Corruption and neglect of duty spread among the watchmen as they illegally sold liquor, failed to enforce the Sunday watch, and brawled with sailors. Independence did not bring an automatic respect for law and order.[36]

Other settlements that grew into towns and cities across the British colonies had similar experiences. Philadelphia, taken over from the Dutch by England in 1671, had at first a constable day watch, then later added a night watch in 1700. By 1751, a citizen-based watch patrolled the city but suffered similar problems to those in Boston, New York, and Charleston. This ineffective system remained in place until 1833, when a formal police department was organized.[37]

In Virginia, Richmond followed a similar pattern, although, by comparison, it was a much younger settlement. Founded in 1737, Richmond had only one thousand inhabitants by the 1770s. A sheriff and a night watch kept relative peace but had no power to make arrests and did not try to prevent crime. Like its larger counterparts, Richmond was affected by war and revolution. Crime increased dramatically during the war for independence and forced Richmond to institute a more formal, paid constabulary and watch with the power to arrest criminals. Crime became so bad, that in 1796, the mayor of Richmond authorized the city militia to form patrols to assist the city watch. Like Charleston, the threat of unruly, even rebellious, slaves occupied much of the watch's time. Not until after the War of 1812 did police reform begin, and even then it was not until the 1820s that a formal police department was formed in Richmond.[38] These same trends can be found across early America, especially in urban areas and cities.[39]

CONCLUSION

War and revolution brought an increase in crime across the colonies. Assaults, murders, theft, breaking and entering, counterfeiting, and the like plagued cities and rural areas alike. Drunkenness continued unabated. There simply was no well-organized, effective law enforcement in place to deal with crime mostly brought on by severe economic troubles, namely, monetary inflation and scarcity of goods. Corruption, poor-quality watchmen and constables, and an overall disregard for the duty continued to plague law enforcement effectiveness. The widely varied local practice of self-policing no longer sufficed.[40]

The constabulary and the watch were not the only aspects of the criminal justice system that suffered. Criminal courts continued to prove ineffective at dealing with criminals already arrested. Ignorance of the law, corruption, inconsistency, and basic neglect of duty characterized courts in early America. As long as the spoils system ruled selection of judges, nothing would change in the courtroom to help those trying to keep peace on the streets.[41]

Be it a sign of rebellion against the centralized rule of the British government or enthusiasm for democratic republicanism run amok, citizens of early America had a distinct revulsion to authority and rule of law. Nowhere was this more typified than in American attitudes toward law enforcement. Fear of a standing army, suspicion of centralized authority, and a growing tradition of individual liberty all contributed to this phenomenon. Changing these attitudes would be a challenge indeed and one necessary to reform law enforcement across the country into effective police agencies.

The Development of Municipal Policing in the Northeast

INTRODUCTION

The history and context in which policing developed in the northeastern part of the United States is fertile ground for examining several policing strategies that were later adopted by police departments nationwide. Emerging from the watch and ward systems of early America, many of the significant political and organizational decisions affecting the development of municipal police departments can be traced to Boston, New York, and Philadelphia. During the first half of the nineteenth century, these three police departments initiated innovative law enforcement strategies—some failed, but others became the very foundation for police departments of today. Each of these major northeastern cities approached the need for police service from a different perspective under the direction of slightly different forms of local government, all in response to a variety of community problems and concerns.

The United States changed dramatically from the beginning of the nineteenth century to the Civil War. Economic growth and territorial expansion combined with a shift in political thought and class stratification to force major changes in American society. Prosperity broadened in the 1820s as more Americans found financial stability from the transportation and market revolutions. The country itself doubled in size with the Louisiana Purchase and increased even more with the addition of Texas and the Mexican Cession, all of which provided more economic opportunity while putting predominantly white Protestant Americans in conflict with nonwhite cultures. Politics changed as the electorate expanded, finally bringing democracy to the nonpropertied "common man" (at least the "white" common man). As a consequence, the old guard of Federalist and Republican elites that had dominated government since the Revolution gave way to a new class of democratic politicians who preferred the power of the federal government to that of the states and the rights of the individual to the power of government.

Immigrants from abroad, namely, the Irish escaping the horror of the Hunger, poured into American cities. By the 1830s and 1840s, ethnic conflict in major American cities had become a serious problem. Of course, by 1850 the southern half of the nation would rely totally upon black slave labor to support a credit-based agrarian economy, while the northern half began the road toward mass manufacturing using wage labor to sustain a consumer market economy. In this atmosphere, individuals realized the opportunity to pursue their happiness and take advantage of newfound political power. They lashed out at special privilege and the archaic, oppressive class structure. Cities teemed with ambition and greed and boiled with ethnic and racial conflict. Thus, they became the center stage for clashes between the "haves" and the "have-nots."[1]

The pre-Civil War period is crucial to the development of municipal police organizations. Responding to crises in the cities, municipal governments would gradually create organized police departments. Boston, New York, and Philadelphia provide excellent snapshots of this evolution. Additionally, experimentation with police oversight was also an established trend by the end of the Civil War. These advancements set the stage for the even greater challenges of policing a more industrialized and urbanized nation during the latter half of the nineteenth century.

THE CONTEXT OF MUNICIPAL POLICE DEVELOPMENT

The study of public administration often uses comparison as a tool for evaluating the effectiveness of public organizations. Dwight Waldo, Max Weber, and others have been intrigued by this approach.[2] Identifying a model that is representative of "defined concepts, or clusters of related concepts" allows the evaluation of "administrative means" with "administrative ends." The model guides the process of recognizing organizational structure, problems, and successes.[3] By applying this evaluative process to a modern police department, clusters of ideas and organizational strategies can be observed. The same process can be applied to nineteenth-century police organizations, which can help identify the ideological roots of modern police departments.

A modern police department and a nineteenth-century department may not seem comparable at first glance. The modern police department immediately brings to mind visions of uniformed officers on patrol in clearly marked police vehicles. The modern community retains an unchallenged expectation that police officers will respond to calls and react to crimes that are committed in their neighborhood. When serious crimes occur, more seasoned and experienced officers, working as criminal investigators, will assume responsibility for the crime scene and the investigation. As this process unfolds, criminals are arrested and prosecuted according to the rule of law. This modern image of police behavior and police department structure is designed to support that very behavior and can be traced to the nineteenth-century police departments of Boston, New York, and Philadelphia. These three original police organizations heavily influenced the modern American police department.

When considering the origin of police departments in the United States, it is important to consider four concepts that center around the political, social, and ideological atmosphere of the time. First, as the northeastern urban centers of the United States, including Boston, New York, and Philadelphia, continued to grow, the problematic transformation from town to city overwhelmed these rapidly developing urban areas. Commensurate to population growth were issues of public safety and public order.

The northeastern population centers clung to their traditional desire for local governance, a trend left over from the rebellious atmosphere of the American Revolution. Early fears of centralized authority made the new ideology of republicanism and decentralized control both appealing and essential in forming municipal governments during and after the American Revolution. This apprehension toward centralized authority became exaggerated in those elements of government that had direct authority to detain citizens, search and regulate private property, and enforce laws. Along with the fear of centralized authority was an equal if not more intense suspicion of standing armies and state police. England had used the military as a domestic police force in the colonies after the French and Indian War, the memory of which caused the colonists great anxiety as the new nation decided its military and police policies. The excesses of the French state police during the French Revolution only enhanced those concerns.[4]

Second, the commitment to the principles found in republicanism and representative government were omnipresent in early nineteenth-century America. From Boston to Chicago, the support for republicanism was so strong that it occasionally materialized in the form of vigilantism. In the post-Revolutionary War decades, the idea of forming a national police force, which England would do in 1829, was deeply at odds with the American ideal of self-governance and republicanism. Although the concepts of public police and a commitment to crime detection and crime prevention found some support, the fear of a centralized or national police was a consistent stumbling block to change.[5] From 1829, when Sir Robert Peel's Metropolitan Police Act was put into effect in London, to 1845, when New York City became the first city in America to adopt elements of the Metropolitan Police Act, citizens in the major cities of the northeast clung to the hope that self-governance would eventually sustain public safety and control crime.[6]

Third, a strong undercurrent of nativism and racism pervaded northeastern cities. These prejudices against foreign-born immigrants and people of African descent often resulted in incredibly violent riots.[7] Philadelphia's nativist movement exploded in riots in 1844. In New York City, the destructive year 1834 became known as "the year of the riots."[8]

People of different backgrounds found support among riotous crowds based on their shared fears or hatreds. Many people new to the demands of urban life took to the streets in protest or riot. Often led by respected local citizens, mobs attacked African American and ethnic neighborhoods. Religious intolerance, often anti-Catholic, resulted in riots that destroyed churches and even convents.[9]

Rioting was both a form of protest and uncontrolled civil unrest that oddly blended with republicanism. As these problems escalated, it is important to mention that the established forms of policing, the night watch and the marshal's office, were not designed to control riots, prevent crime, or even detect crime. At the beginning of the nineteenth century, policing lacked the legal authority, manpower, and conceptual understanding necessary to effectively handle riots and the expanding crime problem. Fear of centralized authority had not yet overcome fear of disorder.

Finally, in Boston, New York, and Philadelphia, the problems created by patronage and ethnic consolidation were growing and directly influencing decisions regarding the development and implementation of police departments. From the selection of police officers to the delegation of law enforcement authority, decisions became intertwined with the political and social environment as well as with the political successes of a given political faction. The nativist impulse made it difficult for immigrants to find employment as police. If an ethnic group dominated the political party in power, however, members of that ethnic group easily found positions in the police department. As patronage and partisan conflict expanded, these problems became indigenous to ethnic neighborhoods and spread to the community at large. This political, social, and ideological atmosphere directly influenced the formative years of police departments in the northeastern United States.

There is no single police department or police organizational strategy that can be identified as the sole source or cornerstone that influenced the establishment of police departments in America. During the first half of the nineteenth century, a collection of important ideas and issues influenced the development of municipal police departments in the urban northeast. Many of these early innovations, and some of the resulting problems, continue to influence modern police departments. For example, the long history surrounding the local control of police departments is so entrenched that many municipalities, no matter how small, have formed police departments that are inefficient and costly. Yet, the desire of small city governments to maintain a police department, often as a symbol of autonomy, remains among the more sacred and established truths in American municipalities today.

There is inherent pride in being "first" in any discipline or professional field. Boston, New York, and Philadelphia are each mentioned in the scholarship of early American policing as being the first police department in the United States. But what does being the first "police department" really mean? In essence, being a department implies a particular bureaucratic organization and function. The broad nature of public safety is open to several different police strategies. The difficulty lies in determining which city first formed a police organization that mirrors modern police departments. Boston, New York, Philadelphia, and other American cities have pieces of the puzzle, but no single police department is responsible for the development of all of the pieces. None of the early northeastern police departments precisely replicate modern-day police departments.

These early police departments do, however, represent the genesis of modern police organizations. The increasingly critical need to control public disorder in the cities guided the drive toward more complex policing systems. As northeastern cities developed and grew, the problems generated by a large number of people living together in restricted spaces created ever-increasing problems and responsibilities for local governments. As political influence and control expanded at the local level, elements of regulatory control were designed to deal effectively with human behavior and other problems created by growth. These regulatory controls were put in place to handle community difficulties critical to fair and efficient local government. Many government functions taken for granted at the beginning of the twenty-first century did not exist in America in the early nineteenth century. The problems and fears created by uncontrolled disease epidemics, poorly functioning sewer and water systems, the sale of alcoholic beverages without licensing regulations, the control of horses in public areas, the regulatory control of firearms, and so forth, were either handled by disconnected levels of government or were not regulated at all.

In the development of early policing in these three cities, the regulatory functions of disconnected municipal departments came together under primitive police departments. From health codes and building permits to licensing taverns and brothels and the execution of arrest warrants, what had been carried out by independent departments now came under the authority of police. This was a critical step in the birth of police departments. Boston, New York, and Philadelphia were the first cities to undergo this centralization of municipal functions.

BOSTON AND THE CITY MARSHAL CONCEPT

At the beginning of the nineteenth century, Boston was the fourth largest city in America. With an expanding population of over fifty thousand people by 1820, the problems of disease, crime, and public disorder increased to alarming levels.[10] The expanding population placed more pressure on municipal government to effectively handle Boston's urban problems. Many of these difficulties directly contributed to the need for more effective law enforcement and were beyond the ability of the "watchmen" system of policing that Boston had relied on for decades.[11]

Ineffective to begin with, the "watch" certainly had its hands full as the need for public safety increased. With no training and limited supervision, watchmen slept on duty, failed to patrol their assigned areas, and often drank on patrol. Boston town records testify to the problem: "Feb. 3: At one o'clock visited South Watch: constable asleep. One and one-half o'clock at Center Watch found constable and doorman asleep. Two o'clock at North Watch found constable and doorman asleep and a drunken man kicking at the door to get in."[12] In response to the inefficiencies of the watch system, an ordinance was passed in 1801 giving the mayor of Boston the additional title of "Superintendent of Police." As superintendent, the mayor inspected municipal work projects and supervised government departments, as well as carried out the implicit duties of chief administrator of police. Through this 1801 ordinance, Boston became the first major city in America to place police responsibility directly on the shoulders of the mayor.

Police organization in Boston underwent more change in 1822 when Boston was incorporated as a city under a strong-mayor system. The ability of the mayor to effectively supervise all the functions expected of municipal government and fulfill the responsibilities of "Superintendent of Police" became impossible in a city of fifty thousand people. With the obvious limitations on the mayor's ability to enforce ordinances and laws, combined with the continuing inadequacy of the watch system, steps were taken to expand the manpower and resources available to the mayor for public safety.

The first new mayor of the now incorporated city of Boston, Josiah Quincy, established a supervisory police position called "Marshal of the City." The marshal was in effect a glorified constable, charged with enforcing laws and ordinances and required to patrol the city once each week to personally see the problems of Boston's streets. Benjamin Pollard was appointed the first city marshal of Boston in 1823. Administrative authority for policing no longer was the direct responsibility of the mayor. The marshal's authority and responsibilities, not bound by statute or tradition, were capable of expanding the will of both the mayor and the council. Pollard carried out his duties with great enthusiasm, relished the role of arresting officer, and often prosecuted cases himself. The marshal's most important duty may have been as health officer, but a myriad of other duties were gradually added to his daily tasks, including licensing dogs, arresting poachers on the Boston Common, coordinating fire brigades, and planning parades and processions. If the duties were too much for the mayor to handle as superintendent of police, they certainly would prove too much for a single marshal. The result would be the creation of multiple city departments with specific functions and oversight. A police department would be among the first.[13]

This was indeed a significant development in the evolution of municipal government. The fact that the marshal had to walk the streets to inspect and ensure compliance of a long list of ordinances set the stage for contemporary police responsibilities. In a modern police department, for example, if a water main breaks at two o'clock in the morning, the first municipal government employee on the scene is a uniformed police officer responsible for the beat or district where the water main broke. It was much the same for the Boston city marshal.

Although the marshal's office assumed many municipal responsibilities, the problem of dealing with crime was not thought to be a direct responsibility of the marshal. Unruly crowds, vice activities, and criminal conduct in general were considered to be the problems of the night watch in Boston. Many city leaders believed that the primary responsibility of city government was to facilitate business, not to fight crime. The building and development of the city was directed toward the facilitation of commerce. Crime was seen simply as a hindrance to the primary responsibilities of city government, just like public drunkenness and disorderly conduct. These nuisances were not yet perceived as serious enough to require the attention of a large independent department of city government.

Neither the night watch nor the marshals were involved in patrolling the city of Boston to look for or prevent crime. The marshal's work was embroiled in public health issues and the regulation of community concerns associated with population growth and commerce. The night watch dealt with unruly crowds, watched for fires, and kept peace in the city during the hours of darkness. They did not patrol the city looking for crime or think in terms of crime prevention. The public environment of this period was filled with social and political uncertainties. From economic depression, stinging debates over slavery, waves of immigrants, anti-Catholic and anti-immigrant sentiments, and sporadic rioting, Boston, like many northeastern cities, was indeed violent and filled with public safety concerns. The concept of policing that is commonplace today had yet to be developed or even recognized.[14]

Boston established an independent day watch as a police force in 1848, which in turn created friction between the day force and the old night watch. The Massachusetts legislature amended the Boston charter to consolidate the watch and ward system in 1854 into a single police department. This established an organized police structure under the control of a "chief" appointed by the mayor and the town council. Thus, before the Civil War, Boston, like Chicago (1851), New Orleans (1852), Cincinnati (1852), and Baltimore (1857), had an organized police structure that far exceeded the watch systems of old.[15]

Boston made significant strides in developing an American style of policing. The strong-mayor form of municipal government effectively controlled police leadership and police functions for the first time. Substantial regulatory control was placed in a marshal's office that eventually evolved into a police department. As the functions of animal control, crowd control, and crime were handled effectively via the marshal's office, they evolved into the responsibilities of the Boston Police Department.

NEW YORK AND THE NEED FOR POLICE REFORM

New York City grew dramatically from 1790 to 1820, increasing from a population of 33,000 to 123,000 in thirty years.[16] Included in this rapid growth were a substantial number of foreign immigrants. Because of cultural differences and economic hardships, many immigrants found comfort in forming ethnic neighborhoods. As New York City's population expanded, however, the social controls that bound a small community together began to disintegrate. Ethnic communities grew beyond neighborhood boundaries and merged with other groups. Combined with the dissension created by the blending of different cultures, social stratification became more pronounced as the "rich segregated themselves from the poor." This tumultuous and restless environment proved to be a fertile breeding ground for all sorts of urban problems. Despite this, for a few decades the moral fabric of New York community life managed to tolerate a fairly high level of crime and civil unrest.

In the early nineteenth century, the New York watch system seemed sufficient to make citizens feel relatively safe. As urban problems created by rapid growth took hold, however, riots and crime became serious threats to social stability. Writing in 1806 about New York City, British criminologist Patrick Colquhoun warned that "The evil propensities incident to human nature appear no longer restrained by the force of religion, or the influence of moral principle." This mounting disorder was new to people accustomed to policing themselves. Yet, a sense of community pride grounded in republicanism slowed the acceptance of major change to the policing system. During the early decades of the nineteenth century, giving up on the notions of protecting one another through self-policing and the traditional fear of centralized authority made public action to change the system rather difficult for the people of New York to accept.[17]

As the problems of urban life grew intolerable and threatened economic stability, the inefficiencies of the police system became a focal point for government and business leaders. Influential business interests motivated the effort to reorganize the New York City police. Driven by business-oriented newspapers of New York, editors and articles demanded better "riot control" to protect economic interests.

As the political and business elites followed the transformation of the police in London, the work of Sir Robert Peel became a popular model for New York City. Peel's Metropolitan Police Act of 1829 declared that police existed to "prevent crime and disorder as an alternative to the repression of crime and disorder by military force and severity of legal punishment."[18] It was an old idea finally articulated in formal, official terms. There is a substantial amount of scholarship praising the Metropolitan Police Act as a model for municipal police organization in the northeastern United States, but there was a major problem with the Metropolitan Police Act for Americans. The Metropolitan Police Act created a national police force, an idea abhorrent to the very ideals and traditions of American republicanism. Giving powers of arrest, search and seizure, and so forth to a national or federal police force in the United States was simply impossible in an age when Jacksonian democracy sought to limit the already expansive powers of federal and state government and promote the rights of the individual.[19]

With the failure of the watch system becoming more apparent with each act of civil unrest, support for the reorganization of the police system, based on the ideas found in Peel's Metropolitan Police Act, grew. The lack of confidence and fear peaked in 1834—the infamous "year of the riots."[20] During 1834 and 1835, riots and looting occurred numerous times in New York City, culminating with the "great fire" of December 16, 1835. This fire destroyed several factories and businesses and leveled several surrounding blocks. Looting only worsened the already horrible situation. To stop the looting, one of the techniques feared by American citizens was utilized: military troops were called in to subdue the mob, arresting about three hundred looters.

New York City political leaders still resisted major changes in the police even though the watch system had obviously failed. A September 1836 report to the New York City Common Council based on a review of police actions during the "year of the riots" and the "great fire" concluded:

> Though it may become necessary, at some future period, to adopt a system of police similar to that of London or Liverpool; yet they believe the present system, with some alterations, may be made amply sufficient for this city, for many years to come. The nature of institutions is such that more reliance may be placed upon the people for aid, in case of emergency, than in despotic government.[21]

Even with the disorder of the previous year, the traditional fear of a strong, centralized government proved so pervasive that the proposals for change were either unacceptable or ignored.

Ironically, it would be a single, relatively less destructive event that would instigate reaction for change. The infamous unsolved murder of Mary Rogers in 1841 rekindled community concerns that police were incompetent, seeking reward for their work, and not organized to handle complicated criminal cases.[22] The murder of Mary Rogers was in the news for several weeks and even inspired Edgar Allan Poe's *The Mystery of Marie Roget*. The sensational crime had several plots. Rogers left her mother's boarding house at approximately ten o'clock on Sunday morning, July 25, to visit her sister. Her body was found in the Hudson River near Hoboken on July 28. It was first suspected that she had been kidnapped and raped before being strangled to death. The second plot had Miss Rogers voluntarily taking a ferry to Hoboken with a dark-skinned young man who then strangled her for some unknown reason. The third plot was more provocative. She might have indeed died from an ill-fated abortion, and those responsible dumped her body in the river. New York police proved unwilling to take serious investigative action and the murder went unsolved. Covered thoroughly by the newspapers and kept alive by Poe's work, the case became a significant motivating factor in the development of the New York City Police Department.

Governor William H. Seward cited this murder case in his annual address of 1842 and called for improvements in the New York City police. From 1842 to 1844, numerous plans for reorganization were presented but rejected for a variety of reasons, mainly political. One plan in particular would have created a day and night police force, and the plan itself, according to Raymond B. Fosdick, became the foundation for a modern police organization in the United States. The New York City Common Council had the authority to accept or reject police reorganization plans passed by the New York state legislature, and considering the contentious political relationship between New York City and Albany, the likelihood of the council adopting a legislative plan for police reorganization seemed nil. Moreover, the political issues in New York City at this point in time were not focused solely on the police. Anti-immigrant and anti-Catholic activities dominated both the Whig and the Democratic parties. Both parties sought the votes of "Native Americans" to maintain the supremacy of native-born Americans over foreign newcomers.[23]

In 1845, Democrats won over the nativist vote and as a consequence were able to temporarily resolve the conflict with the state capital to adopt serious police reform measures. Mayor William F. Havemeyer, a Democrat, called for the adoption of the latest legislative version of police reform. The new law did not replace any existing agencies responsible for police protection. Rather, it instead created a force of two hundred men known as the "Municipal Police" to act as a night and day watch. The mayor would choose members of the police force, with approval of the Common Council. This "law of police reform" was grounded in the principles of Peel's Metropolitan Police Act. Sixteen years after the act was adopted in London, New York became the first city in the United States to make the formal transition from "citizen" police to "public" police.[24] The one major difference, however, was that the New York police remained a local force, whereas Peel's "bobbies" were a national police.

As the newly formed police department hired officers and assumed responsibility for public safety, rapid population growth and political squabbling continued. In the ten years from 1845 to 1855, New York City grew from 250,000 to 629,000 people. Over half of the 629,000 were foreign-born. In 1855, there were still only 800 police officers on the newly formed police department to enforce the law in this rapidly growing and changing city. Staffing and patrol patterns in response to population growth continue to be major issues in American policing. In addition to the difficulties created by growth were the problems created by the political reality of police officers being appointed by elected officials. Saloonkeepers, gamblers, and others wanting special considerations from police used their political connections to ensure that laws controlling their businesses were not vigorously enforced. New York newspapers described the political environment and the quality of policing in less than glowing terms: "We have no right to look for saintliness in blue uniforms and pewter badges when their wearers receive $25 to $30 a week." Because of low pay and political corruption, the papers continued, police officers were ". . . compelled to associate with vulgarians and scoundrels of all grades; are exposed to every species of temptation; act unfavorably on each other, and have not restraining influence beyond their own intelligence, which is not very great, and their fear of exposure, which is not probable."[25]

The corruptive influence of politics on the New York Police Department did not go unnoticed. Through the 1850s, constant calls for reform of the police force came from the press and concerned citizens' groups. From the difficulties created by political interference, the continued growth in the city's population, and the persistent crime problems in poor immigrant neighborhoods, the press consistently and negatively attacked the police department. As a political football, kicked about during every election, controversy became part of the status quo for the police department. In 1857, the New York legislature, responding to strong criticism of police effectiveness, assumed state control of the New York Police Department. The state of New York would run the city of New York's police department until 1870, when the state police board was abolished. This was as close as New York police would get to recreating the Metropolitan Police Act. The Metropolitan Police of New York would effectively protect and serve New York citizens through the bloody Civil War draft riots, but would succumb to the pressures of boss politics as the nation entered the Industrial Age.[26]

Like Boston, the development of a police organization in New York significantly contributed to the evolution of American policing. New York police would be the first in the country to wear a police badge, in this case a star. Badges and later uniforms proved very unpopular among policemen, who believed that these symbolized centralized authority and militarism, and of course exposed police to criminals on the street. Nonetheless, police were forced to accept the badge and then the uniforms.[27] More importantly, however, New York was the first city to place executive authority over the police in a distinct department. In the process of controlling the discipline of police officers and in attempting to remove political considerations from the police, ordinances gave the responsibility for appointing watchmen, inspecting watch houses, and reporting to the mayor and council to a single person, which set in motion the concept of a police executive under the direction and control of the mayor, who was responsible for the discipline of officers.

PHILADELPHIA AND PUBLIC ORGANIZATION

In many ways, the evolution of policing in Philadelphia followed a path similar to that of the Boston and New York police departments. In 1797, the Pennsylvania state legislature gave the mayor of Philadelphia the authority to create a paid "night watch" and to appoint night watchmen. Within the scope of the mayor's responsibilities were several additional elements of public safety. From the regulation and enforcement of health ordinances and the control of fires to supervising the night watch and day watch, the mayor of Philadelphia was by both state law and city ordinance given responsibility for public safety.[28]

In 1797, Mayor and Superintendent of the Watch Hilary Baker became the first public safety employee of Philadelphia to die in the line of duty. Ironically, he did not get killed while attempting an arrest. As superintendent of the watch, Baker was responsible for enforcing the health code and personally inspected places rampant with disease. In the process he contracted "yellow fever" and died. These broad areas of public safety responsibility can be clearly distinguished in contemporary municipal governments, but at the end of the eighteenth century these ideas were fairly new.

Philadelphia's drive toward an organized police department continued in the early nineteenth century. While England adopted the Metropolitan Police Act of 1829, the public records of Philadelphia clearly point out that as early as 1814 the Philadelphia mayor had appointed a police captain and lieutenant to be in charge of the "night watch" with a paid salary from "Common Council" funds. In 1827, watchmen began taking an oath, swearing to do their duty to protect and serve the citizens of Philadelphia.[29] Philadelphia had organized police long before Peel came onto the scene in 1829.

Nativism and racist attitudes toward African Americans emerged as serious problems in Philadelphia in the early nineteenth century, just as in other cities. In 1829, Philadelphia had its first major race riot, the first of several that ripped apart the city through the early 1840s. Historian David R. Johnson points out that the impact of nativism and racism on urban life in Philadelphia was indeed serious. Rioting was the most visible manifestation of this phenomenon, as nativist fear and racial hatred ran deep in the veins of urban life. Nativism affected the temperance movement, rivalries among fire companies, and gang wars; whereas racism fomented conflict surrounding the abolitionist movement, clashes between neighborhoods, and violent assaults by one race on another. Philadelphia's South Street exemplified all of these problems.[30]

A collision of values occurred, as the commitment to republicanism clashed with the distortions inherent in nativism and racism. Political leaders in Philadelphia felt that giving power to a police organization would be in opposition to republican principles of decentralized government. What if police could not be held accountable or abused their power? At the same time, the need to control riots and increasing crime demanded that elected officials do something.[31] With growing vigilantism on one side and increasingly violent crime and public disorder on the other, Philadelphia was forced to make uncomfortable decisions regarding police authority and organization.

To address these problems, Philadelphia Recorder Joseph M'Ilvaine proposed a "regular police" with three distinct duties: the collection of information regarding crime, the investigation of all details necessary to prepare a legal case, and the arrest of the culprits. M'Ilvaine's ideas for police found support when a prominent Philadelphia citizen, Stephen Girard, passed away in 1833 and left over thirty-three thousand dollars from his estate to "provide more effectually than now . . . for the security of the persons and property of the inhabitants of the said city by a competent police." With funding supplied by a private citizen, Philadelphia moved forward in the development of a police department by appointing a special committee, which included M'Ilvaine and two former Philadelphia mayors.

This committee studied the works of the Englishman Peel, as well as those of the police organizations in Boston and New York. Sensitive to both political issues and citizen concerns, the committee recommended the "establishment of an efficient preventive police." They presented their proposal in terms less threatening than what citizens might have feared in a Peel-like police force. The committee reassured the public that Peel's principles actually created a police less arbitrary, less oppressive, and less powerful than the current Philadelphia watch system. Interestingly, the committee also recommended establishing a special constables branch to pursue and apprehend professional criminals. As in both New York and Boston, the new ideas were watered down because of traditional fears of centralization and abuse of authority.

In 1833, an ordinance established four police districts across the city. A captain commanded each district, along with four lieutenants and four inspectors. Overall, Philadelphia now had 24 policemen patrolling the streets during the day and at least 120 patrolling at night. Although it was a step in the right direction, it was hardly adequate. By comparison, London had 3,389 policemen, or about 1 "bobbie" for every 434 citizens. Philadelphia had a whopping single patrolman for every 3,352 people. Police organization was formalized in 1841, when a city ordinance created a "Department of Police." Station houses were built in two of the four districts in 1848, giving the new police department a more permanent physical presence in the city.[32]

In 1850, additional steps were taken to strengthen the police force. Similar to the public safety position in Boston, a "police marshal" was appointed to oversee Philadelphia police districts. The 1854 "Act of Consolidation," passed by the Pennsylvania assembly, expanded the size of Philadelphia from 360 acres to 83,000 acres. The city grew instantly from approximately 2 square miles to 129 square miles. This obviously added substantial responsibility to the Philadelphia Police Department. In 1855, Samuel G. Ruggles was appointed as the first chief of police for Philadelphia and brought military structure to the police department. With nine hundred police officers, Ruggles established patrol areas that covered six hundred miles of roadway and over sixty thousand dwellings. From 1856 to 1861, Philadelphia developed a police telegraph system, issued "complete" police uniforms and badges, and appointed Joseph Wood as the first chief of detectives. Philadelphia also became the first police department in the nation to have a special riot squad of over sixty officers. Shortly thereafter, the Civil War brought homeland security issues to Philadelphia, as one hundred Philadelphia police officers were assigned battlefield gear and sent to defend the state capital at Harrisburg.[33]

Philadelphia's experience with creating organized police mirrors those of Boston and New York. Philadelphia established one of the earliest publicly paid police agencies. And as in other cities during this time, city leaders were reactive rather than preventive in responding to crime and public disorder that plagued pre-Civil War society. Through a more effective and efficient police organization, Philadelphia was able to preserve order by the 1850s. Philadelphia was also the first major police department in the United States to have a detective branch, demonstrating that methods for solving crime were beginning to change.

THE ADVENT OF POLICE OVERSIGHT

One of the most intriguing and significant police developments before the Civil War was the advent of the police oversight board. With city services of all sorts, including police, overstretched and poorly administered, city governments began appointing oversight boards to help administer city services. These included school boards and poor relief boards but would later expand to include hospital boards, civil service review boards, and other boards to oversee the ever-increasing services provided by city governments.

The earliest reference to a "police board" came in the aborted 1844 New York law to create and combine the day and night police force. This board (consisting of the superintendent, two sub-superintendents, and four directors who administered each of the four police districts) had the straightforward duty of administering the New York Police Department. Because the 1844 law failed passage, the police board never convened in New York. The idea, however, did not die. Philadelphia created a short-lived police board in 1850 to write rules and regulations for police and to oversee the upkeep of the main police station in the city. The police marshal and the heads of the various town boards that came under the jurisdiction of Philadelphia police districts served on this board.

New York finally created a board in 1853 and became the first to call board members "police commissioners." The three-member board (the mayor, city recorder, and a city judge) had broad authority, including appointing and dismissing officers, approval of the mayor's selection for chief of police, and general administrative functions. New York's police commissioners would run the New York police department until 1901.

As with so many police developments, New York set the standard for others to copy. Both the failed 1844 law and the 1853 board of commissioners heavily influenced police around the nation. New Orleans created a board in 1853. In 1859, Cincinnati, another forward-looking department, adopted a board of commissioners consisting of four members jointly appointed by the mayor, the city auditor, and the police judge. San Francisco also established a board in 1859, made up of the police judge, the president of the city board of supervisors, and the chief of police. Detroit, St. Louis, and Kansas City established boards in 1861. Buffalo and Cleveland added board oversight in 1866. Southern cities even joined the board bandwagon as part of the Reconstruction in the 1870s. Size, method of appointment, partisan make-up, and responsibilities of police boards varied widely, but the central purpose to oversee the function of police in a city remained constant.

Changing conditions in cities and police problems warranted some form of oversight. Police departments had inconsistent hiring and promotion practices. Dismissal procedures often left the dismissed with no recourse. Informally tenured officers seemed accountable to no one. Moreover, as the nature of city conflict became more violent, charges of police brutality and abuse grew more frequent. Regardless of their motivation, city leaders obviously wanted to stamp out any blight on their communities caused by those charged with maintaining law and order.

Interestingly, Peel's concept of a state-run police force did finally win converts in the United States. Several cities overcame the traditional abhorrence toward centralized, state-controlled policing and turned over their city police to the administrative oversight of state police boards. New York led the way in 1853 by creating the New York Metropolitan Police, which encompassed New York, Queens, Brooklyn, and even Westchester County. Baltimore relinquished control to a state board in 1860. St. Louis and Kansas City, both of which created local police boards in 1861, switched to state boards the same year. Kansas City remains under the control of a state-appointed police board to this day. Cleveland, Detroit, Charleston, and later Boston all turned to state boards.

Most of these did not last, however. Two problems brought about the downfall of state boards. First, the nature of corrupt party politics that erupted into bitter rivalries between city and state bosses caused too much friction for state-appointed boards to effectively run city police forces. Second, the traditional urge for "home rule" returned to city politics, again mainly because of the corruptive nature of city political machines. Detroit, New Orleans, Cincinnati, Denver, and others that experimented with state boards abandoned the efforts by the turn of the century. Even bipartisan boards failed to overcome partisan politics. Assessing the development of police organizations in 1920, Raymond B. Fosdick criticized state oversight of city police departments as a tool of "party success rather than an instrument of public service. Regarded as the legitimate spoils of victory at the polls, it has been prostituted to base and selfish purposes."[34]

CONCLUSION

The development of these big-city police organizations before the Civil War shows how attitudes toward policing had shifted from a fear of centralized authority to a grudging acceptance of organized municipal law enforcement. This was a reactive development, as towns became cities in a relatively short period, nativism created a conservative political environment, and ethnic and racial prejudice reached increasingly higher levels of violence. These developments in police organization set the stage for how police would respond to the massive urbanization of the post-Civil War era, which would see many old concerns continue but also witness the advent of new problems and challenges for the police.

CHAPTER 3

POLICING RACE AND VIOLENCE IN THE SOUTH

INTRODUCTION

It is an uncomfortable fact that American police in the South actively pursued slaves and that slave patrols proved to be an integral step in the development of southern police organizations. Hubert Williams, president of the Police Foundation, and Patrick Murphy, former commissioner of the New York Police Department, are correct in asserting that "slave patrols of the South were America's first modern-style police forces." Unlike Boston, New York, and Philadelphia, where the concept of patrolling was not initially accepted or understood as a police function based on the ideas of crime prevention and detection, slave patrols, as the term implies, "patrolled" areas for exactly this purpose. They sought to both detect and prevent runaways and insurrections. The idea of preventing crime and investigating criminal activity by patrolling was not conceptually developed in northeastern police departments. From walking a beat for the prevention of crime to helicopters assisting modern-day police officers in the pursuit of a fleeing suspect, the police function of patrol was first accepted as a police practice by slave patrols in the South.[1]

The exaggerated support for Peel's 1829 Metropolitan Police Act as the sole source for American police organization and theory has overshadowed the history of police in the South and the origins of the controversial relationship between the African American community and the police. The influence of slave patrols on police departments in the South is a cornerstone of the institutional racism that continues to plague American police departments. By the time Peel's ideas of policing based on crime prevention reached the South, police departments from Virginia to Mississippi had entrenched policing concepts grounded in racial violence and an ingrained police culture rooted in slavery. Peel's "Principles of Law Enforcement," which begins with the prevention of crime and ends with measuring police efficiency by the absence of crime, is substantially more comfortable and acceptable to those in policing than the reality that some current police functions evolved from slave patrols and the enforcement of slave codes.[2]

From back-country "regulators" to slave patrols, police departments in the South developed under the culturally imposed conditions of slavery and violence. With a race-based social order driven by a slave-labor-based agricultural economy, the provincial structure of the South created public safety problems uniquely different from those experienced in the other parts of the country. In this rather isolated provincial environment, runaway slaves and the nightmarish fear of slave rebellion combined with exceptionally violent crime to make the South a very dangerous place indeed.[3]

Like other parts of the country, the history of the South is unique, and popular perceptions remain filled with myth. Agriculture ruled the economy and credit financed the system. As a consequence, cash was always in short supply and in demand. During the seventeenth century, white indentured servitude gave way to black slaves as a source of farm labor. Economics and evolving social structure promoted the change. The shift to slave labor dramatically altered Southern politics; Southern states probably would not have agreed to adopt the Constitution in 1787 were it not for the compromises on slavery. Cities in the South remained small relative to their Northern counterparts, and the reliance on agriculture and slave labor prevented a manufacturing, consumer-based economy from developing. Gradually, a landed aristocracy rose to the top of the sociopolitical ladder, with white yeoman farmers, poor Whites, and black slaves finishing out the downward steps.

Large plantations with hundreds of slaves, *a la* Tara from *Gone with the Wind*, were the exception rather than the rule. In 1860 there were over four million slaves across the Southern states, centered mostly in Virginia and in the Deep South. Several states approached or slightly surpassed having a population that was half slave. Only three thousand families of the so-called planter class owned more than one hundred slaves; seven thousand held between fifty and one hundred. As a result, over half of all slaves belonged to planter-class families. Yet, 88 percent of slave owners held less than twenty slaves, 72 percent less than ten slaves, and astonishingly 50 percent of slave owners owned less than five slaves. In fact, the typical white Southerner was more likely a non-slave-owning yeoman farmer who worked his land with his family rather than with slave labor. Thus, most white Southerners had no direct connection with slavery, but they indirectly relied on the institution for social and economic standing. With Blacks bonded in slavery, Whites had less competition for wage-earning jobs. Moreover, no matter how bad off the White, according to the social caste, he/she was still above a slave. As a result, non-slave-owners had a vested interest in defending the system.[4]

This "peculiar" situation in the South continued after the great Civil War of 1861 to 1865, even though slavery had been formerly abolished and full civil rights granted to free Blacks and freed slaves as a result of the horrific conflict. Southern Whites found ways to defy Reconstruction, preserve their social order, and thus continue to unwittingly limit economic growth. The "humiliation and subjugation" of Blacks continued through the enforcement of Jim Crow laws, economic and educational segregation, and the acceptance of lynching as means of social control. The slave codes of the antebellum era simply became the black codes of the late nineteenth century. Ironically, white Southerners justified the system because it upheld their sense of "honor."[5]

It was within this socially and racially stratified system that over the course of two centuries police organization evolved in the South. Although the Northern experience with immigrants in the cities is similar, it is only remotely so, for the

Southern experience with race is a much more intense, deep, and embedded phenomenon. The nature of crime and violence in the South, the development of slave codes and slave patrols, and the Civil War and Reconstruction experience all contributed to the development of police in the Southern United States.

CRIME AND VIOLENCE IN THE SOUTH

From colonial times through the twentieth century, the South has been filled with crime and violence. During the colonial period, conflict between white settlers and Native Americans reached horrific levels. During this same time period, the murder rate in the South was four times as high as that of densely populated Massachusetts. These rates continued through the twentieth century. Journalist and scholar Fox Butterfield found that statistically "the South, not the 'Wild West' as popularly believed, was the most violent region of the United States." One estimate from 1880 found perhaps as many as forty thousand homicides had been committed in Southern states from the end of the Civil War to that year, whereas a statistical study of violent crime in the South during the early 1920s found the homicide rate in the South was two and one-half times greater than that in the rest of the United States. From 1841 to 1843, the Montgomery circuit court heard eighty-nine separate cases involving violent crime, and this from a county of just less than three thousand white males over the age of fifteen. Pre-Civil War Savannah was rife with murder, assault, and theft. "South of the Smith and Wesson line" was certainly more than just a jestful saying. Homicide found extremely flexible legal support in state laws that defended killing in self-defense and protecting property and in judges who ignored the law to affirm extralegal violence.[6]

Violent behavior in the South touched almost everyone and was indiscriminate. Violence was, indeed, part of Southern culture.[7] Insults and other personal or familial affronts frequently instigated violence, even murder. An entrenched need to defend one's honor resulted in many a bloody affair. Dueling, which was legal in most Southern states until the Civil War, settled many questions, but more often less formal fights to the death ensued, with the results left ignored by law enforcement authorities. Murderous feuds between families and individuals could be found at all levels of the social strata. Law and order did not rule in the South. Instead, a code of honor based upon violent retribution maintained a semblance of order under white rule. These insults included challenging the reputation of a woman, accusations of theft or criminal acts, cheating (Andrew Jackson once fought a duel over the results of a horse race), and other perceived insults to one's "honor." More serious crimes of rape and murder aroused similar demands for vengeance. Although much violent crime involved Whites and Blacks, it frequently manifested itself in attacks of Whites on other Whites and Blacks on other Blacks. From duels to whipping slaves, both criminal and legal or socially accepted violence was commonplace.[8]

This rather dark past of crime and violence remains a public safety problem. At the beginning of the twenty-first century, violent crime rates in the southern states are higher than those in any other region in the United States.[9] Moreover, the number of police officers injured or killed has been and remains consistently higher in the South.[10] There is still a higher rate of firearm ownership in the southern United States than in any other section of the country.[11] The historical combination of crime, violence, and racism confirms the reality that modern-day police departments in this region of the United States developed in a uniquely different environment.

Another universal phenomenon of southern violence was that of the mob. Mob violence pervaded the South much more so than it did the North, where it was indeed quite common. Southerners accepted mob violence as an effective although extralegal means of social control. By using lynch law and the charivari (a mocking ceremony designed to shame the victim), mob action often missed the guilty party by a wide shot. Law enforcement authorities often failed to protect those subjected to mob violence, and in fact, they frequently led or joined the mob. Nonetheless, as long as those to whom the point was directed got the point, the action was justified.

Historian Bertram Wyatt-Brown outlined three factors that made popular white rule based on mob violence more or less permanent in the South. First, the social and power elite accepted and occasionally even led mob action. Second, shaming deviants as an example to others preserved the social order. Third, lynching as a ritual was effective in keeping Blacks under control and in line with white social supremacy. A fourth could be added: law enforcement accepted all three of these factors and did little to dissuade mobs of "citizens" from enforcing the social code. It would not be until the 1930s before these mob acts would become federal crimes and begin to be punished on a consistent basis. The civil rights of Blacks and others who were accused by the mob simply did not exist, before or after the Civil War and Reconstruction reforms.[12]

The punitive charivari type of mob violence took several forms. Normally reserved for lesser offenses, the charivari dated back to ancient Europe as a method of community policing. The purpose was to inflict a lot of shame with a heavy dose of pain. Tar and feathering was popular, as was riding a rail or pine pole through town. Beating often accompanied these shame rituals, along with all sorts of taunts and jeers. In many cases, the charivari was legal, often handed down as punishment from a court of law. In 1796, a South Carolina law allowed for a woman pregnant with a bastard child to be paraded through the town to receive the mob's abuse, mainly sticks and stones and some creative name calling. In Windsor, North Carolina, in 1838, disguised townspeople took drunks from a local tavern on a rough ride in wooden boxes around the village, convincing the deviants that their behavior was not acceptable to the local populace. The use of disguise by the mob was common and traditional and partially explains the hoods of the nascent Ku Klux Klan after the Civil War. As late as 1920, an Arkansas girl was "drummed out" of her community for allegedly sleeping with the husbands of several local wives. She was never seen again, and her family accepted the action as community justice.

Lynching, on the other hand, raised the bar of violence to its ultimate end—death. The purposes were the same, that is, to shame and humiliate, to reap vengeance, and to send a clear message to Blacks and other minorities that Whites remained in control. Blacks more often than not found themselves at the end of the lynch mob's rope, but Whites met the same fate for violating the strict yet informal rules of Southern society. White gamblers caught cheating in Vicksburg, for example, were hung by a mob in order to restore "honor on the insulted citizens." But it was African Americans that bore the brunt of the extralegal violence. From before the Civil War to as late as the 1930s, lynching took place across the United States, but particularly in the South. In many instances, the black victim of a lynching was supposed to have violated a white woman's "honor," when in fact several of these instances, when they actually even occurred, were consensual liaisons. The social code, however, could not allow black "brutes" to have their way with honorable white women.[13]

Police and other local law enforcement authorities, including the courts, did little to stop these extralegal acts. In fact, they often acted as "mediators" between the mob and the local legal institutions. The nature of crime and violence in the South was not reflective of "frontier society" or of lack of established law enforcement organizations. It was, rather, indicative of the traditional custom of community policing and vigilantism that Southerners held on to in order to maintain their unique social order. The same occurred in Northern urban areas as urbanization threatened the established order. The scale, of course, was far greater in the South.[14]

SLAVE CODES AND PATROLS

As police departments formed in the Southern states, the function of "law enforcement" became a consistent task within the listed duties carried out by slave patrols, "white militia," and eventually by city police officers. Included in the list of laws enforced by developing Southern police departments was a substantial number of criminal violations directly supporting slavery, enumerated in slave codes adopted by colonial, and later state, legislatures. Slave patrols became the police organization put in place to ensure that the codes were enforced and that the Southern economic mechanism of slavery was preserved. As the formal tradition of slavery was legally abolished as a result of Union victory in the Civil War, black codes emerged to replace the slave codes in order to sustain Southern society. Southern police departments, as with all police departments, supported and enforced the laws of their jurisdiction. In the words of criminal justice professor Samuel Walker, slave patrols were a "distinctly American form of law enforcement" and constituted the "first modern police forces" in the United States.[15]

Spanish and French slave codes of the seventeenth and eighteenth centuries were designed to protect the slave from his/her master, whereas slave codes in America were meant to do just the opposite. Slaves were a valuable and integral aspect of Southern society, but their condition was indeed precarious. For white slave owners, the worst fear was slave insurrection. A lesser but still serious inconvenience was that a slave, a piece of property according to the code, would run away. Slave codes, then, were designed to keep the slave in his/her place and prevent loss of property and the collapse of the system through insurrection.

Maryland and Virginia were the first to develop slave codes in the 1660s. For the first time in America, black slaves were made slaves for life, as were the children of black female slaves. Over the next fifty years, the codes evolved to define a black slave as a piece of property, giving masters the legal authority to "control" their property through physical discipline (punishment). Interracial marriages were banned in order to prevent mixing of the races—the delineation between White and Black had to be clear and without any blurred lines of racial lineage. A Black came to be defined as a person who had one black great-grandparent. These early codes preserved the social order in which Whites dominated Blacks.

By the mid-nineteenth century, codes across the Southern United States made clear that slaves had no rights as citizens because of their status as property. Even the United States Supreme Court would agree with this interpretation of slaves being human property. In the infamous Dred Scott case (1856), the high court ruled that Dred Scott, a black slave, could not sue for his freedom in a federal court because he was not a citizen; in other words, Scott was a piece of property and therefore not a person and therefore not a citizen. On the other hand, the rights of slave owners were duly protected. All slave states had harsh penalties in place for stealing slaves. Virginia sentenced slave stealers to two to ten years in prison, whereas Tennessee would put away those who dared to steal slaves for up to fifteen years. In some states, stealing slaves was a capital crime.[16]

Again, the federal government concurred by passing the Fugitive Slave Law (1850), which required that runaway slaves captured in free states be returned to their owners. As Boston abolitionist Samuel J. May wrote, it required Northern police officers to ". . . conform that their states should be made the hunting-grounds, and themselves the bloodhounds of Southern oppressors in pursuit of their fleeing slaves."[17]

In Boston just after the Fugitive Slave Law went into effect, U.S. marshals arrested a runaway slave in, of all places, a Cornhill Street coffee shop. When the marshals suspected trouble from an increasingly belligerent crowd of former slaves and free Blacks, they called for assistance from Boston police marshals. Boston city marshals Bigelow and Turkey refused to help. The runaway slave had to be confined in a very insecure federal courtroom. Boston police ignored the situation and looked on with indifference as a mob of free Blacks stormed the courtroom and freed the runaway slave. The conservative press furiously attacked the Boston police for not enforcing the law of the land, whereas liberal and abolitionist newspapers surely applauded their inaction.[18] It should be noted that Bigelow and Turkey were instrumental in creating the organization that became the Boston Police Department.

Even though they had no civil rights, slaves convicted of a capital offense, such as murder or rape, could be and often were executed. In keeping with chattel status, owners of executed slaves were compensated by the state for the loss of their property. Codes forbade a slave from raising his/her hand against any White, in particular his/her master. Slave movements were closely regulated by codes, as was the assembly of slaves off the master's property. In many states, the assembly of five or more slaves away from their owner's land was illegal. Other rules of the code included: forbidding slaves to learn how to read or write; not allowing slaves to preach off of the owner's land; not allowing slaves to own or possess guns, drums, or horns; not allowing slaves to practice medicine; not allowing slaves to possess liquor, gamble, trade with Whites, own animals, or raise their own crops. All of these violations were directed toward two goals—preventing slave insurrection and maintaining the social order.

As with any piece of property, states had what amounted to consumer protection laws worked into their slave codes to regulate the buying or selling of slaves. Along the same lines, slaves could be seized like any other piece of property for nonpayment of debts. In essence, slaves became dehumanized, impersonal objects to be bartered, seized, and sold as mere pieces of property.

Violations of these codes by Whites and Blacks alike were subject to varying enforcement by police, sheriffs, and courts. Many offenders were flogged, sometimes with over one hundred lashes. The death penalty, however, was also common and used extensively on slaves convicted of attempted murder, murder, attempted rape and rape of a white woman, rebellion and attempted rebellion, poisoning, robbery, and arson. Striking one's master was automatic death. Whites who were found guilty of violating these rules in any way were subject to large fines, imprisonment, or flogging. Any White found assisting a slave in escape received the death penalty. Aiding in slave insurrection resulted in the same end. Again, the message was clear—maintain the social order and prevent slave rebellion.

Slave codes did at least try to protect the slave from cruel punishment and unjustified death. The 1740 South Carolina code outlined fines of seven hundred pounds or seven years imprisonment with hard labor for willfully killing a slave. Murdering a slave was not a felony in Georgia and North Carolina until the 1770s. Virginia made murdering a slave the equivalent to murdering a freeman in 1788. North Carolina followed with a similar provision in 1791, and by 1840, most Southern states had like conditions in their codes. Cruelty to slaves was a bit slower to evolve in the codes, however. It would not be until the 1850s that masters and overseers would be fined up to one thousand dollars for inflicting unjust or excessive brutality on slaves.[19]

The following examples just touch the surface of Southern state laws and city ordinances designed to control Blacks and support slavery. In 1842, the U.S. Court of Appeals affirmed the decision of a lower court that fined a man fifty dollars for violating a trading-with-slaves regulation and added one week's imprisonment to the man's sentence. In 1859, Memphis passed an ordinance, common across the South, that made the sale of liquor to "Negroes, slave or free" a criminal offense. The Nashville recorder listed that "one McGoldrick (be fined) $3.00 on each of five charges of selling liquor to slaves." There are countless other examples that cover the range of possible offenses. Gradually, however, these codes fell into the dilemma that, although these slaves were property, they were also human beings. This complicated matters greatly for lawmakers and those charged with enforcing the law. Many states allowed slaves to have public trials, and the constitution of the Republic of Texas even provided that slaves should have trial by impartial juries. It looked good on paper, perhaps, but practice assuredly was another matter.[20]

It is important to recognize that these laws were primarily the enforcement responsibility of Southern police departments, such as they were before the Civil War. The innovative yet dreaded method used to enforce the codes among these rural areas was the slave patrol. Slave patrols became commonplace by the early eighteenth century and were often combined with local militia and police duties. As it became apparent that individual masters and sheriffs could no longer control slaves in a given region, a more organized method of control was necessary. Like the codes themselves, slave patrols were designed to maintain the social order, but their most important function was to root out and prevent slave insurrection.

Slave patrols varied in size and organization but rarely in purpose. Early patrols were usually small and associated with local militia. On horseback, these small groups of well-armed men could cover wide ranges of territory in a relatively short time. Many patrols were mandated by the state, but most had local origins. The local judge could put a patrol into service when needed, and members of the patrol, like the old watch, were paid from the community treasury, usually one dollar per day and five dollars plus any reward for apprehended slaves.[21]

South Carolina's slave patrol law of 1690 dictated that each patrol have ten men under one captain of militia. All white males of age were obligated to serve. From 1737 to 1819, only privileged slave owners could serve, making the patrol a symbol of affluence and honor. In 1819, South Carolina reverted to making all white males eligible for service. Organized in "beat companies," South Carolina slave patrols were split into districts under the supervision of three commissioners to cover territory more efficiently. Each patrol had to inspect each plantation within its district at least once a month and seize any contraband in possession of slaves in violation of the slave code.

Tennessee's patrol system began in 1753 and was administered through county courts. Each court appointed "searchers" to inspect all plantations within the county four times a year. (In 1779, this was changed to once per month.) In 1806, the search system became a patrol system. Each county's militia commander organized and controlled the patrols in his county. Police commissioners in each town, as well as justices of the peace, were also authorized to appoint patrols when needed. By 1856, the Tennessee slave code further mandated that all slave owners patrol their own properties.

Kentucky used its slave patrol system as a traditional police mechanism. In addition to patrolling for runaway slaves, Kentucky slave patrols also roved the territory for highwaymen and other threats to the peace. In some counties, the patrols operated twenty-four hours a day, seven days a week. A tax of one dollar per slave was levied on slave owners to pay for the patrols. North Carolina's police patrol system was legislated in 1794. Under the control of justice of the peace and attached to local militia units, North Carolina's patrols visited each plantation in their districts every two weeks. Flogging was allowed, but the lash limit was set at a comparatively humane fifteen on any slave caught in minor violation of the slave code. In 1802, the patrols were detached from the militia and placed under the sole jurisdiction of county courts. Police on these patrols were paid through a slave levy similar to that in Kentucky and were exempt from jury duty and even given a break on county taxes.

Georgia enacted its police patrols in 1757 and was organized like North Carolina's patrol system. Mississippi's patrols started under the jurisdiction of federal troops and state militia units but were transferred in 1831 to county police boards. Each board appointed patrol captains who in turn commanded five-man detachments. At least a portion of each detachment had to be slave owners, and those citizens refusing to serve on patrols were subject to fines. Runaway slaves captured by patrols netted thirty dollars, one-fourth of which was paid by the state and the other three-fourths of which was paid by the slave's owner. Alabama's patrol system was similar and required from three to five slave owners for each patrol.

Slave patrols and militia often acted as police in cities and towns where no formal police had been organized, mainly for the purpose of keeping an eye on Blacks. In fact, patrols often evolved into police forces for cities, becoming permanent paid forces in places like Richmond, Raleigh, Charleston, and New Orleans. These police systems often accounted for the largest expenditure for city budgets. Blacks caught by police patrols or watchmen on city streets after dark were promptly arrested and subject to public whipping. With the heavy presence of patrols and police guards throughout the city, Charleston, according to one foreign visitor, resembled a military post after dark. When a city reached a size where the old citizen patrol system no longer proved adequate, a paid patrol force became the de facto police.

Often, poor Whites served on patrols, giving them a false pretense of security by keeping Blacks from challenging their position on the social ladder. These poor Whites often abused slaves while on patrol and even set up slaves in illegal trade schemes and other violations of the slave code. Masters and slaves alike often complained about the brutality of these patrols. Yet, the patrols did their job well and instilled terror among slaves. Poor Whites often made up patrols because many slave owners were able to buy out their required service for a nominal fee, much like the wealthy could do to avoid watch service in the colonial period. Without slave owners on patrols consistently, poor Whites were more apt to abuse their service.

Slave rebellion, of course, dominated much of the patrols' time, as rumors spread constantly about possible insurrection. Most of the time, white vigilance

Woodcut scenes of Nat Turner's rebellion, Southampton County, Virginia, 1831.
(Library of Congress)

prevented insurrection from ever taking place, but when it did break out, such as in the case of Nat Turner's rebellion in 1831, slave patrols, the militia, and local law enforcement sprang quickly into action with brutal results.

The concept of the slave patrol was an amazingly effective system for maintaining social order and preventing slave runaways and rebellion. Considering that slave patrols operated through the American Revolution and the creation of the United States, when securing individual rights against the fear of centralized authority was at its height, the very idea of organized patrols that had the power and authority to enter private property without cause or warrant is astounding. Moreover, the brutal nature of slave patrols against Blacks and the assumption that all Blacks off their owner's property were up to no good directly influenced the behavior of police departments, many of which were organized during the time of slave patrols. The violent racism of slave patrols and the separate and unequal treatment of Blacks through slave codes became institutionalized in Southern policing. With that in mind, it is important to point out that the largest law enforcement organization in the United States in 1837, seven years after Peel's Metropolitan Police Act and before the widespread organization of police departments in the Northern United States, was in Charleston, where the slave patrol had approximately one hundred members. The Civil War and the lengthy Reconstruction that followed, unfortunately, did little to alleviate this state of affairs.[22]

CIVIL WAR AND RECONSTRUCTION

During the Civil War, the Confederacy not only fought the Union from without but also faced the serious threat of widespread slave rebellion and public disorder from within. This forced the Southern states to invest more money and manpower into slave patrols, which were both badly needed for the Confederate armies. As Union forces occupied Confederate territory and freed slaves, the police function of slave patrols grew increasingly questionable. Some patrols simply turned into bands of marauding terrorists, whereas others just disintegrated. Police in the cities likewise came under great stress as Union armies took over police duties. During Reconstruction, police took the place of slave patrols in preventing insurrection by free Blacks and maintaining the social order. The tradition of detection and prevention by patrol was sustained. Indeed, the war served to advance the transition from slave patrol to police force.[23]

Richmond and Charleston typify the Southern police experience during the war. Richmond's population tripled in less than a year after becoming the Confederate capital in 1861. Richmond police patrols grew accordingly to handle the growth. By December 1861, Richmond had eleven day patrolmen and seventy-two men working the beat at night. Crime increased, which took police attention away from their primary duty of watching the city's black population. In fact, police arrested many more Whites than Blacks during the war years. Still, Richmond police could not keep pace with growing crime and public disorder, forcing Confederate President Jefferson Davis to declare martial law in March 1862. A military police force took over law enforcement duties and commanded the Richmond police department. Police under a provost martial worked fairly well in Richmond, as the increased size of the police force and the expanded police powers of martial law allowed Richmond finally to control both slaves and crime with some success. Charleston underwent a similar transformation, turning urban slave patrol duties over to a provost marshal. City guards were ordered to arrest any Black without a pass in and around the city. Militia units helped police in patrol duties. In both Richmond and Charleston, civil defense made policing crime and slaves a difficult but feasible undertaking.[24]

Atlanta's police experience during the war is of special note. Perhaps the most important city in the Confederacy next to Richmond, Atlanta served as a major railroad hub and supply center for Confederate forces. With troops and refugees flooding in and out of the city from late 1861 through the end of the war in 1865, policing the city was indeed a challenging task as police faced the problems brought by war while having to maintain the traditional social order through the slave code at the same time.

Surprisingly, controlling Blacks in Atlanta did not prove that difficult. Cases involving runaways and other violations of the slave code did not change dramatically until mid-1864, just before Atlanta fell in the path of General William Tecumseh Sherman's Union forces. Runaway slaves found sanctuary in the chaotic suburbs and often were able to hide out for weeks before being apprehended. Whites openly violated the slave codes by hiring Blacks for wage-paying jobs normally held by Whites. War had made it a necessity, yet city leaders worried that the social order might be under threat as Blacks took more liberties and often flaunted their newfound but still weak earning power.

The more serious problem was white rowdyism, vandalism, and theft. The large influx of poor white refugees threatened public order much more than Blacks did. The Fulton County court dealt with cases involving many more Whites than bonded slaves and black refugees. Larceny and burglary became the most popular crimes and often involved Confederate soldiers on post in Atlanta. Rowdyism more commonly involved soldiers and white juveniles in the city, which should come as no surprise considering the explosion of gambling houses, saloons, and dens of prostitution. Murder rates rose, but not dramatically. The only blip in the rates came in the first three months of 1864, when seven people were violently killed in the city.

Civic leaders knew their city was in trouble but often reacted too late to stem the growing tide of disorder. A "Committee of Safety" met with little success and lasted only a short time. More watchmen and police were hired, but with most worthy candidates gone to war, the pickings proved rather slim. As a result, Atlanta had a police force made up of the poor, elderly, and the not-so-honest element. By mid-1862, the crisis had reached a point that many citizens began calling for martial law and military police to maintain what little order remained in Atlanta. Military police took over in June 1862 and immediately issued an order prohibiting the sale of alcohol. Such policies were hard to enforce, however, and over the next several weeks military police waffled back and forth on closing saloons and regulating the sale of intoxicating liquors.

General Braxton Bragg finally declared martial law in August 1862. Policing Atlanta became the top priority, as military decrees now overrode local ordinances. It did not last, however, as the traditional fears of centralized authority and standing armies rekindled the desire of local citizens to regain control of military police in the city. By the end of September, martial law was done. Nonetheless, the situation worsened, as civic leaders gradually lost control over the military police. By early 1864, the military police operated independently of command structures and even began looting while on patrol.

The regular Atlanta police had a rough time of it during the war. The force doubled in size, from fourteen to twenty-eight. The largest obstacle facing police leaders was again finding qualified, trustworthy men to serve. Though the force never exceeded thirty men at any one time during the war, forty-eight policemen were found guilty of misconduct; twenty-two were dismissed. Charges ranged from drunkenness while on duty to extortion and illegal arrest. In 1864, Atlanta appointed a city marshal to organize patrols to assist police, but the attempt to adapt a rural police method to the extreme conditions of a large, wartime city failed miserably.

Although Northern cities made steady progress in police development during the war, Atlanta and other Southern cities failed to make substantial advances in organization and effectiveness and often ended up worse off than they were before the war. This failure is certainly understandable, however. The extremes of wartime conditions and the complete lack of support from state and national governments, both of which were focused on other issues, contributed to the failure of city police to effectively maintain order.[25]

The Civil War may have ended in 1865, but the former states of the Confederacy continued the fight in a lengthy and violent political battle against the radical Reconstruction policies of the Republican-dominated Congress. In the end, reconstruction failed, allowing the former Confederate states to pass laws designed to maintain control of recently freed Blacks. These new black codes and Jim Crow laws creatively, if not blatantly, deprived Blacks of their newly won civil rights. Once again, enforcement of these laws fell to police and other local law enforcement agencies.

The black codes forbade interracial marriage, prevented Blacks from testifying against Whites in court, made it illegal for freed slaves to own firearms, and gave arrest authority to Whites in situations where Blacks left their place of employment before their contract was completed. To assist with the enforcement of black codes, provisional Mississippi Governor William L. Sharkey proposed the formulation of "Volunteer Companies" to patrol each county. These "extralegal posses, gangs of white men empowered to discipline African Americans outside the law," were nothing more than a continuance of the old slave patrol system in organization and purpose.[26] Like the slave patrols of old, these new volunteer companies often brutalized Blacks for no cause and often overreacted when making arrests.

THE RIOT IN NEW ORLEANS—THE FREEDMEN'S PROCESSION MARCHING TO THE INSTITUTE—THE STRUGGLE FOR THE FLAG.
[SKETCHED BY THEODORE R. DAVIS.]

THE RIOT IN NEW ORLEANS—SIEGE AND ASSAULT OF THE CONVENTION BY THE POLICE AND CITIZENS.—SKETCHED BY THEODORE R. DAVIS.
[SEE PAGE 504.]

Images from *Harper's Weekly* of riots protesting the Freedmen's Convention in New Orleans, August 1866, in which police and a white mob attacked the convention hall. (Library of Congress)

Police departments across the South either organized for the first time or reorganized to meet Reconstruction standards. In many cases, police officials under the prewar system simply took up their posts again. The militia-like nature of slave patrols and volunteer companies survived the war in the newly organized police departments. Blacks during Reconstruction probably had more contact with white police than with any other government entity. In addition to maintaining public order, police therefore also became the upholders of white supremacy in their communities.[27]

The official histories of Southern police departments, when they even go back to the Civil War period, often glorify the fact that a Confederate officer served as police chief, marshal, or commissioner, but say little of the racial and social attitudes that were subsequently perpetuated in police organizations. Savannah, Georgia, provides a good example. Organized in 1852, the Savannah Police Department had eighty-six men under a police captain operating both a day and a night watch. Often criticized as ineffective, efforts to improve the force met with little success. The night watch was disbanded in 1859, but by 1860, the Savannah police had not yet lived up to their potential. The Civil War forced the issue. During the war, Yankees threatened the city more than criminals did, as police spent more time drilling than preventing crime. Union troops occupied Savannah in 1864, replacing police and local militia, who were forced to surrender their arms. After the war, Confederate General Robert Anderson, a West Point graduate, reorganized the Savannah Police Department and served as its chief until 1888. Riots broke out during the 1868 presidential election, killing two Savannah police officers. The end of the war did not end political conflict between North and South by any means.[28]

Mobile, Alabama, had a similar experience. In 1850, the fledgling Mobile police force had thirty men under three marshals. In 1856, Mobile appointed its first chief of police, Stephen Charpentier. Charpentier left to serve in the Confederate Army in 1861, leaving two interim chiefs to run the department during the war. He survived and returned as chief of police in 1865. In 1867, as part of the Union military occupation of Mobile, Union General Charles Dimon took over the Mobile police force until 1870. From that point, a series of former Confederate officers served as chief of police until the 1880s.[29]

The Savannah and Mobile experiences were typical, as officers of the Confederate army frequently served as police chiefs or captains in reorganized departments, just as they became mayors, congressmen, senators, and governors. These leaders brought their prewar values on white authority and race to municipal policing, which in turn served to perpetuate institutional racism in Southern police organizations. Even the rank and file of police during this time reflect the continuation of these values in policing. In New Orleans, police superintendent D. S. Gaster began his police career in 1867, just as Reconstruction began. In 1870, he was promoted to corporal and soon after to sergeant. By 1877, he had become a detective, and in 1879, he was assigned as an aide to the chief of police. He continued in this assignment until 1890 when the Board of Police Commissioners elected him Superintendent of Police.[30]

Reconstruction should have preserved civil rights for freed Blacks and established proper civil and police institutions, but it did not. Instead, the Reconstruction era saw unparalleled violence against Blacks and Whites who sympathized with their plight by marauding gangs reminiscent of slave patrols, the most infamous of which was the Ku Klux Klan. Some police departments reluctantly hired Blacks on their forces to satisfy demands brought on by Reconstruction. Montgomery and Vicksburg actually had large numbers of Blacks on their police forces for a brief time, but most places, like Norfolk, had only a token few. As would be expected, black police officers made Whites extremely nervous—a black police officer directly threatened the white-dominated social order. White citizens taunted black policemen and often paid them no heed. A Columbia, South Carolina, incident in 1876, just before Reconstruction ended, foreshadowed the end of black police in the South for the near future. A shootout between black policemen and white civilians resulted in the death of one white man. The city could have erupted in a race riot, much like would occur in the early twentieth century, but fortunately, calmer heads prevailed. Groups of white vigilantes rode through black sections of town but met no resistance or provocation. Blacks equated the vigilantes with the old slave patrols and dared not oppose them. Whites had made it clear that they would continue to use violence and fear to keep Blacks intimidated and under control. Black police were, for the time being, forgotten.

Reconstruction failed because Northerners grew sick and tired of the lack of progress and Southerners refused to accept total defeat. By 1876, in order to preserve unification, a congressional deal had to be cut to declare a winner (Rutherford B. Hayes) in the presidential election and end Reconstruction. By prematurely ending Reconstruction, Southern state and local governments were able to return to business as usual. Southern Reconstruction was the victim of America's inability to endure. Thus, the first national attempt to resolve the question of minority rights was abandoned in just over ten years. Rights for the minority were sacrificed for decentralized authority and local home rule, both traditions in American political development. Police fit this paradigm, as control returned to local citizens—white citizens. Although slavery had been abolished and constitutional rights were established for Blacks, the structure and thinking of Southern society had changed very little, and would not change again for one hundred years.[31]

Racism was not limited to the postwar South. An Indiana rhyme written in the 1880s "for young Democrats" reflects the level of racism in post-Civil War America:

> "Sing a song of shotguns,
>   Pocket full of knives,
> Four-and-twenty black men;
>   Running for their lives:
> When the polls are open
>   Shut the nigger's mouth,
> Isn't that a bully way
>   To make a solid South?"

The problems of racism during the late 1800s and early 1900s, were pervasive in America.[32] Many police departments crystallized their organizational structure, operational theory, and values during the years surrounding the Civil War and Reconstruction and could not escape the plague of racism that survived the Civil War and Reconstruction. Selective law enforcement based upon race continues to this day.[33]

CONCLUSION

The Southern police department paradigm has existed for a long time. Institutional racism in Southern policing has arguably spread to other parts of the country. From the 1700s through the Civil War and Reconstruction and even today, Southern police departments have been functioning within this paradigm. American police have been influenced by several important factors from the Southern police experience. First, from the active patrol function of slave patrols, Southern police departments utilized patrol as a policing technique for crime prevention. Although this important policing concept occurred in the historical setting of Southern slavery, it has developed into a major police function. Second, a strong commitment to states' rights and suspicion of centralized authority have contributed to the Southern dedication to local control over police functions. Third, with almost unlimited authority, combined with a lack of training and supervision, the racial abuse of power by those with police authority has been a constant problem.[34]

The modern principles of police officer discipline and discretion were not in place as Southern policing developed. Experience and necessity in preserving the social order and preventing slave insurrection became the only acceptable guides to developing police functions in the South. If slaves and criminals resisted or used violence, their resistance was overcome with stronger violence. Force was met with overwhelming force, the consequences of which were rarely viewed as inappropriate or illegal. There were few written police policies or procedures, which left individual regulators, slave patrols, and police officers to use their own independent judgment.[35] The use of words, lashes, clubs, or firearms rested solely with the individual officer. In the end, preserving both the system and the white rule overcame any squeamishness about civil rights and racism, and the work of the slave patrols evolved into the primary purpose of Southern police. Still, it is important to understand that although institutional racism in police departments can be traced to the slave patrol and police experience of the South, much of the recent problems between Blacks and police are more a reflection of contemporary misunderstandings than of leftover historical conflicts.[36]

CHAPTER 4

POLICING THE AMERICAN WEST

INTRODUCTION

The history of law enforcement in the American frontier West represents an interesting chapter in the story of American police development. The rugged transition from frontier culture to urban society provided fertile ground for crime and violence. Establishing and sustaining effective police was indeed a challenge for newly settled citizens. The development of law enforcement practices and organization, the nature of violence and crime in the West, and the path of vigilantism and police reform provide an interesting examination of the frontier West. This is a period in American history, much like colonial times, when regional differences, social conflict, and economic competition played such a dominant role in building community in an untamed land.

The men and women of the westward migration moving across the Great Plains into Nebraska, the Dakotas, Colorado, Wyoming, Montana, Utah, and Oregon brought with them preconceived ideas about law enforcement but found little organization in that regard when they arrived and began settling small communities and towns. Building a sense of community often guided the development of law enforcement in the American West, as settlers became citizens, often using unorthodox means to rid their towns of crime. When American settlers crossed the frontier in the 1800s on their way to Texas, the Southwest, and California, they found nonnative people already established, complete with organized communities and a system of justice. For Americans moving into areas occupied by Hispanics for well over one hundred years, early law enforcement development represented an amalgamation of cultural ideas regarding justice and policing the community.

In the other regions of the West, settlers encountered indigenous peoples with no sense of order that they as foreigners found adaptable. Native communities often utilized police systems that relied on rehabilitation instead of on extensive punishment. Police in native groups varied. Although the Comanche, for example, had no recognizable police, the Cherokee had an organized force of "regulators," and the Choctaw Nation used a highly effective band of mounted police. Because many of these peoples were nomadic, the more familiar icons of European justice, such as court buildings and jails, were impractical if not impossible. Serious offenses often resulted in some sort of social isolation for the accused. "Lynching," in the American sense of the term, was rare in native communities, as those charged with serious crimes, such as murder, were quickly isolated from revenge-seeking villagers. These concepts of justice and policing proved beyond the cultural and racial acceptance of the new settlers coming west. Thus, left to their own experience and common sense, these new settlers gradually overcame lawlessness to establish order and civility in their communities in their own way.[1]

Among the significant developments for the future of law enforcement in these Americanized lands, several stand out as the West transformed into a settled normalized community. First, the nature of crime and violence in the West influenced how citizens responded to lawlessness. Second, regional development, exemplified by the merging of Mexican and American law enforcement and justice systems in conquered areas during the War with Mexico, influenced the transformation of law enforcement in the Southwest. Third, establishing order through vigilantism is one of the more fascinating social phenomena of the frontier West that played an important role in law enforcement development. Fourth, the reform of police forces in the West is an important part of the transition from frontier society to stable communities and is an experience shared with the rest of the nation during the Progressive Era. Related to this was the attempt to establish Native American police forces on reservations as part of the civilizing process of federal Indian policy. Of course, no law enforcement history of the American West would be complete without mentioning the United States Marshals Service, a fixture of the lore and legend of the West, and private security agencies that came with the railroad. Finally, the development of the first state police force west of the Mississippi, the Texas Rangers, remains distinctive as an example of communities moving beyond local law enforcement.

THE NATURE OF CRIME IN THE WEST

The lack of community organization and law enforcement made proactive policing in the modern sense extremely difficult in the West. Settlers had to be reactive, thus ignoring causes of crime and violence. The nascent police reform movement in the East simply did not apply to frontier conditions during the early stage of community development. Crime came from similar sources in the West as it did in the East, from where many settlers originated. Political rivalry and socioeconomic conflict caused most of the problems either unilaterally or in combination. Crime varied from theft, prostitution, and arson to assault, rape, and murder.[2]

Social and economic conflict came readily as predominantly Anglo-American settlers clashed with the many ethnic groups that were already either in the West or migrating alongside Anglo-Americans. Competition for natural resources and economic gain brought Anglo-Americans into conflict against Mexicans, Chinese, Native Americans, freed Blacks, Irish, and even Scandinavians. In some cases, these ethnic groups turned on each other, as did Anglo-Americans. This competition went hand in hand with ethnic prejudice, occasionally resulting in violence. Many Mexicans lost their land and homes following the Mexican Cession to the United States and were subsequently treated as second-class citizens. The Chinese suffered cruel discrimination, particularly in California. Clashes between Chinese and Irish, especially during the building of the transcontinental railroad, sometimes reached tragic proportions.

Social and economic conflict often went beyond ethnic differences. Simple economic gain provided many opportunities for disagreements, even for small wars, over economic resources in the West. The classic example remains cattlemen and sheepherders, but more often than not it was powerful cattle barons battling less powerful ranchers over grazing lands and access to water for herds, such as the Johnson County War in Wyoming. Mining was another battleground, pitting miners against mining corporations. Just as unions organized and fought for better pay and working conditions in the factories of the East, so too did the miners of the West. In addition, just as in the East, strikes occasionally turned violent, as in the Ludlow, Colorado, incident in 1913.

Political conflict could be violent as well. Many settlers moving west after the Civil War, and even before, brought political baggage from the North and South with them to the new settlements. Disagreements over slavery, states' rights, economic policies, and other regionalized issues easily sparked arguments that sometimes exploded into blazing fits of violence. The most extreme case was "Bleeding Kansas" of the 1850s, as proslavery gangs battled abolitionist forces in what amounted to a civil war, killing hundreds. Political conflict also manifested itself in local power struggles, often intertwined with social and economic issues.[3]

Western mythology, however, continues to confuse a more accurate popular understanding of crime and violence on the frontier. A particular example is the cattle towns of Western legend. Abilene, Dodge City, Fort Worth, and other end-of-the-trail railroad hubs for getting cattle to the slaughterhouses of Chicago and other Midwestern cities are notorious in popular culture as places of extreme violence and death. In fact, these cattle towns averaged only one and one-half homicides per year during the peak cattle drive years of the nineteenth century, and no cattle town recorded more than five murders in any one year, a remarkable statistic considering the presence of some of the worst outlaws and "gunslingers" in American history.[4]

Mining camps and towns followed a similar path, except for homicide. Homicide rates for places such as Bodie and Aurora, both in California, far exceeded any community in the West at the time, as well as any city in the United States today. Bodie boasted a murder rate, converted, of 116 per 100,000 population. The average today in the United States is around 10 per 100,000. The best studies of violence and crime in mining communities have been conducted in Bodie and Aurora and in several similar communities in Colorado. Ironically, again going against the myth of the violent West, crimes common by today's standards, such as burglary, assault, and rape, were exceedingly rare in these communities. Homicide, on the other hand, was abnormally high. Most murders in both Bodie and Aurora are attributed to fights caused by excessive drinking.[5]

The law and law enforcement faced difficult tasks in bringing these conflicts under control. Both were often part of the conflict, through corruption, conflict of interest, or political favoritism. Many sheriffs and marshals obtained their positions through corrupt political appointments or irregular voting practices. The local judge, for example, could be the largest landowner in the area. There were indeed many opportunities to corrupt attempts to deal effectively with social, economic, and political conflict in the West. Historian Richard White described this situation this way: "The reality of social conflict in the West creates another reading of Western history. It is a more mixed story of how law and government repressed some violence and provoked other violence."[6] Dealing with crime and violence in the West was indeed an intrinsic part of building communities and creating society in the West.

SPANISH AND HISPANIC INFLUENCES

Justice and law enforcement in frontier New Spain and later in Mexico (Mexico won its independence from Spain in 1821) carried a heavy paternalistic realism in practice and tradition while serving a socially and economically stratified community. Wealthy land-owning *patrónes* sat atop a feudal-like system of peonage, with indebted *peones* (or peasants) working small plots of land or as wage laborers on the large *haciendas*. At the bottom of the socioeconomic strata were local native peoples, many of whom had adopted Catholicism and spoke Spanish.

To maintain order and administer justice in this frontier society, the Spanish government instituted the traditional *alcalde* (or chief governing official) system. Spanish territorial possessions, including what would become the American Southwest and Texas, were divided into *alcaldías* (or jurisdictions). Each jurisdiction had an appointed *alcalde mayor* (or magistrate), who acted as both mayor and judge in criminal and civil cases. (Important cases were normally forwarded to the territorial governor, who would then act as judge.) The *alcalde* was usually a local *patrón* who had extraordinary power in local affairs, including justice. In this case, judge and sheriff were one and the same. The system's record was spotty, stained with inconsistency, corruption, and abuse of power, particularly by the *alcaldes*.

Independence in 1821 brought a predictable desire to distance the new Mexican state from its Spanish colonial predecessor. Accordingly, one of the first areas the new government reformed was the administration of justice and law enforcement. Many Mexican citizens, especially those of the lower classes, wanted judicial and law enforcement functions separate from the executive duties in the *alcaldías*. The corruption of the *alcaldes* remained fresh in their memory.

The Mexican government responded with well-intentioned judicial reform. Territories, including New Mexico and California, were divided into large districts (New Mexico, for example, had three districts), with a prefect overseeing each area. The *alcaldes mayores* continued to administrate *partidos* (or subdistricts) within the district. At the precinct level, *alcaldes ordinarios* acted as judges and became known as *juez de paz* (or justices of the peace). *Alguacils* (or bailiffs) acted as law enforcement officers in each precinct and subdistrict.

On paper, this all looked well and good, but the reality in frontier territories proved to be quite different. The central government in Mexico City remained out of touch with conditions in the far-off territories. In what remained a relatively sparse frontier population, men with legal training were few and far between. Moreover, the new Mexican republic was too weak to oversee its reforms effectively in the faraway territories; thus, corruption and petty influence with inconsistent justice and law enforcement remained. Still, local communities were apparently satisfied with the status quo as the *alcaldes*, justices of the peace, and bailiffs, despite their lack of training, used common sense and local custom to solve disputes and enforce, although occasionally selectively, the law. The system was administered reasonably well considering its shortcomings. Despite the local politics that occasionally influenced justice, the people felt safe.[7]

BLENDING OF OLD AND NEW

Enter here the American migration west. Land-hungry settlers from the United States began pouring into Mexican Texas during the 1820s. The Santa Fe Trail opened New

Mexico to foreign (American) trade in 1821, bringing traders and trappers in greater numbers from the United States and Canada. By 1835, the new Texians, as they called themselves, were well on their way to gaining independence from Mexico. By 1848, what had been the Mexican territory in the Southwest, including Texas, was annexed by the United States by statehood for Texas in 1845 and by the huge Mexican Cession resulting from the American victory in the War with Mexico (1846–1848).

Arizona and New Mexico represent areas in which law enforcement grew from a cultural mix brought about by conquest. The American conquerors who occupied the Southwest during and after the War with Mexico took what was already in place, put an American stamp on it, and then let an already working system continue to function with minimal modification. This experience was similar to that of the Roman Empire, where the practice of using local customs that work and placate the masses proved quite successful.

The man behind this process during the War with Mexico was Brevet Brigadier General Stephen W. Kearny. Marching through the Southwest to secure California, Kearny claimed New Mexico and Arizona along the way. His Army of the West occupied Santa Fe peacefully in August 1846, a significant feat made possible in large part by an already thriving community of American traders that had been in and around Santa Fe and on the Santa Fe Trail for many years. The governor of New Mexico, Manuel Armijo, put out a call to arms, but his people had no stomach for conflict and readily accepted American occupation. Armijo fled south to Chihuahua in disgrace.

Kearny immediately set about trying to soothe the fears of the now-occupied civilian population. Upon entering Santa Fe, he issued a proclamation explaining to the population that the laws of the United States now had jurisdiction in New Mexico and that the Americans had come as "friends, not as enemies, as protectors, not as conquerors."[8]

Exceeding his orders but acting in a practical manner considering the situation and lack of communication with Washington, Kearny installed a civilian territorial government made mostly of Americans who lived in Taos and Santa Fe. He provided the new government with a constitution and legal code, collectively known as the Kearny Code. The new code borrowed freely from law codes in Missouri, Texas, and Mexico. From the Kearny Code, new law enforcement regulations and jurisdictions were created.[9]

Kearny used the same Mexican districts and *partidos* to create new judicial and law enforcement jurisdictions in New Mexico territory. The three districts became judicial circuits, whereas the seven *partidos* served as counties. Kearny kept the prefect office to administer each district and maintained the *alcaldes*, though with fewer powers. The old offices of the Mexican system simply changed titles: the *alcalde ordinario* was now the justice of the peace; the *soto alguacil* was now the constable; and the *alguacil mayor* became the sheriff. Precincts and justices of the peace provided the foundation of the new system.

The new territorial governor, Charles Bent, appointed sheriffs, including four Hispanics, to each county. The Kearny Code outlined the duties and conduct of the sheriffs. They issued warrants and subpoenas, maintained order, operated the county jail, and had the power to organize the *posse comitatus* when the need arose (and well it might, considering that the smallest county then in New Mexico was 1,961 square miles, whereas the largest was 125,508 square miles). They also collected taxes, for which they had to file a bond to ensure proper collection. Terms were for two years with an annual salary of two hundred dollars plus a take on collected fees. Constables had similar duties and equal power but only within the precincts of the county and were designated deputy sheriffs. To further illustrate the extent of cultural blending, through 1912 (when New Mexico achieved statehood), of the 349 men who served as sheriff in New Mexico, 206 were Hispanic.

Arizona, so sparsely populated and wild, was left alone, except for the presence of a few U.S. Marshals, until the territory was officially organized in 1863. Three judicial districts served alongside four counties, each with a sheriff. The major difference, however, was that the Anglo-Americans of Arizona removed all vestiges of the old New Mexico territory from its civic administration. English became the official language for law courts and other civic business, and Hispanics were shut out from community participation. The roots of Arizona's organization, however, reflect the framework of the Kearny Code.

Under this system, sheriffs and constables functioned fairly well. With the help of the U.S. Army busily fighting Indians, sheriffs and constables were able to focus on their immediate duties, which included keeping the peace and occasionally chasing *desperados*. As we know from the more colorful history of the American West, that, in and of itself, was a full-time job. This system stayed in place throughout the territorial periods of both New Mexico and Arizona, and even statehood did not change the duties much, as both remained predominately rural, sparsely populated areas.[10]

ESTABLISHING ORDER—VIGILANTISM

In the Rocky Mountain region, the Great Plains, and the Northwest, where Spanish influence did not extend, American settlers moved onto virgin soil as far as justice and law enforcement were concerned. Seeing little that might be adaptable in Native American justice systems, these settlers relied on their own knowledge, experience, and common sense to establish order and build communities. In these areas, and even in places previously occupied by Spain and Mexico, citizens took matters into their own hands through committees of vigilance, an extralegal method of administering justice and law enforcement.

A lawless element often either preceded the westward movement or arrived hot on its heels. Cattle towns, mining camps, and trail stations all had rough beginnings. As more people moved West to make their living, however, tolerance for lawlessness became less accepted. With the absence of already established law enforcement, citizens had to take matters into their own hands until normalized law enforcement could evolve and maintain order. Thus, the story of law enforcement in many regions of the Western frontier followed a path of vigilantism on its way to normalized police forces based upon models more common in the Midwestern and Eastern United States.

Committees of vigilance could be found throughout the newly settled West, exercising extralegal authority in the name of establishing order. Law enforcement by citizenry was not an idea unique to the American frontier in the latter half of the nineteenth century. Vigilantism followed the frontier all the way from the earliest English settlements on the Atlantic seaboard. This phase of enforcement, occasionally justified and often abused, may be the one thing that unites the law enforcement experience of the entire nation.[11]

The lynching of John Heith at Tombstone, Arizona, February 1884. Heith was implicated along with five other men for killing three men and one woman during the robbery of a Goldwater-Castenada general store in December 1883. The other five men were apprehended later and legally hanged in March 1884. (National Archives)

Scholars continue to study vigilantism on the Western frontier. Far from being isolated incidents of "lawlessness and disorder," so-called lynch parties and committees of vigilance were more a response to the rapid growth of Western settlements and the desire to organize stable communities. Economic and social development seem to be the generally accepted concepts to explain why honest citizens, sheriffs, judges, lawyers, and others, tolerated extralegal activities to repress crime in their communities. Although familiar with the law, during this disorderly phase of community development, few in positions of authority had the patience for due process when their towns suffered from hooliganism, overcrowded jails, and expensive courts. Allowing the local citizens to take matters into their own hands often proved the more convenient, economically viable solution. This socially constructive vigilantism was effective in many instances. Reacting to disorder that the absence of police or other established law enforcement could not seem to handle, citizens did not reject law and order in turning to vigilantism: they simply became the law, judge, and jury, and on occasion executioner. Consider that a town trying to attract new businesses, a railroad depot, or the like, could ill afford a reputation as a den of outlaws. Community vigilantism often provided a quick fix to run miscreants out of town when the stakes for economic and community development were indeed high.[12]

The popular notion of vigilantism centers on mob rule and the horrible scenes of lynching in the early twentieth century. For many communities across the Western frontier, this was simply not the case. For example, in California during the gold rush years following 1849, popular action was widely accepted as the best and surest way to deal with the rapid growth of gold fever wrought upon small communities and towns. Newspaper accounts rarely referred to the people's court as "the mob." It was not until the 1860s, when community economic and social development advanced enough for prominent citizens to frown upon vigilantism, that the word "mob" began to appear in a derogatory fashion. By then, with better organized law enforcement, judicial circuits, and the decline of the wild-camp-like character of many of these localities, the anxious need to establish order had subsided.

Nevertheless, while it flourished, vigilantism challenged law enforcement authorities and in some cases defied sheriffs, police, judges, and even governors. The accused were hauled out of courtrooms, taken from jails, and occasionally given punishment without ever being arrested or formally charged. In most cases, the unfortunate criminal was simply run out of town. Still, extralegal punishments and executions, notably hangings, were all too common as violations of due process. Crimes included vagrancy, drunkenness, lewdness, prostitution, theft, and arson. Of course, horse or cattle theft and murder were the most serious offenses that earned the fury of vigilant citizens.[13]

Two of the worst periods of vigilantism in the American West occurred in the latter half of the nineteenth century. In 1884, vigilantes in northern and eastern Montana claimed thirty-five lives. In Texas, from 1880 to 1896, the San Saba County "mob" executed twenty-five men. Other major movements included such places as Las Vegas, New Mexico; Seattle, Washington; the Niobrara River area of northern Nebraska; the Creek Nation in the Indian Territory (Oklahoma); and Johnson County, Wyoming. At least 150 persons fell victim to vigilante justice in the 1880s and 1890s.[14]

It is important to remember that despite this extralegal violence the people's court had the best intention in mind: that is, to establish and maintain order in their communities. Overall, vigilantism did not approach the maniacal anarchy depicted on the Hollywood screen. The closest vigilantism came to destroying local societies was after order had been established and local law enforcement was recognized as legitimate and functional. Only then did citizen justice achieve its fearful potential. In these cases when concerned citizens returned to popular justice, incidents of this brand of vigilantism proved sporadic. It would not be until the early twentieth century that vigilantism would take on its more popularly known character of widespread racially and ethnically motivated executions.[15]

One of the more interesting cases of vigilantism at work in the American West is the committee of vigilance of San Francisco. Experiencing rapid population and economic growth resulting from the gold rush of 1849, San Francisco became a haven for thieves, gamblers, prostitutes, conmen, among other unpleasant sorts. Overburdened and corrupt police and courts failed to deal with the growing crime problem.

In 1851, concerned citizens of San Francisco decided to take action and formed their first vigilance committee. Fearing that San Francisco's growing reputation as a "den of sin" would hurt business, local merchants organized this committee to

Lynch law at work in San Francisco as depicted by the *Illustrated London News* of July 12, 1856. (Library of Congress)

clean up the town. Over seven hundred vigilantes participated as police and in courts, and over several months forced a decline in crime with the public's approval and gratitude. It all started out innocently enough, but more immigrants settling in the area and a return of crime changed the scene.

By 1856, the city had come under the control of a Democratic political machine using immigrants, particularly Irish, as its base of political support. Corruption and crime were again on the rise. Local citizens, led by merchants and other businessmen, organized a new committee of vigilance to take action. Whereas the earlier committee sought to clean out crime, this committee struggled to take political power from the machine. A murder provided the impetus to organize, but the committee's activities went far beyond seeking justice for this one crime. Over eight thousand people ultimately participated in this tide of vigilantism.

The committee organized into paramilitary units under the leadership of William Coleman, a local merchant. Coleman's units defied local law enforcement authorities, performed illegal search and seizures, arrested hundreds, including many Irish, and conducted its own trials. Amazingly, only four hangings took place amidst all this fervor for justice. To ensure that corruption would not again infect their city, the vigilantes elected one of their own as mayor and several others as aldermen in that fall's elections. The end result was that one political machine was overthrown by another. Crime, however, did not decline.[16]

The Western frontier was ripe for vigilantism. Lack of communication, huge distances, and sparsely populated regions proved fertile ground for localism. This localism manifested itself to a great extent in community preservation and urban development. As more people populated the West and technology brought better communication, civic institutions normalized. Regular law enforcement supplanted the need for popular justice as it had originally developed. Perhaps modern law enforcement ideas from the East had a good deal to do with this shift from vigilantism to a professionalized civic system of crime prevention. Police forces increased in number and effectiveness. Courts improved and expanded jurisdictions. The study of criminal behavior also helped overcome the excesses of popular justice. In the end, it is interesting to contemplate the vigilante route taken in the American West and that democratic society actually inadvertently promotes such behavior.[17]

POLICE REFORM IN THE WEST

Police departments and county sheriff's offices gradually achieved permanent standing in towns and cities as communities became more stable and had the financial resources to support regularized law enforcement. What began as practical reactions to crime and violence became police reforms to rely on legally mandated authorities to maintain law and order. It is important to understand that lawlessness did not end with the closing of the frontier. Crime remained in the form of corruption, vice, and violence.[18]

Ruins of one of the first jails in Montana Territory, Bannack, Montana, 1942. (Library of Congress)

Sheriffs and local police marshals actually spent little time chasing bandits with large posses across the desert landscape. Much of the time, they were busy with a variety of duties as well as keeping the peace. They collected taxes, maintained streets, cleaned sidewalks, served civil papers, inspected livestock brands, and housed drunks in the local jail, which they also maintained. It was hard and often thankless work, which is why some communities turned to so-called "gunfighters" to serve as sheriffs and marshals. "Wild Bill" Hickok and "Bat" Masterson are among the most famous of the gunmen who wore the star. Rarely, however, did these two or any other peace officer face down a gunman in the street, as depicted so often in American popular culture. Gunfighters were generally avoided whenever possible. In fact, many communities adopted ordinances banning weapons, again contrary to popular mythology. Gun control actually enjoyed great success as a limiter of violence in the American West.[19]

Reforming police to combat these evils was part of the wider reform movement in America during the Progressive Era. Professionalization of law enforcement occurred alongside that of education, medicine, law, and other professions. With this movement came a faith in government to solve social ills; thus, government was entrusted to police communities more so than ever before. Progressive law enforcement meant many things. For some, it was a better organized force, complete with an administrative bureaucracy. For others, reform meant utilizing the latest science and technology in fighting crime. Most agreed that crime prevention could be best achieved not through reaction, which had been the norm, but through police social work and the idea of community policing. This movement left its mark on Western police forces just as it did on police in other parts of the United States.[20]

By the 1890s, communities turned toward police reform measures that were being adopted with success in midwestern and eastern cities, such as Chicago, Philadelphia, and Boston. Even in Montana, which was still sparsely populated, Helena and Bozeman were organizing police forces based on Eastern models. Dallas organized in 1881, and even Portland had officers in uniform as early as 1872. The idea was that a professionalized police force would serve the public and not be the tool of special interests that had plagued police work so much in the past. Salaries, benefits, and pension plans helped get the best officers. Probation periods under civilian oversight ensured quality hiring practices. Police began to wear uniforms to gain a more noticeable presence in the community. Police chiefs joined state- and nationwide police organizations. Law enforcement officers from several western cities and towns even attended the National Association of Police Chiefs conferences in the 1890s. As evidence that police in the "Wild West" were often in the forefront of progressive change, the Portland Police Department became the first department in the United States to hire a woman police officer, Lola Baldwin, in 1905.[21]

Police departments in the West began to grow, increasing the ratio of personnel to population. In 1893, Austin had a force of 17 for a population of 28,000; Colorado Springs had 10 for a population of 17,000; Dallas had 47 for a population of 42,000; Los Angeles employed 74 officers for a population of 72,000; Oakland had 48 officers for a population of 60,000; Ogden had 16 men in uniform for a population of 15,000; San Francisco used 456 men for a population of 350,000; Seattle had a force of 62 for a population of 60,000; and Stockton, California, had 15 for its 16,000 residents. Each of these forces was uniformed, organized around an appointed police chief, and used some type of police signal system.[22]

Along with more people in uniform and managerial organization came better policing methods. New communications technology made rapid response more a reality than a catch phrase. Other technology, including new fingerprinting methods, helped solve crimes through detection. Automobiles and motorcycles replaced horse patrols on city streets. Community action programs helped better relations between police and the neighborhoods they served. Regular patrolling was instituted. Still, these methods did not work everywhere, nor were they implemented throughout the entire West. Some areas simply did not have the funding to obtain new technology or pay higher salaries to keep good professional officers. Others continued to suffer from political corruption, and the use of "third-degree" tactics by police remained widespread. Despite these problems, the advancements made by police forces in the western states were truly extraordinary considering that a little more than fifty years before, most areas had no law enforcement at all.[23]

NATIVE AMERICAN POLICE FORCES

Native American issues are among the more controversial in American history. The policy of "civilizing" the American Indian was mostly well intended but often misdirected. Beginning in 1871, the United States government began a legislative program to break up the power and cultural identity of centuries-old tribes and enlighten Indians to the wonders of individual liberty and the pursuit of happiness that so many white Americans valued. Indians would no longer be treated collectively as sovereign nations, as had been the case in America since the 1600s, but would now be considered as individuals by the U.S. government. This policy shift involved the creation of reservations, funding for education, farming, health, economic development, and the like, all designed to prepare Indians for individual independence. Much of this experimentation proved futile, but some of these attempts had long-term benefits. One of these was the attempt to teach Indians about democratic law and order through the establishment of police forces.

The idea of Indian police on reservations came from Indian agents. The U.S. Army had maintained order on reservations but was overstretched because of long-range patrols and ongoing Indian wars. As part of the civilizing process to teach Indians the value of the rule of law and individual liberty, agents toyed with the idea of Indian police officered by Whites. Moreover, crimes and assaults on reservations had become a serious problem, forcing agents to seek a practical solution—have the Indians police themselves.

The Indian agent to the Iowa, Sac, and Fox tribes of Nebraska first established an Indian police force in 1869. Agents also organized a Navajo mounted guard in 1872 to patrol reservation boundaries and recover stolen horses and cattle. By 1874, the Winnebagos, Santee, and Sioux used their own people to police their communities under the direction of the local Indian agent.

Occasionally, agents used Indian police to weaken the influence of the military in reservation affairs. John Clum, Indian agent for the San Carlos Apache reservation, did just that when he created an Apache police force for the reservation in 1874. Clum hoped to regain control of the reservation as Indian agent from the local military commander. His small force, to which he paid fifteen dollars per month, proved effective at keeping the peace. Within two months, the military was no longer needed to patrol the reservation and withdrew.

This same Apache police force arrested Geronimo in 1877. Clum and an expanded force of over one hundred Apaches tracked Geronimo after the renegade had led raids on several Arizona settlements. Geronimo, along with fifty followers, holed up in a warehouse at the Warm Springs Agency. The Apache police cunningly made Geronimo think that he had a numerical advantage and through surprise overtook the building with little violence, capturing perhaps the most famous of the Indian warriors.

Despite the success, these early Indian police forces had no Congressional authorization or funding. Agents and commissioners testified before Congress in 1876 to obtain funding for Indian police. Three years later, Congress appropriated thirty thousand dollars for 450 privates at five dollars per month and 50 officers at eight dollars per month. The salary proved problematic, as Indian scouts for the Army earned fifteen dollars per month and Clum's Apache policemen earned the same amount. For Indian police on reservations without a food ration, the salary was not enough for subsistence. In 1881, Congress upped the appropriation to seventy thousand dollars, and in 1883 increased it to eighty-two thousand dollars, improving monthly salaries and increasing the number of policemen.

Occasionally Indians resisted their own police forces for cultural reasons or by claiming that those Indians who joined the white man's police force were traitors and turncoats. At the Colorado River Agency, Mohave Indians refused to join the agency police force because of a traditional reluctance to "denounce" each other. In 1879, men under the leadership of the local chief attacked the police barracks at the Lower Brule Agency, killing livestock, breaking windows, and ultimately forcing policemen to renounce their pledge of service and return to the tribe at gunpoint. Often, Indian police became confused as to whom they should obey, their chief or the agent in command of the police force.

Sioux Indian Mounted Police, Pine Ridge Agency, Dakota Territory, 1882. (National Archives)

For the most part, however, Indian police proved effective and gradually were accepted by their tribes. Many tribes already had internal policing, and some, like the Cherokee, had elaborate criminal justice systems already in place. Their service to native communities included guarding supplies and warehouses; rooting out horse and cattle thieves; maintaining order at food distributions; arresting those accused of drunkenness, assault, and murder; and acting as eyes and ears across the reservation for Indian agents. As part of the civilizing program, Indian police wore white man's clothing, even uniforms, practiced monogamy, and were supposed to be role models for the fellow tribesmen in adopting the ways of the white man.

By the early 1900s, Indian police forces were well established. In 1907, Congress budgeted two hundred thousand dollars for Indian police forces, raising monthly salaries to twenty dollars for privates and twenty-five dollars for officers. Although they often used outdated, shabby equipment, Indian police forces functioned with effectiveness. Indians accepted the role of police and courts in their societies. To this day, the Bureau of Indian Affairs continues to administer law enforcement in cooperation with local Indian police on the reservations.[24]

U.S. MARSHALS

U.S. Marshals had been around for decades before achieving fame in the American West. Created under President George Washington, U.S. Marshals were the first federal law enforcement service. As the United States organized western lands into territories, U.S. Marshals often represented the only law enforcement presence until territorial governments were able to organize county law enforcement. These presidentially appointed lawmen had extraordinary authority, including appointing their own deputies and deputizing regular U.S. Army units. Their jurisdictions were usually huge, and, being undermanned, U.S. Marshals faced difficult, trying challenges to maintain law and order in the territories.

Arizona and New Mexico proved to be the most violent jurisdictions for U.S. Marshals. Both territories provided perfect havens for all sorts of fugitives and criminals. Deputy marshals often bore the brunt of tracking down outlaws in the territories, spending weeks in the saddle traveling through some of the most remote, rugged, and dangerous terrain in the world. Indians, the elements, and their prey only added to the danger these few men faced.

Marshals and deputy marshals themselves were not always that far removed from the wrong side of the law, as finding willing appointees was often difficult. Some were nothing more than bounty hunters in cahoots with inexperienced, corrupt territorial judges. For the most part, however, U.S. Marshals and their deputies performed well under these extreme conditions. Many were hard working, courageous men who believed they were helping tame a frontier. African Americans in particular served well as marshals and deputy marshals. Although many emancipated slaves came West and became cowboys, some joined the Marshals Service.

Like other law enforcement officers, U.S. Marshals served a variety of functions. In addition to tracking down criminals, U.S. Marshals served warrants, subpoenas, collected fines, and impaneled juries for territorial courts. They guarded mail and stage routes as well as railroads. As the population increased in the territories, deputies took on more field responsibilities, leaving marshals to take care of growing demonstrative duties in their communities. Often, marshals appointed brothers and cousins as deputies, and their wives were normally hired to run the office. Low salaries were always a problem, forcing marshals and deputies alike to supplement their income through bounty hunting, extra court duties, or working jobs on the side.

According to historian Jacqueline Pope, U.S. Marshals had three loyalties motivating their service: collecting extra fees, protecting their communities, and serving the federal government. The latter two show the delicate role that U.S. Marshals played in defending American democracy. Appointed by the president and funded by Congress, marshals were not wholly civilian, nor were they military; thus, they acted as a barrier protecting one from the other. There have been times when this position proved delicate, if not uncomfortable. At the outset of the Civil War, U.S. Marshals across the South, Texas, and New Mexico chose to side with their communities and broke their oath of loyalty to the federal government. On the opposite extreme, U.S. Marshals helped to forcibly put down mining strikes in Colorado, Nevada, and California, thus siding with big business interests against their communities.[25]

PRIVATE SECURITY AGENCIES

Many are familiar with Pinkerton detectives in the American West through Hollywood films, notably *Butch Cassidy and the Sundance Kid*. "Pinkertons" were indeed a major part of the law enforcement history of the West. Private security developed quite naturally in the West with the absence of established law and order, especially on the railroads. Gold and silver shipments from mines, payrolls for miners and ranch hands, and other valuable goods tempted many an outlaw in the largely unpoliced West.

Stagecoach companies actually set the precedent for private security west of Missouri. Henry Wells and William Fargo established American Express and later Wells Fargo to transport valuable shipments by stage. Their green, ironbound strongboxes surrounded by heavily armed agents became easily recognizable trademarks in the West. Wells and Fargo became the first to employ their own police to pursue those who dared to rob American Express and Wells Fargo stages.

As rail replaced stage, crime naturally shifted to the source of appealing goods. Accordingly, railroads used political influence in Western state and territorial governments to let the railroad companies police the railroads. Enter Allan Pinkerton in 1855. Pinkerton saw the need for security on railroads in the Midwest and established the Northwest Police Agency to police the rails for six Midwestern railroads. In 1857, Pinkerton expanded his business as more railroads pushed across the Midwest. Pinkerton Protection Patrol Company offered private contract interstate police service, a first in American history. As railroads spread across the American West, so too did Pinkerton's business. Of course, through the end of the nineteenth century, the all-seeing eye of the Pinkerton Detective Agency would experience fame all over the United States as an effective detective agency and police-for-hire service. The Agency would also help many mining companies put down strikes.[26]

STATE POLICE—THE TEXAS RANGERS

The idea of a state-supported police force to defend a frontier or act as a state law enforcement arm was not new, nor was it distinctive to Texas; but the Texas Rangers do represent an interesting episode in the development of law enforcement in the American West. Considering the Americans who settled in Texas during the pre-Republic of Texas years and shortly afterward, it is not surprising that a ranger force would develop in this hospitable but untamed land. According to historian Charles M. Robinson, the predominantly Southern Anglo-American settlers of Texas were already frontiersmen with a "ranging tradition." These people shared characteristics from their common frontier experience, including community, personal honor, martial spirit, and strong family and social traditions. Such characteristics served the newcomers well in a new land with a "foreign" culture.[27]

The Texas Rangers actually came into existence under the aegis of Mexico. Indian raids, particularly from Kiowa and Comanche, harassed Spanish, then later Anglo-American, settlers across the Texas frontier. With the opening of the Anglo-American settlement into Mexican Texas in 1821, the Mexican government found a possible solution to the Indian problem: Let the settlers take care of themselves. As the leader of the Anglo-American settlements in Texas, Stephen F. Austin considered creating a ranger-like militia to defend the new settlements from Indian attacks. Before he could get permission from Mexico City to create this force, the Mexican governor of Texas, Colonel José Félix Trespalcios, preempted Austin by ordering the Anglo-American colonists to establish a frontier police corps. Based on the traditional militia model, local citizens organized armed companies to maintain law and order in and around the settlements and defend against Indian attack when necessary. This was not a permanent around-the-clock force but rather one that operated on an as-needed basis.[28]

In order to keep the Anglo-American settlers in Texas and instill a greater sense of community, the Mexican governor also allowed the Anglo-Americans to elect an *alcalde* as well as officers for the ranger militia. Ironically, the new *alcalde*, John Tumlinson, was killed by an Indian while on his way to the territorial capital in San Antonio to request more ammunition for the new ranger unit. By 1823, when Austin's grant was formalized and he was authorized to form a unit of "national militia" for defense, the volunteer militia and local ad hoc police forces gained official standing. In 1826 the force gained permanent standing and the territory was divided into six military districts. From this grew the Texas Rangers, though they were not officially called as such.

The militia spent much of its time fighting Indians. Throughout the 1820s and early 1830s Indian raids and threats of Indian attack required near-constant attention. Indians alone, however, did not fill the plate. Outlaws from the United States, so-called "border ruffians" and other undesirables, kept the ranger militia busy as well. Horse theft was the most prominent crime and was just as serious as Western mythology maintains.

Under the deal struck by Austin with the Mexican government, the Anglo-Americans were allowed through their *alcaldes* to handle their own cases except for capital offenses, which were dealt with at the territorial level in San Antonio. Here is where differences of opinion concerning "justice" began to show between the Anglo-Americans and the Mexicans. Rumors spread that capital offenders were

Woodcut engraving of a
Texas Ranger, ca. 1848.
(Library of Congress)

often set free on their own recognizance and that Mexican authorities made little effort to detain escapees. The Texians began to see justice as uneven and selective, and usually not in their favor. Gradually, the Anglo-American settlements began to administer justice on local terms and without approval from the Mexican government. It was one of the first cracks in the Mexican–Anglo-American relationship that would result in the Texas revolution of 1835–1836.[29]

Although many die-hard Texans would never admit it, the Rangers saw little action during the Texas War for Independence (1836). Except for serving as rearguard for the exodus of civilians fleeing Santa Anna's army and keeping the Indians at bay on the frontier, military matters were left to Sam Houston and the Texas Army. After the war, the Rangers served a similar function during the Republic period (1836–1845). They had indeed become an outstanding Indian fighting force. The annexation of Texas into the Union and the subsequent War with Mexico saw the continued use of the Rangers as a quasi-military force.[30]

During the Civil War, the Rangers provided frontier defense, mainly against Indian attacks.[31] After the war, both the Rangers' role as a military force and as Indian fighters ended. Reconstruction meant Union occupation of Texas, which meant no force that had existed in Confederate Texas would be allowed. Consequently, the Rangers ceased to exist, despite state legislation that formally recognized the "Texas Rangers" (the first time they were called this). With the U.S. Army guarding the frontier and reconstructing Texas, there was no apparent need for the Rangers. Scattered efforts to revive the force for frontier defense during Reconstruction represented only nominal attempts to fight the Apaches and made little headway against resistance from the Army.[32]

It was during Reconstruction, however, that the Texas Rangers were indirectly ordained for more traditional police service. E. J. Davis, a Republican carpetbagger, was elected governor of Texas in 1870. Voted into office by enfranchised former slaves and disenfranchised Confederates, Davis ranks as one of the most unpopular governors in the history of the state. Realizing that his position was tenuous because he was an outsider, Davis had the legislature create a state police force that he used somewhat as the secret police were used by the Tsar of Russia. Under the command of Adjutant General James Davidson, the state police consisted of 150 officers, plus all local peace officers (who automatically became members of the force). Propaganda from Davis's Reconstruction government praised the effectiveness of the state police, claiming it had arrested 973 criminals from a wanted list of 2,780 during the first five months of the force's existence, which was an exaggeration at best.

Because martial law was still in force, Governor Davis allowed the new Texas State Police to run roughshod whenever and wherever it pleased. In wanton abuse of its power, the Texas State Police hunted down criminals and many innocents with ruthless efficiency and carried out its own brand of justice, which even the handful of Texans in favor of Reconstruction found difficult to accept. "Killed in attempt to escape" and "killed while resisting arrest" plagued the force's reports. State Police officers illegally confiscated property, using the martial law decree as a tool of convenience. Walter Prescott Webb, the leading historian of the Texas Rangers, called the brief history of the Texas State Police "a story of official murder and legalized oppression." After almost three years of offensive injustice, corruption, and violence, the Democratic Texas legislature passed a bill disbanding the Texas State Police, which the governor promptly vetoed. The legislature overrode the veto, disbanding the force in April 1873.[33]

In 1874, the state legislature brought back the Texas Rangers to essentially take the place of the defunct and discredited Texas State Police. This mission brought the Rangers closer to what they would ultimately become—a state-supported law enforcement agency. While the Rangers along the Rio Grande fought a series of border wars with Mexican *banditos*, other companies were formed to deal with the steady stream of outlaws that found Reconstruction-era Texas both a haven and a place ripe for the picking. The "Big Four"—Ben Thompson, Bill Longley, John King Fisher, and the infamous John Wesley Hardin—represented the worst of the lot of bad men that could be found across Texas. Ultimately, the Rangers cleaned the "Big Four" out. (Thompson, Fisher, and Hardin were killed; Longley was hung after sentencing.)[34]

Success on the Mexican border and in dealing with the *badmen*, along with the end of the Indian wars in Texas, could have proved to be the end of the Texas Rangers. Were they still needed? The answer was a resounding "yes." As law enforcement agencies across the nation reformed in the 1880s and 1890s, so too did the Rangers. The image of the gun-slinging bands of Rangers faded into legend. The new Rangers, with the frontier all but closed, found new problems and new crime to deal with as the twentieth century dawned. The emphasis on court-administered justice as opposed to that given by the Texas State Police and others on countless occasions, plus the vast improvement of local police forces throughout the state, freed the Rangers to deal with statewide crime. Border troubles, however, kept part of the force tied to the Rio Grande during the seemingly constant state of revolution Mexico found itself in during the earlier decades of the twentieth century. Prohibition- and Depression-era gangsters also kept the Rangers busy during the 1920s and early 1930s.

It was the end of an era, however, as science and technology created criminology, replacing the man on horseback ranging the frontier forever. The Texas Rangers adapted, and today they are a force of over one hundred highly trained and specialized men and women scattered across Texas, leading investigations and assisting various federal, state, and local law enforcement agencies in a variety of ways. Other states in the West created state police forces based on the Ranger model, including the Arizona Rangers and the New Mexico Mounted Police.[35]

CONCLUSION

The history of law enforcement in the American frontier West is colored in myth and legend by kernels of truth. Building communities in an untamed land populated by one of the most heavily armed peoples in history was indeed a challenge. Law and order, however, won the day as settlers became citizens and used their experience and common needs to lessen the scope and frequency of social, economic, and political conflict. Police in the West evolved from nonexistent to reformed forces based on Eastern models and their own experiences, borrowing from already established communities when needed.

CHAPTER 5

URBANIZATION, PROGRESSIVISM, AND POLICE

INTRODUCTION

After the Civil War, the United States experienced the rapid and dramatic changes brought on by the Industrial Age. The country would transform from a predominantly rural society with agrarian values to a nation of urban centers that brought new challenges and new moral standards. Economic growth, industrialization, consumer capitalism, and immigration, among other factors, served as catalysts for the urbanization of American cities. Crowding, corruption, and poor city planning created a situation demanding spirited reform.

Police in America would ride these same trends. Urbanization changed the mission of police, as well as the nature of crime. Corrupt city politics heavily influenced how police functioned. Progressive reform set police on the path of professionalization and community-oriented policing methods that would achieve fruition in the second half of the twentieth century. In order to understand the police during this period, it is important to briefly discuss the causes and effects of urbanization, as these have a direct bearing on police development. It is also imperative to examine the advent of the Progressive movement, its characteristics, and its impact on solving the ills of urbanization. With this review, the initial development of police as a profession can then be placed in historical context, as police rose from the depths of political corruption to near the surface of the Progressive reform movement. By 1900, police were experimenting with civil service, training, and sharing experiences through organizations—in other words, police work was becoming a profession.

THE IMPACT OF URBANIZATION

The urbanization of American cities continued a trend that began in the 1820s and 1830s. The ability to mass-produce consumer goods through factory systems stimulated industrialization in the Northeastern and Midwestern United States. By the

Civil War, the corresponding need for wage-earning laborers to produce these goods in increasingly larger factories caused a migration to American cities from the countryside. Immigrants from abroad, mainly Europe, turned the migration into a flood, as thousands inundated the cities each year. Transportation also greatly impacted this phenomenon. By the 1880s, railroads provided transport for goods and mobility for people all over the United States. Even within cities, the development of railed mass transit made urban sprawl possible, as workers and middle-class managers could live outside the city core but still work in town centers using trolley systems and later commuter trains.

From the beginning of the Civil War to the end of World War I, the number of people inhabiting cities with a population of at least 8,000 ballooned from 6.2 to 54.3 million! By 1910, New York City boasted a population of 7.7 million, including 1.9 million foreign-born Whites, 1.8 million native born of foreign or mixed decent, and 91,000 Blacks. By 1920, more Americans lived in urban settings than in rural areas for the first time. Immigration from abroad also fed the urban labor mill, as hundreds of thousands of immigrants looking for work, predominantly from Europe, flooded industrializing cities. Migration within the United States, notably the mass migration of African Americans from the rural South to northern and midwestern cities looking for better jobs and less discrimination (finding mostly disappointment on both counts), also increased the size of industrialized cities. Thirty-two cities in 1900 had African American populations of over 10,000, and, of African Americans living in the North or West, over 70 percent resided in urban areas. African American urban populations increased across the country—Memphis, Atlanta, Dallas, Detroit, Chicago, and even Los Angeles experienced an influx of African Americans from rural areas.

The immense immigration of the post-Civil War era probably had the greatest impact in dramatically changing the look of American cities. Escaping oppression, seeking economic opportunity, or simply having no other place to go, immigrants from Europe and Asia poured into the United States and settled mainly in cities. Irish, German, Scandinavian, Asian, and Eastern European immigrants brought different, and to some, threatening, social and cultural lifestyles. Religion perhaps reflected this difference more than any other thing. The United States went from a predominately Protestant nation to a country of Protestant–Catholic churchgoers. Jews from Eastern Europe and Russia added to the flavor. Religion mixed with the economic diversity of immigrants, creating a volatile recipe for racial and ethnic conflict in American cities. Add to these the migration of African Americans from the South to northern and midwestern cities throughout this period. Foreign-born and African American immigrants often settled in inner-city areas, taking the place of prosperous, middle-class Whites who moved to new suburban areas now available because of mass transit. Religious, racial, and ethnic ties created strong, tightly bonded inner-city neighborhoods.

This enormous influx and the physical growth of cities created equally massive problems. Housing, health care, and city services such as water, sewer, and trash collection all could not keep up with crowding and uncontrolled growth. Poverty, vagrancy, street children, and the like were only a few of the many problems created by this rapid process. What few city services existed became so overstretched that some city governments simply broke down. Native-born city dwellers were content to blame these problems not on growth or industrialization but on the immigrants and newcomers themselves. This nativist backlash against cultural and social differences had dire consequences, not the least of which was mob violence.[1]

Violent crime among individuals, however, declined, whereas arrests for lesser offenses such as drunkenness and petty theft significantly increased. Vice increased as well, as inner-city residents sought entertainment to take their minds off the drudgeries of long hours of work. The common association between increasing urbanization and an increase in crime is not so clear-cut. A better description would be that as legitimate economic opportunities increased, violent crime decreased, and as police departments professionalized, arrests for what used to be tolerated by society increased. Industrialization and the advent of the boss system, which took ethnic conflict off the streets and into the realm of politics, contributed to this trend.[2]

The main reason cities were inept in coping with the problems of urbanization was the boss system. Boss machines are famous in American history and are even considered by some a highlight of American democratic practice. The Tweed ring of Tammany Hall in New York is the best known; but Irish-dominated machines in Detroit, Chicago, Boston, and New Orleans also achieved notorious notoriety. Smaller cities, like Omaha and Memphis, also developed boss machines that held court over local governance for decades.

In keeping with the basic ideals of republicanism and decentralization of authority, city governments during most of the nineteenth century remained small and increasingly ineffective. As a consequence, boss systems easily took control of city politics. By promising political favors in exchange for votes, boss machines teamed up with neighborhood businesses to manipulate city governance for their own political and financial gain. Patronage was the name of the game. Contributors, family members, friends from the neighborhood, and so forth, landed upwardly mobile and often lucrative city jobs as firefighters, police officers, inspectors, board members,

Image from *Harper's Weekly* of fights at the polls, November 7, 1857. (Library of Congress)

and the like, all regardless of ability. As long as everyone played along, everyone got what he or she wanted out of the system. For many years, the system was popular and fairly effective, considering the corruption involved. Bosses provided relief where city government failed and gradually became professionals at providing "city" services. If government existed to serve the needs of the people, then bosses indeed took the place of government. Bribes, voter fraud, and intimidation were the bosses' main tools. City inhabitants tended to let the system work because the tangible benefits seemed to improve conditions in the inner-city neighborhoods. Immigrants tended to support the machine strongly. Bosses gave them jobs, places to live, social mobility—things they had come to America to achieve—all in exchange for votes. "Vote early and vote often," as the saying went, was not a joke!

Addressing any grievances and serious problems that threatened the machine, however, was problematic. Widespread corruption overcame American cities, as building inspectors, fire marshals, public works contractors, and even police, came under the controlling grip of the boss system. With a vicious cycle of votes, bribes, and payoffs in place, republicanism suffered—how could any public official or employee be held accountable in such a system? The fine line of public virtue had long been crossed by partisan boss politics. Doing what was best for the public good at the expense of one's own interests had always been a tricky aspect of republicanism. In post-Civil War America, the concept was lost in the cities, as politicians looked out for themselves at the expense of the public. Irish machines often ignored the needs of other ethnic groups. Blacks became totally lost in the machine system. Critics charged that the boss system was destroying American democracy, and time-honored values such as the individual pursuit of happiness were in danger of extinction.[3]

POLICE UNDER THE BOSS SYSTEM

Police under boss systems during the latter half of the nineteenth century experienced, if not enjoyed, unprecedented levels of political corruption. Police became one of the plums of boss patronage as well as a sure means to economic security for the individual policeman. The corruption of beat patrolmen, the corruption involved in police organizations, and how bosses and others used police to build amazing fortunes are central themes to police history during the age of industrialization and progressive reform. Yet, in spite of all this sordid activity, police managed to give the false appearance of effective protection of the lives and property of citizens.

Criminal justice professor Samuel Walker suggests that the nineteenth-century beat patrolman was more a "political operative" than a professional policeman serving the public good. This is certainly an apt description, for patrolmen held their appointments through political patronage and payoffs, and a bad result at the polls on election day could cost a cop his job as a new party brought into power cleaned house to make room for its appointees. Cincinnati, for example, dismissed 219 of 295 policemen in 1880 after an election brought a competing political machine to power. The Democratic victory over Republicans in Chicago in 1897 turned out many native-born American cops for an influx of Irish American policemen. In 1889, Los Angeles Republicans ousted the Democratic machine, throwing most Spanish American officers off the police force in the process. In these circumstances, it is easy to see how stability, accountability, and effectiveness in policing would suffer over time.[4]

By most accounts, patrolmen did the job for the money, not as a career, and as long as one's machine was in power, the potential for earnings was great. Becoming an officer was not easy. Competition for such a lucrative position was intense, and an appointment normally demanded good standing in the local machine. Bribes did not hurt: an appointment to the New York Police Department required the blessing of the local Tammany Hall block boss plus a $300 bribe.[5] An average annual salary of $900 ($600 in San Francisco, $1,200 in New Orleans for the 1880s) awaited those lucky enough to get an appointment. By comparison, a skilled craftsman earned around $800 per year, whereas a factory worker might get $450. The financial gain from corruption sweetened the plum even more. In addition to the money, the social standing that came with the uniform made police work a desirable position.[6]

Policemen of this period in American history tended to come from working-class neighborhoods and were themselves often immigrants or at least first-generation Americans of a variety of ethnic backgrounds. Fabled is of course the Irish beat cop. There is plenty of evidence to support the historical existence of this mythical icon of police. Irish-born Catholics came to dominate many police forces across the northeastern and midwestern United States off and on through the 1920s. By 1880, Boston's police department had over 100 Irish cops. Chicago, Cleveland, and San Francisco each had a greater proportion of Irish police than the proportion of Irish in the local population. Many cities, including Omaha, even had Irish-born police chiefs. The perception of foreign-born, and Irish at that, patrolmen dominating police forces irritated nativist undertones that occasionally resulted in mob violence. And the Irish police themselves inadvertently promoted antagonism by their prejudice against other ethnic groups, particularly Italians. Yet, studies show that Irish cops managed to keep the peace and were not bent toward preferential treatment of their own, as they were said to be more aggressive in arresting fellow Irishmen for public disorder than they were in arresting any other group.[7]

German Americans also had considerable representation on police forces in the United States. In Cleveland, Cincinnati, and St. Louis, German-born police officers made up a large proportion of police departments. Cleveland, for example, had thirty-five German-born officers along with thirty-one Irish-born and forty-six American-born officers. Immigrants from other nations provided multitudes of policemen across the country. Scandinavian Americans made up one-fifth of the police department in Minneapolis. In Chicago, New York, Cleveland, Minneapolis, San Francisco, and Milwaukee, about one of every two policemen was born outside the United States in 1890. Adding those whose parents were born outside the United States increased the ratio even more: five of six in New York, nine of ten in Milwaukee, four of five in Chicago, and three of four in St. Louis.[8]

Ethnicity in police departments fed the boss systems. Ethnic neighborhoods had political interests and supported the local boss, which in turn represented those interests to the next level of the machine. Police appointments came under the control of the bosses, who in turn made appointments based on who could serve them best, that is, help line their pockets with illicit profits. Corruption in police departments was possible because of the way the system was organized. Few police departments were autonomous; most had political supervision that controlled appointments, promotions, and discipline. The decentralized nature of police departments during this period promoted corruption. Precinct captains often had more authority than the police chief. Thus, the boss system could capitalize on ethnic politics in communities to control law enforcement, which quickly became corrupt and further fed the vicious cycle of corruption. According to Robert Fogelson, as long as the local precinct kept the peace and controlled (not eradicated) vice and crime, city and state government leaders were content to let police basically operate as adjuncts of political bosses and the machines.[9]

Saloonkeepers and madams of illicit houses paid off local bosses to appoint "sympathetic" precinct captains. The captain and his beat patrolmen would ensure that businesses were left alone in return for additional payoffs. Corruption was big money, and anyone willing to get in on it could make a fortune of whatever size he wished. New York provides some colorful examples. Captain Alexander "Clubber" Williams commanded a precinct in New York's red-light district in the 1880s, where he quickly amassed a fortune in money and political influence. Saloons, brothels, and gambling houses paid Williams off in return for the salutary neglect of local police and protection from prosecution. Williams even had the houses selling bottles of his own special brand of whiskey. Williams did so well that by the 1890s, he boasted a house on fashionable East Tenth Street, a Connecticut estate, and a fifty-three-foot steam-powered yacht. Williams accumulated over 350 formal complaints against him for everything from brutality to neglect of duty. He was fined by city commissioners over two hundred times, the fines no doubt paid by bosses or by his immediate clientele that survived only through his protection. Investigative boards and grand juries could not touch the politically well-connected Williams. He even managed to get promoted from captain to inspector despite his long record of abuse. He met his match in Theodore Roosevelt, who in 1895 headed the famous Roosevelt Board that forced the infamous Williams to quit the force.

Another New York precinct captain, Timothy Creeden, paid fifteen thousand dollars for his promotion to captain, borrowing the money from not so legitimate creditors. Captains in New York made three thousand dollars a year, and Creeden had been a sergeant. Creeden hoped to use the graft of his position with local "businesses" to make payments on his loan. His first assignment, however, was not in such a lucrative location, so his creditors had the local boss transfer Creeden to a better location so he could pay off his loan more quickly. Both Creeden and Williams provide excellent examples of how the system could result in big money for the industrious. The profits trickled down the line, as beat patrolmen and detectives often acted as "bagmen" to collect bribes and encourage those behind on their payments. Because patrolmen and detectives often owed their appointments to the captain, loyalty contributed to their willingness to participate in illegal activities.[10]

Chicago also had some colorful characters involved in corruption and graft. Whereas in many departments precinct captains had more power than chiefs, Chicago's system was more centralized, giving the chief control over captains as well as detectives, who made up a separate branch directly under the chief. Serving less than one year, Chicago police chief Jacob Rehm made a fortune from graft across Chicago. Beginning his brief term with widespread arrests of prostitutes and raiding several gambling houses to impress city leaders, Rehm then backed off and allowed many to return to work under his protection, the cost of which was quite high. Greed brought Rehm down in the end, as his involvement in the infamous Whiskey Ring proved one step too far for city officials.[11]

Police graft easily influenced politics and even determined elections. Obviously, police tended to support the party machine that nurtured their pockets. Accordingly, police would do what they could to benefit their party at the polls on Election Day. Intimidation was commonplace. Supporting the Democrats in the 1894 election, Chicago police stood idly by as Democratic thugs intimidated voters and in some cases actually went inside polling booths to make sure voters chose the "right" candidate. Prominent Republicans found themselves "arrested" the day before the polls opened, then suddenly released the day after the election. The Chicago *Tribune* decried this gross infringement on the right to cast a ballot unhindered, criticizing police for their blatant interference with the election. Similar scenes occurred in Baltimore in 1875, Kansas City in 1894, and in Philadelphia the same year. New York police openly promoted the standard "vote early and vote often" motto of the machines. Perhaps one of the oddest scenes happened in New Orleans in 1888. A reform-minded group called the Young Men's Democratic Association actually armed themselves and surrounded polling sites to keep police from harassing voters! So much was at stake in an election: graft, influence, even a way of life, as a new party or a new ethnic group could drastically change the landscape of city politics and the influence of a religious or ethnic group.[12]

Under these conditions, police did not attempt to rid their beats of crime; rather, police regulated crime with extraordinary illegal authority coming down from the political machines. Problems went unresolved if the solution was not in the interest of the machine. George Washington Plunkitt of the infamous Tammany Hall machine in New York City boldly claimed there was a clear "distinction between honest graft and dishonest graft."[13] So long as Plunkitt and the machines controlled city governance, that distinction in reality remained blurred, and crime continued under this semiregulated condition.

It would be wrong to suggest that all police were involved in corrupt activities. Many policemen wanted no part of graft, honest or otherwise, and were transferred to areas or precincts where corruption was not so pronounced. Besides, local bosses did not want police who were not team players in their schemes; thus, it was in the interest of the machine to get potential "do-gooders" out of their profitable precincts.

As police continued to be by design ineffective at eradicating crime, suburbanites began to lose patience for what had been traditionally tolerated behavior in society. It was perhaps this latter point that kept crime levels relatively low. As new people moved into urban settings, they brought with them value systems and a brand of civility that the cities of pre-Civil War America lacked. Thus, police did not affect crime rates; rather, it was the change in the nature of society that altered how crime and antisocial behavior were perceived. Public order came from schools, social organizations, religious institutions, and the like, not from police. Concerned citizens came to see the police, not criminals, as a central problem of the new, urban American city.[14]

PROGRESSIVE REFORM

By the 1880s, upper-middle-class suburban Whites began to take on the boss machines. Believing in pragmatism, legal realism, social gospel, and humanitarianism, the so-called Progressives set out to reform society at the expense of the bosses and those they served. Most of all, Progressives wanted to remove the evil from the democratic system of American governance, a system that was not evil in and of itself but that had been corrupted by greed and power. These upper-middle-class reformers feared the boss machines, especially because immigrants and the working classes under the thumb of the machines had become so vital to city politics. Balance needed to be restored. Progressivism also spurred the movement toward professionalization, which involved education, service, a code of ethical behavior, and the establishment of organizations to promote these virtues within a "profession." With these ideals in hand, Progressives embarked upon a daunting voyage to reform city government and use that new government to right the ills of urbanized society.[15]

Reformers managed to restructure city government through state legislative mandates. Not so much in the debt of city machines, state politicians proved more open to reform because they were accountable to a wider body politic and often at odds with city machines. New charters weakened city councils and aldermen, gave more power to mayors and later city managers, and allowed the appointment of expert commissions to recommend policy on a range of city issues and problems and oversee city services, such as police and fire departments. Voting practices also came under the gun of Progressive reformers. By the early 1900s, cities across the United States had voter registration systems in place, election boards provided oversight of elections, and voting more than once became illegal. The primary result of city government reform was the decline of the role of political parties in city politics. Citywide elections diminished the power of ethnic neighborhoods as partisan voting blocks. With the institution of civil service and other reforms, voters came to realize that party affiliation had nothing to do with school superintendents, hospital boards, running public works facilities, and other civic services, including police departments.

By taking patronage from the bosses and removing party politics from city elections, Progressive reformers thought they had achieved a great victory for democracy. In reality, those on the bubble of disenfranchisement found themselves almost totally without a political voice. Changes in city electoral policies drastically changed the make-up of city government, as ethnic groups found their collective political power weakened under new districts and wards. This was common—places like Pittsburgh, Los Angeles, and Dayton made it possible for more upper-class professionals to get elected to office, often replacing middle-class Progressives in the process. Progressives had done their work too well.[16]

Progressive efforts to reform police actually predate the Progressive Era by several years, and in some cases by decades. Reform actually began with putting police in uniforms—an effort to make police more visible and to give police a sense of camaraderie on the job—and continued with adding women for the first time to police forces. The more important reforms would tackle organization, oversight, and professionalization.

Uniforms aroused controversy and were a product of the industrial age and progressive era of reform. Up to this time, the only thing denoting a police officer was the badge, which many departments only began using in the 1840s. Early badges were made of leather, then from copper, thus, the term "copper" or "cop."[17]

Common sense dictated that uniformed police would be more visible to citizens in distress. Those concerned with discipline noted that uniformed police would be less likely to take a nip or take a nap on duty because they would be more visible on patrol to supervisors. A major downside for critics was that uniforms would make police more susceptible to assaults and "exposed" to criminals. The logic of a uniformed officer seems apparent today. Uniformed officers deterred crime by their mere presence and made the neighborhood feel secure. Visibility was the key. Victims of crime could easily spot a uniformed police officer. The uniform also brought a certain prestige and efficiency to the job. Uniformed "cops" walking their beats or later driving their patrol cars knew they were visible and that they were causing people to alter their behavior.

Yet, many police resisted the idea of uniforms, as did the public. Both claimed uniforms represented the all too strong presence of centralized authority. Coming fresh out of the age of Jacksonian democracy, the sentiments of individuality and democracy saw little use for an authoritarian-type uniform. On a more practical level, police believed a uniform would give them away to criminals and thus erode their effectiveness on the job. Bosses, on the other hand, came to support uniforms. Uniforms made their power visible and could act as a deterrent to those thinking about challenging their power. As an example of how divisive the uniform issue was, police in New York actually engaged a lawyer to protest the possible adoption of uniforms in the 1850s.

Overcoming opposition to uniforms was not easy. In New York, police commissioners simply announced they would not renew the four-year appointment of officers who would not wear a uniform. Despite near violent protest, New York police commissioners got their way and established the first uniformed police force in the United States in 1853. Philadelphia police similarly resisted uniforms for several years, before finally caving in to regulations in 1860.[18]

Unlike New York and Philadelphia, however, Boston did not have to twist the arms of its police to don uniforms. Many Boston officers already wore a makeshift blue uniform, and all police were formally outfitted by 1859.[19] Portland, Oregon, police put on uniforms in 1872. Dark blue coats with matching vests and pants topped off with a black hat and brass buttons were indeed great steps forward for a city that only thirty years previous consisted of a few log cabins. Portland police also wore a new star badge that same year. Portland Officer Thomas Burke was issued badge number 1 along with the new uniform in 1872. He was certainly qualified for police duty by the local machine: "He was Irish, a loyal Democrat, and his brother was Police Commissioner W. P. Burke."[20] Dallas police adopted a uniform in 1881, as did Orlando in 1892. Wilmington, North Carolina, police patrolled in blue beginning in 1893. Most police departments across the United States adopted uniforms by the 1920s.

Uniforms were only a small part of the reform story. The appearance of women on police forces was also a Progressive move. Reformers believed women could bring "social purity" to communities through police work and help reform police in the process. The gender typecasting is extraordinary but not unusual considering the context of the Progressive movement, much of which was led by women. Policewomen could help deal with female criminals, prostitutes, and vagrants. Those against women in policing cited concerns that women should not be exposed to the filth and vile of society and that police work is a manly business—women did not have the physical or emotional strength to handle the job. Although many males in the Progressive movement balked at women police, they recognized that women had a role in enforcing the law.

Women first became involved in police work as part of the police matron movement during the last half of the nineteenth century. Matrons took care of both the young and the women taken into custody by police, especially those who suffered with mental or emotional issues. Women's groups, such as temperance unions, promoted the movement. New York City appointed six matrons from the Female Reform Society in 1845. Portland, Maine, employed a city-paid matron in 1878 to take care of women awaiting trial in the city jail. Jersey City followed suit in 1880, followed by Chicago (1881), Boston (1883), Philadelphia (1884), Denver (1885), and Cleveland (1886), among several other cities. Both New York and Massachusetts passed legislation in 1888 requiring cities of over twenty thousand people to employ police matrons.

Matrons, however, had no police powers. This would come, though, with Progressive reforms. Portland, Oregon, as previously noted, hired the first women with

Cincinnati suffragettes demonstrate how a policewoman would make an arrest, 1909. (Library of Congress)

police powers in 1905. Los Angeles appointed Alice Stebbin Wells, a social worker, as a police officer in 1910, after Wells presented a signed petition supporting her appointment to the mayor. Wells was placed in charge of supervising regulations for dance halls, arcades, motion picture theaters, and billboards, and frequently advised the police department on matters involving women. Wells proved amazingly successful, and her notoriety spread across the United States and Canada. New York added the first female detective to its force in 1912, promoting Isabella Goodwin from the matrons' division after she helped bring a successful end to an undercover operation. By 1915, over twenty-five additional cities had appointed women police officers.

Like police chiefs, women police also organized. In 1915, policewomen attending the Annual Conference of Charities and Corrections founded the International Association of Policewomen, electing Wells as its first president. Serving as a national voice for women police, the association conducted studies to find out how and where policewomen were used across the country. Although women still did not patrol, they did begin to supervise their own divisions. Dayton, Seattle, Denver, Baltimore, and Portland all had women as supervisors over divisions of policewomen. Milford, Ohio, a village of fifteen hundred people, became the first town in the nation to appoint a woman police chief in 1914. Dolly Spencer, a strong and enthusiastic town advocate, took over the Milford police department when the old regime failed to solve the community's growing illegal gambling problem. She conducted raids on gambling dens and was able to stop the problem for most of her two-year tenure as chief of police.

For the most part, policewomen remained relegated to gender-specific police jobs from the 1920s through World War II. Un-uniformed and rarely armed (some police-women received pistol instruction), they dealt with juvenile delinquency, crimes involving women, and aiding victims of sex crimes. Their contribution to preventing crime, however, began to go unnoticed. Leading reformers such as August Vollmer, O. W. Wilson, and the FBI's J. Edgar Hoover recognized the preventive role women police officers played but saw them as essentially social workers. With the social work theory of policing falling out of favor, Vollmer and his colleagues leaned toward policing as a "war on crime" and had little use for women police officers.

This remained the case through the 1950s. Although police departments across the country hired hundreds of women onto their police forces, these new officers fell into predictable jobs, such as meter maids, clerical assistants, and social workers. Like their male counterparts, policewomen served to prevent crime. They were uniformed and given the title "patrolwomen." Yet, they remained underutilized. Only a handful of departments, namely, New York City, placed women undercover on the streets or used women extensively in police operations. The late 1960s, however, would bring tremendous change to the role of women in American policing.[21]

Uniforms and women police officers represented basic Progressive Era reform ideas, but the more intense efforts to reform police were directed toward organization and supervision. These processes began in the 1880s, before the Progressive Era, with the advent of the police commission. Civil service commissions were indeed a national trend during this time, as government at all levels began addressing problems in their respective bureaucracies. The Pendleton Act, passed in 1883 by Congress to clean up grievances and other issues in the federal civil service system, made this a national issue.

Police commissions attempted to redress these problems at the local level. Under a board of commissioners, usually consisting of the mayor, a city judge or two, and a recorder, administrative responsibility for police theoretically could be removed from the graft-ridden hands of partisan city councils and wardmen, in other words, from the machines. The effort proved unsuccessful, however, as the commissioners themselves became highly politicized. Major cities across the nation tried the police commission model; only Philadelphia did not. By the early 1900s, most cities had done away with the commission experiment. Nonetheless, this development was important in the evolution of policing in America and deserves examination.

New York City had a police commission, perhaps the most famous, until 1901 when it was abolished. Established in the 1850s (and actually administered by the state for a few years), the board of commissioners for New York police fluctuated between fits of sincere effort toward reform and more persistent periods of machine control. The 1890s saw the strongest movement toward reform of the New York board of commissioners and the police department. The Reverend Charles Packhurst (Madison Square Presbyterian Church) began a crusade to clean out the New York Police Department by attacking Tammany Hall corruption. The enduring machine responded by transferring captains and other officers involved in corruption to other precincts and assignments, but this did not quell the call for reform. The Republican Party, now in control of state politics in New York, used Packhurst's evidence of graft and corruption among New York police to take on the Democratic Tammany machine.

In 1893, the Republican state legislature created the so-called Lexow committee to investigate the New York Police Board and the New York Police Department. The Lexow committee's findings were damning: voter intimidation and election fraud; payoffs by local businesses, saloons, and brothels for police "protection"; promotion standards built around the amount of money one could shell out; liquor rings; and many other examples piled high with evidence of the corruptive influence of the boss machines. The Lexow committee recommended appointing a bipartisan police commission, with two Democrats and two Republicans replacing the current board of commissioners. The first Republican appointed was none other than Theodore Roosevelt. Roosevelt was by far the most progressive and aggressive commissioner, and even patrolled city streets at night himself to catch cops shirking their duty in saloons and brothels. Roosevelt's influence, and that of the bipartisan commission, was short-lived, however. As Roosevelt left to become Assistant Secretary of the Navy and then to charge up the hills of Cuba, Tammany Hall regained control of the commission. In 1901, a new investigation did away with the commission altogether and appointed a single commissioner to run the New York Police Department.[22]

Thomas Nast cartoon of police corruption in New York City, from *The New York Gazette,* April 17, 1892. (Library of Congress)

Other cities resorted to state-controlled and appointed boards to oversee city police departments. Cincinnati came under the control of a state-appointed board in 1887, after years of switching from mayoral supervision of police to a commission appointed by the mayor and then to one elected by voters. The state system seemed to work fairly well, but in 1902 the board was abandoned and Cincinnati returned to a four-member board appointed by the mayor and the city council. In 1910, like New York, Cincinnati pitched the board idea in favor of a single-person supervisor of police. St. Louis and Omaha underwent similar experiences. Kansas City is to this day still under the supervision of a state-appointed board of commissioners. The old problem still remained, however. Partisan political machines still had tight control over the rank and file and could infiltrate commissions when it suited them. It would take a major shift in thinking to overcome this problem. The shift would come in seeing policing as a profession and career, rather than as a politically and financially lucrative plum.[23]

Before and during the Progressive Era, police, like many other "professions," moved toward professionalization by cleaning out corruption, instilling a sense of duty and service to the community, following a code of ethics, establishing training and education, converting to bureaucratic consistency and oversight, and building professional organizations to support and lobby for the "profession" of policing. Three areas of professionalization represent the strongest push to reform policing into a "profession." First, cities began to adopt civil service models to administer police departments. Second, police departments began to train and educate their officers. And third, police across the country began to organize professional groups to share and develop ideas on policing as an effective service to protect the public from crime.

Civil service would solve a number of police problems by standardizing disciplinary procedures, appointments, oversight, and promotion. For policemen themselves, civil service provided a fair and usable promotion system. For departments and citizens, civil service established better oversight, which in turn resulted in bureaucratized efficiency for departments, thus improving protection for citizens. Civil service had a chance once city leaders realized that police could provide lines of defense against crime and make the population feel more secure in the growing industrialized cities of the late nineteenth century. By reorganizing departments on a civil service model, police now specialized according to uniformed service, detective service, and crime prevention service. Combined, this new system under civil service was much more efficient, less likely to be corrupt, and enjoyed a more positive image among citizens. By 1920, only ten of the sixty-three cities in the United States with a population of over one hundred thousand did not have a civil service system in place.[24]

To get rid of political appointments, reformers put in place competitive examinations for police positions. This would achieve two things. First, the standard for passing the examinations was at such a level that only those with some education could pass. This, reformers hoped, would ensure an educated police force that would not be under the control of bosses. (It was assumed by progressives that the bosses enjoyed more support from the lower classes because they were poor and uneducated and thus depended upon the assistance of the boss system.) Second, the exam itself promoted progressive values, such as "concern for public interest" and a belief that "public office was a public trust." This would further insulate police from boss influence. More rigorous physical and mental standards were also put in place, and in cities where these standards already existed they would be enforced for the first time. This again would ensure that police would fit the idealistic mold of progressivism.

The results were immediate. The Roosevelt Board in New York enforced physical and mental standards beginning in 1895. For the first time, a police department had strict requirements of height, weight, and even age for new recruits. Also for the first time, New York police actually stopped the common practice of recruits using substitutes to take written police examinations, which tested spelling, penmanship, letter writing ability, and arithmetic. Through early 1896, 55 percent of the over three thousand applicants did not pass the physical standard, whereas 30 percent did not make it past the mental exam. This changed the socioeconomic status of police, as well as the ethnic make-up of precincts and departments. The Roosevelt Board appointed ninety-four native-born Americans out of one hundred appointments in 1896.

Samuel Walker suggests rightly that the enforcement of civil service appointment standards broke the hold of the lower class on rank-and-file appointments and as a consequence broke the hold of the bosses on police. Better educated, more financially stable middle-class police did not need the machine. Still, the standards could be circumvented. Commissioners and supervisory boards often did not have to accept the top candidates and could in essence pick whomever they wanted off of applicant lists. One could lie when asked about syphilis or other socially and morally embarrassing illnesses. Of course, the tried-and-true bribe continued to be a problem, as many applicants still believed they were expected to offer money to get appointed.[25]

If an applicant made it through to get a uniform, he then underwent a probation period, which might or might not result in his termination from service. It all depended on how rigidly the evaluation processes were enforced. As the system became more bureaucratized, it became more and more difficult to weed out unfit policemen. Promotion also had its troubles. Historian James Richardson suggests this was perhaps the weakest part of the civil service system. Examinations for promotion tended to emphasize one's ability to take a test, not how well one performed the job. With the strong tradition of political favoritism still fresh in their minds, reformers were indeed unwilling to evaluate an officer's performance based on the musings of colleagues and immediate superiors, who were actually in the best position to evaluate performance on the job. The trust required to do this did not exist in the early twentieth century in most cities. By taking promotion out of the hands of supervisors, reformers hoped to again distance police from political influence. And again, the effort brought mixed results. The promotion boards established to administer and grade examinations were often politically appointed and thus susceptible to influence.[26]

Oversight went through an important evolution during this period of civil service establishment. Police chiefs, superintendents, and directors of public safety gradually gained control of police departments. Reformers hoped political control of the machines would decline, by giving control to one person as opposed to giving it to a board. With the decline of police boards at the turn of the century, many cities turned the job of running the police department over to a professional police chief. Larger cities often added a civilian commissioner to act as a supervisor. Ideally, the chief would be educated, a professional who commanded the respect and trust of the community. Such was the case in Europe, where chiefs came from the military and had university education. Few European chiefs came from the rank and file. Such was not the case in America, where chiefs often worked their way up the ranks and saw the chief's position as a way to settle out their retiring years. Reformers wanted the European model, whereas reality dictated the American path. American military men and university graduates saw police work from the standpoint of class distinction—it was an undesirable job of low social standing. Thus, for the most part they simply were not interested.

Moreover, since the chief's position did not carry tenure and was appointed at the whim of a mayor, chiefs were never devoid of political influence. The same applied to commissioners and public safety directors. Many cities had strict terms of office for police chiefs, a symbol of the traditional unease of semipermanent, centralized authority. This further restricted the ability of a single person to run a police organization. Civil service protected only a rare few chiefs or commissioners. San Antonio limited the police chief's term to two years; San Francisco and Los Angeles had four-year terms; and Memphis allowed only a single year. Normally, a newly appointed commissioner would appoint a new chief, regardless of where the old chief was during his term. The turnover was chaotic and certainly hindered reform efforts. From 1900 to 1911, San Francisco went through eight police chiefs; Pittsburgh had six from 1901 to 1906. Up to 1919, Los Angeles had twenty-five chiefs in forty-three years; Des Moines had eleven in sixteen years to 1917; and Denver exhausted fifteen chiefs in thirty-eight years, with one serving in the office four different times! There were exceptions—the police chief of Grand Rapids who retired shortly before 1920 had served for twenty-one years; Manchester, New Hampshire's chief was still going in 1920 after twenty-eight years in office; and Milwaukee had the same chief for over thirty-one years. These, again, were exceptions, not the norm.

Raymond Fosdick, a leader in police reform during the early decades of the twentieth century, offered this assessment of the police chief's dilemma in reforming a department under political conditions:

> The impermanent character of the chief's tenure is ascribable, as has been indicated, largely to politics. A Democratic administration wants a Democratic chief, just as a Republican administration insists upon a chief from its own party. It is one of the accepted rules of the game, and the idea of the chief as an expert in a specialized department is subordinated to the conception, difficult to overcome, that spoils belong to the victors and that the police department must be kept in line for the next political battle. Consequently, the chief is the victim of recurring political changes—appointed to his position, losing it, often reappointed and losing it again, as the political wheel registers success or failure for the party with which he is affiliated.[27]

Civil service was far from perfect. It was rigid, rarely allowing for any flexibility in rules or procedures. Moreover, for patrol officers and detectives, it often punished initiative. Those that tried to "think outside the box" in the new bureaucratic system did not get promoted. For the rank-and-file patrol officers who joined up to take advantage of the spoils, civil service reform was a major inconvenience to what they thought was a good, lucrative job. These cops resisted reform as much as they could, even supporting antireform candidates for mayor and occasionally openly defying reformist policies. Under civil service, patrol officers had a more difficult time getting transfers and benefiting from the spoils system. Probation periods and summary dismissals seemed like a violation of their right to have a job of authority. Under the old system, there was protection and security; under the new one, all of that disappeared. For the cop on the street, the reformers were "implacable foes."[28]

Those cities without civil service in place, however, continued the chaotic trends of old. In Louisville, a Republican victory in the mayor's office in 1907 resulted in a new chief, who summarily degraded all Democratic captains to patrolmen and replaced them with Republicans, some with hardly any experience at all. Democrats got their revenge in 1917, taking the mayor's office and subsequently thinning 300 patrol officers from a police force of 429! In Salt Lake City, changeover in police personnel ran as high as 85 percent with each change in office during this period. Supporters stayed behind the new system. Raymond Fosdick claimed, "It is no exaggeration to say that civil service stands between the police and utter demoralization in the cities of the United States." Corruption continued, but in cities with civil service systems, though imperfect, graft and greed were curbed.[29]

One of the more interesting aspects of police reform in the Progressive Era was the trend toward military models of police organization. Progressives tended to apply the ideas of scientific management and corporate organizational models to running city governments. After all, what was a city if not a large corporation that provided the best service at the lowest cost. For police, however, management ideas such as these proved tricky. The so-called "military analogy" seemed more fitting to what the police were supposed to be doing—fighting a war against crime. From President Woodrow Wilson (a great proponent of public administration) to New York Police Commissioner William McAdoo, progressive politicians likened American police in a range of variations to a military force. The analogy may sound extreme, but in the early years of the twentieth century, it resonated throughout the nation. Police warred on crime, a war that was no less terrifying because it was being fought in American cities. New York City Police Commissioner Grover Whalen filled in the players in the analogy: criminals were the enemy; lawyers served the criminals as their diplomats; the police manned the trenches as the last line of defense; civilians played the role of unwilling combatants; and the battlefield was the American city. Unlike World War I, where "peace without victory" was the objective, nothing short of unconditional surrender would suffice in the war against crime. A small minority, including Raymond Fosdick, disagreed with the analogy, but their dissent fell on deaf ears and the analogy became "conventional wisdom."

On the surface, it is easy to see how reformers would adopt the military analogy. Police departments had organized, some as early as the Civil War, according to military structure. Lieutenants and captains commanded battalions and platoons of sergeants and patrolmen who might as well have been privates. Uniforms, sidearms, insignia or rank and unit, salutes, and other superficial symbols supported the analogy. The deeper and more serious symbolism of a war on crime, however, was more poignant. Remember that this was a time when the military enjoyed great popularity—success in the Spanish-American War and World War I, and great heroes like Roosevelt, Dewey, and Pershing, put the military in the public forefront.

Robert Fogelson correctly asserts that the military analogy legitimized the progressive reformers' attempts to separate police from partisan politics. The military itself was not partisan, nor did it come under the corrupt control of party politics (most of the time!). Thus, logically police should be free from party machines to conduct their war on crime in American cities. Like a general who has absolute command of his forces, so too should a police chief have "absolute power" over his department. By presenting police as a military rather than as a political organization, reformers hoped to eliminate the perception that police were just another tool of the machines.

The impact of the military analogy in police reform was most felt in the reorganization of police departments. Los Angeles and Milwaukee, among many other cities, reorganized their departments along military lines and openly searched for former military officers to lead their departments as chiefs. In accordance with military organizations, departments became more centralized, specialized, and staffed with more administrative and operational support, much like a large military unit. Chiefs, like a general does to the president, should answer to the mayor and serve at the mayor's pleasure. Centralization, consolidation, and specialization became the watchwords of progressive reform according to the military analogy.[30]

The great extreme of putting the military analogy to work was the experience of Philadelphia in the 1920s. Mayor W. Freeland Kendrick, a reformist elected in 1923, applied a radical form of the military analogy to clean up the Philadelphia police department. His choice for the job was none other than the renowned Marine Corps General Smedley Butler. Butler was a veteran of the Spanish-American War, the Boxer Rebellion, and other campaigns that had earned him a deserved reputation as a fighter and leader. He was given leave from Marine Corps service by President Coolidge to take the position as director of public safety in Philadelphia. Butler attacked immediately on taking the post. Within forty-eight hours, 75 percent of the thirteen hundred saloons in Philadelphia had been closed. The idea of a war on crime was literal for Butler. He organized a special "bandit squad" armed with armored cars and sawed-off shotguns to raid prostitution houses and suspected crime dens. His attitude toward criminals was not progressive, claiming, "The only way to reform a crook is to kill him."[31]

Butler attacked the police department itself with equal vigor, basically destroying years of reform in one fell swoop. Butler abolished the department's School of Instruction and turned promotion procedures inside out. He was notorious for barging into a station house, locating the nearest sergeant who appeared to have "leadership qualities," and promoting him to lieutenant on the spot. Under Smedley Butler, it was about as close to a battlefield promotion as one could get in the war on crime. Butler's tenure lasted but two years. He was too much, too fast, and showed that reformers using the military analogy had perhaps pushed their case too well. Strong leadership could obviously go too far, and the disregard for civil procedures and for authority that was infamous in the military was not what American cities needed.[32]

The military analogy did prove effective. It helped further the separation between politics and police and weakened the grip of political machines. It made the administrative and operational aspects of police organization more efficient and effective. Above all, however, it helped supplant the traditional civilian orientation of American policing. European police models used military organization, were separate from local politics, and were supervised by the state. Now, American policing was on par with respect to organization and separation. Moreover, the mission of American policing had been narrowed and clarified. Crime fighting (police work) and prevention (social work) now defined the role of police in American cities.[33]

Police training and education also drew the attention of Progressive reformers. Education was one of the most important issues of the Progressive Era. Professions certified educational tracks for law, medicine, teaching, and other fields. Education came to be viewed as one of the ways progressives could cure the disease of urbanization.[34] Progressive police reformers followed suit, seeing police training and education as a way to decrease political influence, increase police effectiveness, and portray policing as a true profession. For reformers, the very thought of police departments putting untrained patrol officers on the streets was an abomination to what the progressive movement stood for. Turning raw recruits into well-trained, effective patrol officers was imperative to police reform during the early 1900s.

The first centralized, uniform training program began in Cincinnati in 1888. The police "school of instruction" replaced earlier attempts in the Cincinnati Police Department to offer training at the precinct level. Each recruit received seventy-two hours of instruction, which was unprecedented in police departments at the time. During the first seven days on the job, recruits took classes for four hours, then spent the rest of the job apprenticing with an experienced cop on the street. For the following three months, they took four hours of instruction per week. Classroom instruction, focused on the department's manual of rules and regulations. After this, recruits were placed on probation for six months, at the end of which they took a physical and a written examination. A grade below 70 percent resulted in a retake sixty days later. If they failed the second examination, they were fired.[35]

Another program similar to that of Cincinnati's police school would come years later. Philadelphia, one of the most corrupt cities during this period, elected a progressive mayor in 1911, who in turn appointed a reformist superintendent of police named James Robinson. Robinson initiated many changes, including the militarization of the police department, but his most important program may have been establishing the Philadelphia Police School of Instruction. Philadelphia had a police manual, dating back to 1897, but it had fallen out of use, and few recruits even knew the manual existed. Robinson revised the manual to provide more than just the "general duties of a patrolman." Using the new manual as the textbook, the School of Instruction opened in 1913. Classes of about forty students took courses that lasted four weeks. Like Cincinnati, Philadelphia recruits had to score at least 70 percent to pass examinations. Those who completed the course were awarded a diploma. One hundred twenty-five police completed the school in their first year. General Butler would abolish this school as part of his whirlwind of retro-reform in 1924.

Despite the apparent success of training schools like Cincinnati and Philadelphia, the concept of centralized police training as an important part of professionalizing police developed slowly. Centralized training schools did not become common until the early 1920s. Decentralized and informal programs could be found dotted across the country, mainly in major cities, during the 1910s. Cleveland, for example, had such a program dating back to 1903 that was administered by captains at the precinct level. These short classes, which met once a week, taught officers already in the force about local ordinances, state laws, and department rules and regulations. This program was later centralized into a school for recruits and officers. An informal gathering that developed in Cleveland in 1910 shows that police themselves were beginning to see the value of education in their profession. Called the Forum Club, Cleveland officers gathered on their own initiative to discuss police issues, the new field of sociology, and law. By 1914, the Cleveland Police Department was organizing lectures given by judges, the mayor, and other officials for officers to broaden their understanding of the criminal justice system.

Still, many schools for police training were ineffective, if not a waste of time. Investigative committees of citizens' groups and other independent agencies (another progressive innovation—to investigate through independent committees to avoid political influence) found these fledgling academies and schools to be grossly inept at pedagogy and at the new science of criminology, and were more adept pounding "unrelated facts into the student's head by constant repetition." Policemen tended to not take courses seriously, and few, if any, actually failed a class because of favoritism and grade inflation. With such a strong condemnation of police training programs, reformers eagerly took on the standard to practice what they preached.[36]

New York's police school was the first in the nation founded as an institution completely independent of the police department. New York had local, decentralized training dating back to the late 1800s. Sergeants would be assigned to teach new recruits the ropes in the precinct as well as out on patrol. This training lasted only thirty days and was rudimentary at best. With no oversight, any consistent training proved impossible, and under the boss machines, it probably was not even desirable. An attempted centralization to combine this localized training with military drill and exercise sputtered along as the School of Recruits for a few years and was finally condemned after a 1913 investigation found the program useless.

This changed in 1914. Police Commissioner Arthur Woods transformed the School of Recruits into the Police Training School, which would not only train raw recruits but also serve as a center for continuing education for veteran officers, especially for those preparing for promotion examinations. Organized like a college, the school had a permanent teaching staff, a curriculum, and an administration to run it. Three-month terms of full class days covered a range of topics: patrolling, observation, crime classification, deportment, ordinances, sanitary codes, homicide, assault, weapons, burglary, court procedures, election law, and other subjects. Part of the day was set aside for drill and exercise modeled after practices used at West Point. Every few days, students were taken to observe at area precincts. Raymond Fosdick claimed in 1920 that the New York school was the "best training system in police work which any American city of size has produced."[37]

Chicago almost took the idea of a "school," or "academy" as it became known, a step further. Northwestern University submitted a proposal for teaching college-level courses to police. Nothing came of it. Such was not the case for August Vollmer in Berkeley, California. After several years of lectures given by faculty to police on forensics and other topics, Vollmer created a permanent three-year program in 1916 that became the first real police academy taught by university faculty at the University of California, Berkeley. A rigorous curriculum covered the social sciences, natural sciences, criminal law, court procedure, and police administration and practice. Having college-educated officers out on the streets was a revolutionary concept. Perhaps the greatest impact came from Vollmer's graduates—as his "disciples," they in turn spread the word as they were hired as police chiefs and supervisors around the country. Vollmer would help create the first school of criminology at a university in the United States.[38]

The strongest support for police training came from another part of the professionalization formula—professional organizations. At a time when the American Medical Association, the American Bar Association, the National Association of Teachers, and other "professional" organizations were either finally gaining momentum or beginning to organize to reform their respective fields, police seemed woefully behind.[39]

Police leadership began to organize under the National Prison Association in 1870, an organization primarily organized for prison officials across the country to improve prison conditions. Police chiefs and other police officials participated in the Association's standing committee on police. From the 1870s to the 1890s, this was the only professional organization available for police. Because of its association with prison work, the standing committee on police spent a great deal of time and effort on crime prevention and rehabilitation as criminal justice policies.

Fortunately, however, the standing committee also recognized other problems already mentioned in this chapter. As early as 1874, the National Prison Association endorsed a professional, nonpartisan police service that would not be subject to the corrupt inclinations of the boss machines. The Association also endorsed civil service as a professional and efficient means to run police organizations and to separate police from the machines. Both were hard sells to cities in the grip of bosses, but these ideas found a national forum in the National Prison Association, which in turn spread these ideas across the nation.

The National Prison Association also supported improved police training. Beginning in 1888, the Association endorsed formal training schools and programs for recruits as well as for veteran officers. As was the case with civil service, it was difficult to convince cities to put training schools in place. Veteran officers resisted the idea, and bosses blocked efforts to fund the schools. Still, the National Prison Association laid the groundwork for police leaders to form their own organization. Important issues were discussed on a national basis, and ideas could be shared on crime prevention, organization, and new technology.

A year after the founding of the National Prison Association, the National Police Convention held its first and only meeting in St. Louis. Under the leadership of both the St. Louis chief of police and Joseph Brown, mayor and head of the St. Louis police board, over a hundred delegates from around the country (twenty-one states were represented, as well as Washington, D.C.) gathered to discuss strategies of crime detection. For three days, delegates discussed photography and exchanging rogues' galleries, using the telegraph in police work, and crime detection methods. Crime prevention also gained attention through sessions on "Social Evil" and "Abandoned Youth." Prostitution, juvenile delinquency, and rehabilitation as an alternative to arrest were other topics discussed in St. Louis that mirrored the agenda of the National Prison Association. It seemed a great start, but planning for another meeting in 1872 fell through.[40]

Oddly, no further attempts were made to gather police leaders for a national meeting until 1892. Omaha Police Chief Webber S. Seavey sent out circulars to every police chief and superintendent in cities across the United States and Canada with populations of over ten thousand people to organize a national organization at a meeting in Chicago, which would take place alongside the Chicago World Columbian Exposition. Seavey hoped to elevate American police to a "much more proficient and high standard" and in turn strike the greatest blow against crime in American history.[41] It was a lofty goal, indeed, but one whose time had come, considering the many problems of political influence, corruption, and lack of professional standards and practices in policing.

Ironically, the new National Police Chiefs Union, which would become the International Association of Chiefs of Police (IACP), did not address the range of issues as had the 1871 meeting in St. Louis and even resisted reformist rhetoric. The meeting itself achieved little, except for the very important task of establishing a national organization for heads of police. As Samuel Walker suggests in his assessment of the founding of the IACP, participants seemed more interested in enjoying the World's Fair than spending long hours discussing important police issues. Another convention was held in 1895, with annual conventions taking place in that year. The organization became a committed advocate for professionalization in 1901, when Richard Sylvester, superintendent of the District of Columbia police department, took over as president and renamed the group the International Association of

Chiefs of Police. He would serve as president for fifteen years, promoting education, civil service, the exploration of new technology, and support for the young science of criminology, among other significant issues.[42]

The IACP led the charge to make the position of police officer a full-fledged profession. Openly recognizing that police leadership should view itself on par with other professional fields, the IACP battled to create a "professional consciousness" among police leaders across the country. Public image was important, and the IACP even condemned the burgeoning silent-film industry for depicting police as buffoons. (The Keystone Cops were not the image police wanted to encourage.) This was one of the first instances when a professional organization accused the motion picture industry of being a negative influence on young people. Other image issues, such as the "third degree" and police brutality, brought the IACP to the defense of police practices. Lynching, of course, was another image issue that often placed law enforcement in an unfavorable light.

The rank and file of police in America also attempted to organize, but not so much for the expressed purpose of professionalization. Fraternal orders and benefit societies for patrolmen had been around since the 1860s and functioned more like trade unions. The St. Louis Police Relief Association began in 1867 to support sick policemen and police widows. Similar groups formed in Denver (1890) and New Orleans (1893). Fraternal groups started out to serve a more social purpose, but as reform and other influences challenged the standing of police on the streets, these groups became politically active as lobbies for police. The New York Patrolman's Benevolent Association was the first to take on this task, beginning in 1891. Its greatest achievement in the early years may have been getting an eight-hour workday passed in 1901. These activities were more in line with the general movement toward unionization of labor in America than fitting in the trend toward professionalization. The rank and file remained more concerned with day-to-day issues than with broad, career-oriented concerns. The Boston police strike of 1919 was a severe setback for police organizations as political lobbies and unions and kept the rank and file from recognizing the benefits of professionalization for many years.[43]

CONCLUSION

The historical period from the advent of massive industrialization through the reactive reforms of the Progressive Era greatly influenced the history of police in America. As the nation changed socially, economically, and politically, so too did police. But change came at a price. As departments turned toward civil service to downplay the influence of politics and enforce professional standards, the subsequent increase in bureaucratization dramatically changed policing. The neighborhood cop, known to all on the block, was in danger of extinction. As police continued to follow the professional model of the 1920s, they risked becoming faceless, nameless servants of the state. The rest of the twentieth-century history of the police in America centers around gaining a balance between bureaucratized management and community service.

CHAPTER 6

THE SHIFT TO POLICE AS PROFESSION

INTRODUCTION

After World War I, America hoped to put behind the experience of war and settle into a time of peaceful progress and economic prosperity. It was not to be, as the 1920s brought dramatic social change and the 1930s plunged the nation into the worst economic crisis in its history. Then, to top it all off, war returned the United States to the world stage, as Europe plummeted into yet another catastrophic conflict. All of these events accelerated the changes in government and society that had begun during industrialization and the Progressive Era. Their legacy would be the modern bureaucratic and welfare state, which reshaped the relationship among federal, state, and local government responsibilities, including law enforcement.

From the end of World War I through World War II, police in America underwent equally dramatic change. Police would fail in an attempt to unionize, which would be accompanied by sporadic but serious violence. In turn, police relations with labor would continue to be edgy, especially as the Great Depression put millions of Americans out of work. Police and race would for the first time become a widespread public issue, as race riots in several major cities broke out with unprecedented violence. The 1920s would be the age of the crime commission, as progressives continued attempts to reform police into more efficient and effective organizations to fight crime, which seemed to be spiraling out of control. Professionalization would continue, and the idea of the cop as a social worker would give way to the popular image of the cop as a crime fighter. Federal involvement in this process would be at a level never before seen in the history of American policing, and reform continued to focus on leadership rather than on the rank and file. By the end of World War II, police would again face a crisis of mission and status that would undergo further dramatic change from the 1950s through the 1990s.

THE "ROARING" TWENTIES, THE GREAT DEPRESSION, AND WORLD WAR II

These issues in policing evolved against the backdrop of the fabled 1920s, the Great Depression, and the greatest war in human history. Understanding this context is vitally important to appreciate the progress made by police during this time. The shocking horror of World War I and the subsequent Red Scare in the United States intensified the anxieties Americans felt as they embarked upon a decade of great change. Prohibition, women's suffrage, an unstable economy hidden by transparent prosperity, and the seemingly incessant moral decay of American society made for what historian Roderick Nash called a "nervous generation."[1]

Faith in scientific and technological progress had failed to stem the tide of disorderly change. Searching for some sort of order out of this chaos occupied the minds and time of reformers and other citizens. Although some Americans chose to find solace in a return to agrarian Protestant values, the reformers who had inherited the idealism of the Progressive Era continued to search for order in a new, organizational society based on pragmatism and professionalism. These ideas influenced all aspects of American society, as minorities, labor, industry, government, and even sports organized to improve the efficiency and effectiveness of whatever it was they undertook as a business, a service, or a people. Police found themselves in the difficult position of being caught between two diametrically opposed forces—those who opposed change and those who supported it.[2]

The Great Depression deeply and profoundly impacted American society. The economic crisis put millions out of work, which triggered all sorts of problems, if not threats, for cities and police. From the pitiful "Hoovervilles," which sprung up outside cities and towns to temporarily "house" transients, to massive, organized demonstrations in places like New York, Washington, and Chicago, and to farmers attacking the banks that had foreclosed on their land, it seemed to many that capitalism and democracy were under siege. Added to this concern was the fact that the people of Germany, Italy, and Spain, not to mention those of the Soviet Union, had turned their backs on supposedly sacred truths of free society in exchange for authoritarian regimes and programs fronted by such stimulating monikers as national socialism, fascism, and five-year plans.

The reactions of the Hoover and Roosevelt administrations to the Great Depression were as different as night and day. President Herbert Hoover believed in the invisible hand of free-market capitalism and was very leery of federal intervention to solve the crisis. As a consequence, the man who promised two cars in every garage and a chicken in every pot did little to stop the steep, downward economic turn. Franklin Roosevelt, taking office in 1933, did the exact opposite. Stretching the Constitution further than it had been stretched since the Civil War, Roosevelt used the power and resources of the federal government to intervene in the economy, put people to work, and give the impression that the government "cared." It was, in a sense, revolutionary. Roosevelt's New Deal programs had an impact on police as well, and the Federal Bureau of Investigation came of age and set the standard for professional conduct and image for law enforcement at all levels in the United States.[3]

Detroit police inspect equipment discovered in an underground brewery, ca. 1920s.
(National Archives)

World War II brought the United States out of the Great Depression, as war industries and enlistments eradicated unemployment and production soared as the government consumed. Indeed, many problems were solved by the war effort, but all was not as rosy as is often assumed. The so-called "Greatest Generation" continued its racist attitudes, went on strike during the war, and bought and sold restricted goods on illegal black markets across the United States. Crime did not cease and desist because of the war. It remained a problem, and police had to deal with it along with many other civil defense duties that suddenly fell under their job descriptions during the national emergency.[4]

Cities underwent another round of urban growth after World War I, which continued through World War II. The famous 1920 census confirmed that the country had become a nation of city dwellers (although the census criterion for a "city" was a population of at least twenty-five hundred people). Six million Americans left their farms for the greener pastures of cities. Northern cities exploded in population as well as in racial conflict as African Americans left the South in droves for better work in the industrialized North. Southern cities experienced great growth as well—Atlanta, Dallas, Memphis, and Houston boomed.

Between war and restrictive immigration laws in the 1920s, the number of foreign-born Americans declined rapidly. Ethnic prejudice and a healthy fear of potentially jobless immigrants flooding already crowded cities promoted the near closing of American borders to people from abroad. Immigrants from Mexico, however, enjoyed unrestricted access to the American labor pool, as Mexicans came across the southwestern border into Los Angeles, El Paso, and San Antonio and spread further to take jobs in Chicago and Detroit. Although significant, the decrease in immigration to American cities did not lessen racial and ethnic tensions within those cities. The ethnic borders of neighborhoods and barrios became more visible and concentrated. Asians, Slavs, Chicanos, Jews, and African Americans found themselves relegated and isolated from predominantly white communities. This increased prejudice among all groups, as each came to see themselves as isolated victims of bigotry and oppression under siege. Gang wars and organized crime took hold of these areas, replacing the boss systems of old. Often centered around illegal liquor distribution and gambling, organized crime flourished in Kansas City, New York, Boston, and, of course, Chicago.

Other ingredients added to the urbanized mix of the American city. Mass transit continued to influence urban growth. The advent of the modern shopping center changed consumer habits and affected downtown areas. Increased traffic, reactive city planning, and the dramatic growth of vice districts all shaped the urban landscape. The American city presented a great challenge to those charged with maintaining law and order. Race riots, gang wars, vice, and labor strikes added to the usual crimes of the city. All of these issues had been problems before the 1920s, but each significantly intensified at different times throughout World War II.[5]

Economic crisis and war again had indeed extended the transformation of American cities. It is within this context that police and police organizations responded to these crises. Many trends of the Progressive reformers continued, but new ideas also surfaced. The nature of crime also shifted. The rank and file of police often ended up right in the middle of these battles.

POLICE, UNIONS, AND LABOR

The rank and file had no need to unionize as long as the boss system took care of police. But with the fall of the bosses and the growing perception of police work as a career as opposed to as a job, the patrol officers on the street began to be aware of their situation and the need to organize to do something about it. Under the old system, police who came to see their job as a hassle would simply quit and seek other employment. As police professionalized, however, and patrol officers came to see their work as both a career and a profession, they were more likely to take greater interest in resolving the hassles as well as other issues.

Unlike factory workers, miners, and other trades, police were slow to unionize. Wages, likewise, failed to keep pace. Although reformers had given their full attention to police organization and leadership during the first two decades of the twentieth century, salaries languished unnoticed. The cost of living had risen 25 percent from 1900 to 1915, then doubled between 1915 and 1920 because of the war. Police salaries, however, remained stagnant. Workers had unionized and, as a consequence, enjoyed increased salaries that in many cases outpaced increases in the cost of living. Police found themselves looked upon as second class to workers in the world of labor. Poor salaries, less than ideal working conditions, the occasional danger, long hours, plus the reputation for corruption, definitely spoiled the image of police.[6]

The rank and file of police had organized in social organizations, such as the New York Policemen's Benevolent Association, but the idea of an actual union of police remained problematic. Police, like the military, considered themselves to be in a tricky position with regard to organized labor. They recognized the dichotomy of public trust. As servants of the public paid by tax dollars, could police in good faith unionize, even strike? Many departments restricted political activities of police and in fact could dismiss a police officer for engaging in such activities. Both departments and officers themselves were unsure about unions.

Unions were also unsure about police. They had, after all, often been subjected to nightsticks and rifle butts when police had been ordered in to break up strikes. The American Federation of Labor (AFL) had been ambivalent toward police unionization prior to World War I, but changed its tune after the war. Samuel Gompers, the famous and influential AFL president, gave in to pressure from several police benevolent associations and fraternal orders that were now taking on issues directly related to police as a career—salaries, benefits, work hours, and the like. In June 1919, the AFL approved a resolution favoring AFL chartering of local police unions. In the two months that followed, sixty-five local police groups submitted applications for AFL charters. Thirty-three were granted.[7]

The action of the AFL took place against the backdrop of two notable police strikes. Cincinnati and Boston both experienced strikes by police, the former relatively peaceful and the latter exceptionally violent. On September 13, 1918, Cincinnati police refused to show up for the second shift. Their demand was simple—an annual salary raise from $1,260 to $1,500. They had not attempted to unionize, but they certainly had solidarity in the walkout, as the mayor of Cincinnati was forced to mobilize the wartime Home Guard to police the city. (Boy Scouts actually joined the Guard in patrolling toward the end of the strike.) Chaos could have easily reigned, for the next day, a large parade of young men who had recently registered for Selective Service was scheduled to patriotically march through the city. With its large German American population, one can see how this situation could have turned ugly very quickly. Fortunately, nothing of consequence resulted from the policeless parade.

In addition to the salary increase, the striking police wanted guarantees that strike leaders would not be put on trial for violating police regulations. The mayor would bend on salaries but not on disciplinary action against the ringleaders. Nevertheless, he promised no action against patrol officers who returned to duty immediately. On September 16, with few assurances on salaries and disciplinary action against striking police, police in Cincinnati returned to work. Weeks later, the city granted the fifteen hundred-dollar salary raise. Incredibly, public disorder did not break out during the strike. The strike did, however, set the stage for strikes in other cities, such as Boston.[8]

Unlike the Cincinnati strike, the 1919 Boston police strike erupted in violence, although it potentially could have been much worse. Like the Cincinnati police, Boston police wanted higher salaries. The central issue, unlike that in Cincinnati, was union affiliation with the AFL. Distinctly different from the year 1918 when

America was at the height of its war experience, 1919 had been a year of disappointment, economic instability, and resurgent radicalism. Socialists and "Reds" frightened government at all levels, and unions came to rightly or wrongly symbolize the trend toward radicalism. Attorney General A. Mitchell Palmer's Red Scare of 1919 gripped the country. Often led by disgruntled veterans, incidents between radical labor groups and conservative citizens broke out in New York, Cleveland, and Seattle. A "law and order" attitude with no patience for police strikes had settled in among middle-class Americans fearful of radicalism. It was an inauspicious beginning for the "nervous generation" of the 1920s.

Boston police, like their brethren in other cities, were concerned about salaries. Salaries had not kept pace with war and postwar inflation. No organized union represented Boston police. A fraternal police organization, known as the Boston Social Club, however, began to promote issues on behalf of Boston police. Talk spread through the Boston police force in late 1917 about salary demands and unionizing under the AFL. Over the course of the next year, the Boston Social Club repeatedly proposed a two hundred-dollar raise on annual salaries to Police Commissioner Stephen O'Meara. O'Meara in return repeatedly denied the requests. The patrolman's salary had been set static at fourteen hundred dollars per year since 1898, despite a 79 percent increase in the cost of living. On January 1, 1919, seven hundred members of the Boston Social club (whose ranks had grown throughout 1918) met at Longfellow Hall in Roxbury, where they voted to demand the two hundred-dollar raise. They did not vote to strike; in fact, striking was not even discussed.

Other issues in addition to salaries brought more Boston police into the fold. Police in Boston worked a seventy-three-hour, seven-day week, with one day off every fifteen days. Night patrolmen worked eighty-three hours! Duties had multiplied to include delivering delinquent tax notices, administering the census, and even watching over Sunday afternoon band concerts around the city. Corrupt captains, despite civil service reform, held up promotions. Worse still was the horrid condition of the station houses. Rats, rotting, and overcrowding only began to characterize these decrepit buildings, many of which were more than thirty years old.[9]

Commissioner O'Meara died in December 1918 and was replaced by the cold and inflexible Edwin Curtis. Curtis's intransigence throughout the spring of 1919 convinced the Boston Social Club to seek AFL affiliation to give more weight to their demands. Boston police regulations, however, prohibited any police officer from becoming a member of an organization "outside the department." The Boston Social Club defied the regulation and petitioned the AFL for a charter. At its June 1919 convention, the AFL voted to extend a charter to Boston police, who accepted it in early August.

The AFL action was a blow to Commissioner Curtis and business leaders in Boston. Fearing the radical influence of the AFL and what that might mean for their police, conservative civic leaders voiced their concern over the trend toward unionization. Things approached a breaking point. The new union met on August 15 and elected officers, each of whom was now in formal violation of the regulation against joining organizations outside the department. All were arrested and brought before Curtis for a formal hearing. At the behest of the mayor, Curtis delayed his final decision and even offered a plan to alleviate the crisis. Boston police could keep their union if they disassociated it from the AFL, and a special committee would be appointed to look into police officer's complaints about salaries, conditions, and other issues. If the ringleaders agreed, then all would be forgotten.

They did not agree and were subsequently suspended from the force on September 8. On the afternoon of September 9, Boston police "deserted" their posts and went on strike. Over eleven hundred police walked off the job, leaving less than five hundred to maintain order in the city. On the morning of September 10, Curtis and the mayor called out a previously organized unit of five hundred volunteers as well as several companies of the Massachusetts National Guard to preserve order in the streets. But it was too late, as Tuesday night proved to be one of looting, destruction, and violent attacks against striking police and other bystanders. All told, eight people were killed with several more injured and over three hundred thousand dollars in damages to property in downtown Boston. Compared to the race riots of the time, these numbers were not so terrible, but the appearance of anarchy in the streets of Boston and its association with a police union struck a deathblow to police unionization. It would take decades for police to recover from the Boston strike of 1919 to again attempt unionization.[10]

The Guard restored order by September 11, but the damage to Boston police had been done. The press and Commissioner Curtis characterized the police union as a group of anarchists who had deserted the trust of the people of Boston. Most of the striking police were suspended permanently and replaced by a new force. Curtis announced that salaries for new officers would be fourteen hundred dollars and uniforms would be free, much to the chagrin of the former officers. The police in Boston came out looking like malcontent radicals who dared to put the citizens they were to protect and serve in the gravest of danger.[11]

Police in Washington, D.C., came close to going on strike while the situation in Boston was developing, but the negative images of Boston convinced Washington police to rethink their strategy and avoid a strike. Many cities admitted a need for a local police union, but like Boston and Washington, D.C., most could not accept a union affiliated with the AFL. Other cities reacted to the Boston crisis by being preemptive. Los Angeles, New York, and other cities raised salaries to keep their police from unionizing and striking. Only a handful of places, such as Oklahoma City, embraced police unions. Most of the local unions that affiliated with the AFL either were forced to give up the affiliation or disintegrated on their own accord. The year 1919 caused a serious setback for police unionization. The International Police Union, sponsored by the AFL in 1920, never really got off the ground. Police shrunk away from expressing a political voice, which resulted in police not really having an organized, formal voice at all.[12]

It is somewhat ironic that police would become vehemently antiradical and antilabor during the Great Depression, after having been so close to unionizing after World War I. Labor organizations grew dramatically during the early years of the Great Depression—an understandable trend considering the loss of jobs, decrease in wages, and substantial economic displacement. Police found themselves in a favorable position during the economic crisis, as salaries actually increased and, after initial consolidation, many jobs remained secure. Police were, after all, a necessary expenditure. Radical labor organizations represented a threat to an already dire situation, and police in many cities agreed. Along the same line, old ethnic rivalries resurfaced to fuel the jealousies and prejudices of the employed against the unemployed, the conservative against the radical, and the nonunionized police against organized labor. Police forces remained dominated by older ethnic groups, such as Irish and Germans, whereas new immigrants to the United States came from Poland, Hungary, and other countries from Eastern Europe. These new immigrants tended to be the foot soldiers of radical labor unions. The old saw the new as a threat to the status quo. Police easily came on board as industrialists, and the press painted the radicals as "communists" and "anarchists."[13]

In few cases was this more apparent than in the infamous 1937 "Memorial Day Massacre" in Chicago. Showing support for United Auto Workers picketing the front gates of the Republic Steel Works, hundreds of Republic Steel workers along with their families and other supporters planned a huge rally for Memorial Day. As the marchers approached the front gates, a police line moved in to block their way, ordering the marchers to disperse and go home. Marchers and police faced each other for several tense moments before someone threw something at the police. Gunfire rang out, and police rushed forward into the marchers, fiercely swinging "billy" clubs and axe handles. One woman, three children, and at least twenty-six others suffered gunshot wounds. Ten men were killed. Over eighty people, including twenty policemen, required hospitalization to tend their injuries. The violence triggered incidents elsewhere. Martial law had to be declared in Johnstown, Pennsylvania, and Youngstown, Ohio. Police killed three workers in a standoff at a union headquarters in Masillon, Ohio. Public criticism took aim at the growing militancy of workers, not at the violent reaction of the police.[14]

The threat of radicalism gave some departments cause to create antiradical units or divisions. The most famous of these was the Los Angeles Police Department's "Red Squad." Active from the 1920s through the 1930s, the "Red Squad" conducted undercover operations to spy on radical groups and suspected "Bolsheviks." Members of the squad excelled at intimidating radical union leaders, so much so that their activities led to Congressional inquiries in 1939.[15]

It is important, however, not to overstate the overall attitude of police toward labor. Police in some cities helped resolve labor problems without violence. St. Louis, Toledo, and Louisville had labor mediation offices. Cleveland, under public safety director Eliot Ness (of "The Untouchables" fame), used a labor relations bureau to coordinate police mediation to end strikes peacefully. It is difficult to assess whether the rank and file agreed with these approaches to labor strife despite the support of such policies among police leadership and city officials. Kansas City Police Chief Otto Higgins even created a special unit act as a neutral "umpire" between strikers and management. New York police adopted a policy of neutrality in strikes but would not hesitate to act against violent strikebreakers.[16]

The police experience with unionization and the development of antiradicalism attitudes had profound and prolonged impacts on the future of police in the United States. These issues would continue to drive the evolution of American policing from the 1950s to the present day.

RACE RIOTS AND POLICE

In addition to disorder associated with labor strife, police also found themselves at the center of an even more volatile and potentially threatening public violence— race riots. Along with lynching, race riots represent one of the darkest episodes in American history.[17] The role of police in these riots is telling of the problems in policing during this time. The race riots of the 1950s and 1960s often come to mind before the bloody affairs of the early twentieth century, but for the history of police these early incidents are no less significant.

Police battle with striking teamsters, Minneapolis, ca. 1934. (National Archives)

The race riots of the early twentieth century often began with a simple rumor, usually involving some attack or affront by a black person upon a White. As with lynching, the white person normally turned out to be female, which only heightened the sense of insult and the desire to avenge honor. This was not an exclusively Southern phenomenon. Consider, as previously mentioned, the large numbers of African Americans who migrated to Northern cities in search of better work, putting extra economic and social pressure on immigrants and on Whites already residing in these places. Surprisingly, it simply did not take much to touch off massive mob violence.[18]

The role of police in these riots is nothing short of controversial. Police openly discriminated against Blacks in race riots, rarely arresting white perpetrators. As a result, Whites came to believe that they would not suffer judicial or any other punishment for their actions against Blacks, which only served to enhance the level of violence. Police were not bystanders in these riots, as they often provoked and led violent attacks against Blacks and other minorities. Seeing no law enforcement to defend against white attacks, Blacks armed to defend themselves, which again only served to raise the level of violence. The riots normally ended as quickly as they began, and often for less reason, but the level of violence that occurred during the riots was truly disturbing. An unwillingness to declare this sort of violence as illegitimate and a willingness to preserve the existing social order contributed to police reaction.[19]

The race riots that occurred during World War I and shortly thereafter did not occur in a vacuum. These riots represented the eruptions of steadily building pressure brought on by competition for jobs, incidents and rumors involving Whites and Blacks, and the general anxiety of this era in American history. The race-related riots in East St. Louis, Houston, Tulsa, and Chicago provide good examples of the nature of race riots and the controversy over police reaction.

The 1917 East St. Louis race riot originated in the mass migration of Blacks into the city during the early months of 1917. Companies looking for replacements for striking white workers found them in Blacks willing to come to East St. Louis. They came in droves, perhaps as many as seventeen thousand. In a city where police effectiveness was questionable at best, this volatile situation of Blacks crowding into a city of discontented Whites set up a dreadful situation. Throughout the spring of 1917, Whites and Blacks clashed in minor skirmishes leading up to a day of escalating violence against Blacks at the end of May. Tensions remained high through June. Rumors flew through the black community that a white attack was imminent on June 30. They prepared accordingly to defend themselves. White kids firing guns into houses while riding pell-mell through black neighborhoods supposedly set off the alarm, and the black community responded.

In a poorly planned move, plain-clothes police arrived in unmarked cars to disperse the crowd. The crowd, quite naturally assuming the cars were more Whites coming in for the big attack, fired on the police. One police officer was killed and three were wounded as the police withdrew, but a mob of Whites gathered to avenge the death of the white officer. Things quickly got out of control, as small bands of roving Whites set fire to black homes and businesses and chased down Blacks in the streets, beating and killing as they went. In the end, police had neither the resources nor the inclination to stop the violence. State troops proved ineffective as well. A congressional investigation cited several instances where Blacks were beaten and even lynched in full view of police and soldiers, who did nothing to try to stop the bloodshed. In four days, nine Whites and at least twenty-five Blacks died in the riots. Countless more were injured. Over three million dollars in property damage made East St. Louis look more like a French village caught between Allied and German artillery. Blacks left East St. Louis en masse.

The congressional investigation was not kind to East St. Louis police. According to the final report, the problem came from the top: "A police force is never better than the police commissioners; and the police commissioners, in turn, reflect the character and wishes of the mayor." Both the mayor and the commissioners were the products of corrupt boss politics, which trickled down to police ranks. East St. Louis police were described as incompetent and venial, and through corruption had, according to the investigation, taken the "reins of the government from his [the mayor's] feeble hands and guided it to suit their own foul and selfish purposes." In at least one instance, police opened fire without provocation on a black woman who had simply walked outside of her home, and in another case police beat a black man to death simply because he had hidden in an old icebox to save himself.[20]

The East St. Louis riot set the stage for other public disorder in places like Coatesville, Pennsylvania; Longview, Texas; Washington, D.C.; and Norfolk, Virginia.[21] The next major riot, however, took place in Houston, Texas. As in East

St. Louis, the atmosphere in Houston was filled with racial tension. The situation, however, was different. In the case of Houston, the racial violence would actually break out between black soldiers and white police officers.

The arrival of several hundred black soldiers in July 1917 to Camp Logan just outside the city precipitated the outbreak of violence. Black soldiers on passes to visit the city eventually clashed with white police officers. The first event involved a black soldier allegedly accosting two white police officers who had arrested a black woman for using abusive language. The police officers had physically abused the woman, and the soldier was arrested and beaten, apparently for coming to her aid. A black corporal later that day attempted to find out what happened to the first soldier and found the same result—he was shot at, beaten, then arrested. Rumor reached Camp Logan that the corporal had been shot and killed by Houston police for no reason. Black troops at Camp Logan organized to attack Houston police in revenge. A captain tried to calm them down and take their rifles, even telling them that the Houston superintendent of police had informed him that the two officers were wrong and had been suspended pending an investigation. It was to no avail, as Houston police had approached the outskirts of the camp, triggering reaction by the already mutinous troops.

Rumors of a race riot spread throughout Houston. Whites heard that black soldiers were coming into town to wipe them out. In reality, the black soldiers were only interested in finding white police officers. Blacks in Houston sympathized with the black troops, but feared white reprisals. It was an unbelievably tense situation, and neither law enforcement nor the military seemed to be taking the necessary action to stop it. Ironically, white soldiers of the just-arrived Illinois National Guard finally restored order. Houston police were powerless to do anything. The mutinous black troops had killed seventeen white Houstonians before being rounded up by the Illinois Guard. Although less property was destroyed, the gunfights were apparently intense and wounded several bystanders. The black troops were immediately shipped to El Paso. At the end of the year, courts-martial for mutiny resulted in the execution of thirteen black soldiers from the 24th Infantry Regiment. Forty-one others received life sentences.[22] It was indeed a frightful moment in the history of public order in America, as the two institutions charged with preserving public order and defending democracy fought each other on city streets because of race.

The East St. Louis and Houston riots were forerunning indicators of political and social change in the United States because of World War I and social revolution in other countries (primarily Mexico and Russia). A fear of mass rebellion or even revolution by radicals, by Blacks, or by some oppressed ethnic group gripped the nation. In an effort to maintain order at all costs, any sign of disorder had to be legitimately and violently put down, or so it seemed to those Whites who wanted to maintain the status quo. The Chicago race riot of 1919 brought to the surface all of these concerns, in particular the apparent acceptance of the state, in the form of police, to accept a "tolerable" level of violence by individuals before taking action.

The bloodiest year proved to be 1919. Filled with several lesser incidents, the first major riot of that year occurred in Washington, D.C. Similar to the riot in Houston, this riot involved members of the military; however, in this case, white sailors and marines attacked Blacks in the nation's capital and police again failed to control the violence. The four days of riots killed dozens, including several white police officers. Both the NAACP and W. E. B. Du Bois called for the reform of

Washington police, criticizing the force for being anti-Black and only intervening in the riot when Whites seemed to be in danger. The police were indeed partial to Whites, giving cause for some critics to call for Blacks to arm themselves for their own self-defense. This was not, of course, the best alternative. Only a neutral police could stop a race riot. Some even suggested that a federal police force be created to police Washington, D.C. and other American cities, an idea that invoked memories of Peel's Metropolitan Police Act of 1829.[23]

The riot in Washington was an omen of things to come. The most serious riot of 1919 broke out in Chicago in late July 1919. Labor problems, corruption in the city government, bomb attacks in several black housing projects combined with what had become the usual assortment of assaults by Whites on Blacks and vice versa to raise the level of racial intensity to the point of eruption. Police managed to disrupt a potentially wide-scale riot on July 4, but conditions were still ripe for an outbreak.

Ironically, it would be police who would inadvertently spark the riot beginning July 27, 1919. Whites and Blacks normally enjoyed the segregated Lake Michigan beach, with Whites on one end and Blacks on the other, divided by an invisible but understood line. A black boy swam over to the white side of the beach and climbed aboard a wooden raft, giving white boys an excuse to throw rocks at him and taunt him. Fearing for his life, the boy refused to come ashore after being forced off of the raft. He drowned. It is interesting to note that Whites and Blacks jointly searched for the boy. Blacks on the beach began shouting for the policeman on duty to arrest the white boys responsible for forcing the black boy off of the raft. The policeman did nothing, and when scuffling broke out between the black and white crowds on the beach, the policeman arrested a black man. The black mob attacked the policeman.

That night and for the next two days, Whites and Blacks fought each other indiscriminately. Gangs of Whites attacked Blacks while gangs of Blacks attacked Whites. Chicago police, all thirty five hundred officers, were mobilized to try to control the Blacks, not to stop the Whites. Mayor "Big Bill" Thompson refused to request state militia from the governor, who was ready to give the order. Finally, on Wednesday morning, Thompson called in the militia, which cooperated with police officials to stop the mayhem. These white soldiers ran into stiff resistance from white citizens as they formed a protective cordon around the black neighborhoods of the South Side.

Once again, state forces proved neutral, whereas local police had taken sides. After the riot died down finally on August 8, those who wanted to remove the base causes of racial conflict urged reforming the Chicago police into an impartial, neutral force. The riot had taken at least thirty-eight lives, including twenty-three Blacks. Hundreds had been injured, many seriously. Rumors persisted that hundreds of dead Blacks had been thrown into a creek to hide the true toll of the riot. Property damage was huge, as entire neighborhoods were burned to the ground.

Unlike the East St. Louis riot, which was investigated by a congressional committee, a privately funded committee of both white and black businesses and social leaders investigated the Chicago riot. The so-called Chicago Commission on Race Relations produced a scathing yet insightful report on not only the riots but also the roots of racial and economic conflict in Chicago. The report recommended that the police create a special plan for riots of all kinds, that police be impartial when dealing with rioters, and that all charges of police misconduct during riots be fully investigated. In other words, police had to be held accountable for their failure to act. Unfortunately, the recommendations fell on deaf ears and had no impact on police.[24]

The May 1921 race riot in Tulsa was the last major riot in this string of violent public disorders. The trigger in this instance was the arrest of a black man who was accused of molesting a white orphan who worked as an elevator girl in a downtown office building. The black man was held in the supposed safety of the courthouse. Rumor quickly spread throughout the black section of town that a white mob was preparing to lynch the man. Armed and nervous, a crowd of blacks gathered around the courthouse that evening to fend off the rumored lynch mob. The crowd resisted police attempts to disperse them, and then someone fired shots at the police.

This caused a white mob to confront the Blacks at the courthouse. Breaking into downtown hardware stores to steal guns and ammunition, the well-armed white mob descended on the courthouse grounds. A white police officer shot and killed a black man who supposedly resisted arrest. As in East St. Louis, gangs of Whites rode through black neighborhoods shooting indiscriminately. The black crowd retreated to their own section of town and prepared for the worst. Unlike Chicago's authorities, Tulsa's municipal authorities quickly realized that police had no control over the situation and petitioned the governor to send in Oklahoma guardsmen, who were sent in the next day.

The militia gained control of the area around the courthouse, but the black neighborhoods came under a mass assault by armed Whites. Fire destroyed much of the area, and Blacks were forced to defend themselves. In the end, at least nine Whites and fifteen Blacks were killed, but the numbers were probably higher. Unlike other race riots, there was no investigation into the Tulsa riot, and therefore no recommendations were made to prevent such a tragedy from reoccurring. In all likelihood white leaders contented themselves that white dominance over Blacks in Tulsa had been restored.[25]

One would have hoped that a reactive scurry of reform would have followed these horrible riots, but nothing came of it. The 1919 and 1920 meetings of the International Association of Chiefs of Police (IACP) did not even bring up the issue of race riots, of police–race relations, or of preventive or preparatory measures. The standard and otherwise excellent works on police reform during the 1920s, 1930s, and 1940s do not even mention the problem of race riots.

Although it is easy to criticize police for their lack of action, the question does remain: What could they have done? Considering the context of police in cities in the 1910s and 1920s, police probably could not have taken much more than the few positive steps they indeed took during these riots. Racism pervaded police departments from the top down. The theory of community policing did not exist. Police training for race riots was not an option, because general training for the police was such a new concept.

Moreover, although lynching continued to be a problem during the 1920s and 1930s, mass race riots subsided after the Tulsa riot of 1921. A 1935 incident in Harlem, although horrid in and of itself, was not a riot on the scale of that in Houston, Chicago, or Tulsa. The problem itself seemed to have gone away despite the inability of police or communities to address it. These riots had been rooted in the black migration to American cities during and after World War I. That migration had now ceased, and Blacks in the cities settled into black ghettos, much like immigrants did in ethnic neighborhoods decades before. In other words, the status quo was no longer threatened; thus, Whites no longer had reason to attack Blacks on such a massive scale.

Scholar Samuel Walker points out that police response to the resurgence of race riots in the 1940s was much more proactive and effective. The cause of these riots was much the same as that of the earlier ones—Whites perceived Blacks had upset the status quo. This time, however, police were better prepared but still suffered from old problems. By the 1940s, most police departments had intensive training for cadets and patrol officers. Specialized units and better police leadership made reaction to the riots of the 1940s much more neutral and effective in restoring order. Professionalization, too, was influential, as officers came to see themselves as representing the profession of policing. Outside experts, in the Progressive tradition, also influenced police in their planning and response to racial issues. Perhaps most importantly, the nascent concept of community policing began to grow during World War II to become the linchpin of police development during the 1960s. Although far from perfect, police came out of the World War II era better equipped in a variety of ways to deal with urban public disorder. Unlike the earlier riots, where police learned nothing from the experience, police departments in these latter riots took serious lessons and reforms from the experience.

The race riots of World War II show that police had improved somewhat but still had a long way to go. The causes were the same: crowding because of migration to cities for war jobs, an increase in crime committed by Blacks and other ethnic groups, and the traditional racist attitudes that had not died away. It is estimated that from March through May 1943, over one hundred thousand work days of production for the war effort were lost due to strikes and riots, most of which were racial in nature. Ten thousand white workers at the Cincinnati Wright aircraft engine plant went on strike to protest the hiring of black workers—the day of the strike was June 6, 1944, D-Day in Normandy. Twenty-five thousand went on strike at the Detroit Packard plant in 1943 over the promotion of three black employees. Police managed to keep the strikes relatively peaceful, but the strikes could easily have gone out of control.

The "zoot suit" riots in Oakland and Los Angeles showed the failure of police to react, as soldiers and sailors beat and murdered Mexican American men who had reacted against white servicemen dating Latino women. Detroit erupted in June 1943 when Blacks and Whites enjoying a Sunday afternoon on Belle Isle turned on each other in several minor incidents. Before nightfall, over five thousand people were in a full-scale race riot on the bridge connecting Belle Isle to Detroit. In the end, thirty-four people were killed, including twenty-five Blacks. Seventeen of the twenty-five Blacks were shot and killed by police. A young NAACP lawyer and later Supreme Court Justice, Thurgood Marshall, wrote a damning indictment of police misconduct during the Detroit riot, citing several instances of police brutality, favoritism toward Whites, and unjustified killings.

New York city exploded in August 1943 when a black soldier and a white policeman came to blows. In Harlem, looting and vandalism broke out in response to rumors that the black soldier had been severely beaten. Five million dollars in property damage, five dead, and over five hundred injured testified to the scale of the violence. The great irony of these events is that they occurred during a conflict that supposedly united Americans as never before against forces representing unprecedented racial and ethnic prejudice, yet in the United States these same problems threatened that very effort.[26]

The police experience with racial violence from World War I through World War II shows the failure of police to react impartially to racial incidents. Attitudes are indeed hard to change—the institutionalized racism among police proved amazingly resistant to social change, as will be examined in the riots of the 1960s and the race-related clashes of the 1990s. Police did, however, begin to see how they could influence race relations in communities, but the road to this realization was long and hard.

POLICE AND CRIME COMMISSIONS

Although mass public disorder escaped the attention of reformers, the crime wave that hit American cities after World War I certainly did not. The entire criminal justice system came under intense scrutiny as reformers and the new professionals tried to improve the effectiveness of the system to curb crime. Unlike the partisan-motivated commissions of the late nineteenth century, business leaders and other elites in major cities across the United States joined forces with local bar associations and academics to study the nature of crime and how to deal with it for the good of the community. Although their recommendations rarely offered anything new and insightful, these commissions refocused public attention to old problems and placed police in the context of criminal justice for the first time. The idea of a crime commission would eventually reach the federal level with President Herbert Hoover's National Commission on Law Observance and Enforcement. The era of the crime commission marked an end to the image of police as buffoon-like tools of political bosses. From this point, police would come to be viewed as an integral cog in the increasingly complex machine of criminal justice.[27]

At their base, crime commissions were reactive, and, as is so often the case, high-profile criminal acts or exposed corruption motivated the appointment of a crime commission. The Cleveland Survey of Criminal Justice, for example, was the result of the criminal activities of a municipal court judge. In 1921, the Cleveland Foundation, a private philanthropic organization, provided funding for the survey, which had strong support from the local bar association as well as from scholars at Case Western Reserve University. Under the direction of famed jurists Felix Frankfurter and Roscoe Pound, legal experts, sociologists, and police administration professionals conducted the research-oriented, nonpartisan survey of the Cleveland criminal justice system. Raymond B. Fosdick would write the report on the Cleveland police department.

The Cleveland survey was revolutionary because for the first time a commission tried to get at the root causes of the failure of criminal justice and police to control crime. Using scientific research methods and academic analyses of statistical data, the Cleveland survey was indeed a fulfillment of Progressive beliefs in the ability of science, technology, and the academy to provide objective and pragmatic solutions to society's problems.

Fosdick's report on the Cleveland police department was, on the whole, positive. He painted a picture of competent police officers who were caught in the restrictive routine of an unguided system that did not reward creativity or imagination in police work or organization. Cleveland police, according to Fosdick, needed the direction of a strong, tenured police chief who was not entangled in the corruptive web of city politics. Under such a chief's leadership, Cleveland could improve its current training program for cadets, develop better retention strategies to make officers see their work as a career, and better enforce what he saw as lenient and inconsistent discipline.

Overall, Fosdick's report was geared toward making the Cleveland police a crime-fighting organization as opposed to a social work organization. Fosdick suggested reorganizing patrols by using more automobile patrols and fewer foot patrols. He wanted more centralization and less administrative waste. His assessment and recommendations forced Cleveland police to become more efficient, to change their view of what their mission was, and in essence to become more professional.[28]

Chicago's experience with crime commissions shows how the clash between the old boss system and the new reformers seesawed back and forth well into the 1930s. A city known for its vice and violations of the Volstead Act, not to mention for its long tradition of machine politics, Chicago was also a center for progressive reform movements (Jane Addams and Hull House, for example). The Chicago Crime Commission had been somewhat effective at getting Chicago police to operate with more administrative efficiency and to focus on fighting ordinary crime. This should come as no surprise, because Chicago businessmen tended to dominate the commission, and the Chicago machine wanted to protect its lucrative vice operations. Reformers hoping to do something about political corruption and vice, and the involvement in both by police, however, found little success.[29]

They would continue to find little success as long as "Big Bill" Thompson was mayor. Thompson epitomized everything the moral reformers despised in corrupt city politics. Although he supported the commission's efforts to fight crime to make Chicago a safe city for business, he resisted any efforts to clean up vice. Reformers got their chance to change this trend in 1923 with the election of Mayor William H. Dever, a reform candidate. Dever tried to get the commission and police to set their sights on cleaning up vice and prohibition violations in addition to fighting ordinary crime. He centralized control and authority in an effort to curb corruption within the police department. Neither the commission nor the police were interested, however, and Thompson ousted Dever in the 1927 election. Thompson ended centralization and returned things to the old ways as quickly as he could. Only through decentralization could the illegal activities of the machine thrive.

The return to the "good old days" was too much, too fast. The crime commission could no longer look at itself in the mirror and feel good about what it was trying to do for the public good while allowing Thompson and the machine basically free reign in gambling, bootlegging, and prostitution. Thompson tried to save his political career by appointing a new police chief and allowing a new commission, the Citizens' Police Committee, to conduct a survey to restructure the Chicago police department. The committee's report was conducted and written by academics from the University of Chicago and Northwestern University, members of the old Chicago Crime Commission, and outside specialists from, for example, the American Institute of Criminal Law and Criminology. The recommendations, published in 1930 and 1931, focused on revamping the police department into an efficient centralized organization. The proposed organization had six divisions (personnel, detective, uniformed force, traffic bureau, records and property, and morals), and each division was under the charge of a chief inspector, who answered to the commissioner of police. In addition, a secretary and a deputy commissioner were given specific functions in support of the commissioner. This brought the number of direct subordinates down from twenty to eight. When implemented, the reorganization effort merely window-dressed the entrenched corruption. It was, however, a step in the right direction, but it would take decades to approach a complete reform of Chicago police.[30]

As in Cleveland and Chicago, the crime commissions of Cincinnati, Baltimore, New Orleans, and Los Angeles turned to outside professionals to conduct and write their survey reports. The first three cities used Bruce Smith and his New York-based Institute of Public Administration. Smith, a renowned public administration specialist and reformer, also directed the Citizens' Police Committee report in Chicago in 1930. For Cincinnati, Smith outlined recommendations for a regional police force encompassing the surrounding counties based on access to highways and railroads. In a bold suggestion, Smith even proposed that Kenton and Campbell counties in Kentucky be included in the regional police force. This of course brought into question all sorts of jurisdictional issues. Municipalities, no matter how small, pride themselves in having their own police departments. Smith was correct to note the problems of such inefficient use of police resources and recommended consolidation, but the traditional need for local autonomy and fear of centralization made implementing the plan impossible. Still, Smith's proposition was a forward-looking solution to the problem of fighting crime in the Ohio River valley.[31]

Smith's Baltimore survey of 1941 was one of the most thorough to date. Covering everything from sick leave to the role of the police commissioner, Smith examined Baltimore's police department with a statistical measure for effectiveness that would become typical in evaluating public administration. He recommended more strict and consistent procedures for promotion, review, and dismissal. He offered plans to reorganize patrols, to use physical resources such as radios and cars, and to implement better recruiting and training programs. He also, as was his custom, recommended that Baltimore completely revamp its police training program.

Smith's most important recommendation, however, dealt with organization. Organizational weaknesses, a consistent theme in Smith's police surveys, caused Baltimore police to suffer from administrative and operational inefficiencies that only reorganization could cure. Baltimore's span of control from the police commissioner down overlapped in places that needed no overlap and did not overlap where connections seemed obviously necessary. Smith outlined a plan that got rid of the board of examiners and placed complete administrative control under one police commissioner, who answered directly to the governor of Maryland. He cut the number of direct subordinates under the commissioner from fourteen to six, consolidating several wasteful redundancies of the previous system. (For example, Smith placed the formerly independent ballistics laboratory unit under the control of the detective division.) Baltimore police, streamlined and consolidated, could now operate with much more financial and operative efficiency and supervision and less legislative tinkering. Smith even authored the legislative bill to reorganize the Baltimore police department.[32]

Smith's 1946 survey of New Orleans police is intriguing because of the city itself and its archaic police department. Although cities like Cincinnati, New York, Milwaukee, and Louisville at least made the effort to keep up with, if not lead, national trends in policing, New Orleans police remained decades behind. In a city of multiple cultural influences with a liberal toleration for gambling, prostitution, and drink, the potential for unprecedented corruption and graft far exceeded what already existed. Smith saw severe and immediate problems. New Orleans police had not even approached training, communication, transportation, and general organizational methods in use by most major city police departments by the 1930s.

Consistent with his other surveys, Smith reorganized the New Orleans Police Department, streamlining operations and getting rid of redundancies. Overlapping lines of authority only muddied the waters. New Orleans had a superintendent of police that changed with each new mayoral administration. A police board of five members and a disconnected commissioner of public safety also served at the discretion of the mayor. Both the mayor and the board had direct lines of control over the superintendent, who in turn had eleven bureaus plus twelve precincts under his direct command. It all made the superfluous Baltimore system look neat and tidy. Under such a system, New Orleans continued to experience the corruptive influences that plagued other major cities decades earlier. As with Baltimore, Smith got rid of the board and placed the superintendent in a semitenured position under the mayor. The twenty-three subordinate bureaus and precincts were cut to eight, with most of the bureaus consolidated under six divisions.

The reorganization of the New Orleans Police Department would only scratch the surface of improving the effectiveness of the rank and file. Inadequate foot patrols, superficial training for recruits, almost no training for veteran officers, illogical precinct boundaries, and other problems would for many make the New Orleans police situation seem hopeless. However, Smith did not consider the situation hopeless; he attacked each problem with what must have seemed to him obvious solutions: add more patrol officers to the streets with redesigned beats; build and maintain training programs for recruits and provide continuing education for veteran officers; consolidate precincts for better use of resources; and most importantly, address salary and benefit concerns of the rank and file to improve morale. It was a tall order, perhaps the tallest Smith prescribed in his career surveying big-city police organizations.[33]

Finally, another of the more significant surveys taken during this era was August Vollmer's examination of the Los Angeles Police Department in 1924. Los Angeles brought the famous Vollmer in from Berkeley as the panacea to solve all of Los Angeles's police problems. Los Angeles was not Berkeley, although Vollmer attempted the same reform in Los Angeles that he had worked for so many years to achieve in the small university community. He tried to bring together police training and local universities as he had done so successfully in Berkeley. Reorganizing divisions and restructuring patrol areas met stiff resistance from police bureaucrats and beat-patrol officers, respectively. Vollmer simply was not prepared for the deep-seated bureaucracy and political influence that controlled the Los Angeles Police Department. This failure, combined with a personal scandal that undermined Vollmer's authority, made for a brief and hellish tenure for Vollmer in Los Angeles. By 1925, he was back at Berkeley.[34]

Fighting crime and enforcing prohibition laws had become such an issue that the federal government stepped in to offer its own study of crime and police effectiveness. President Herbert Hoover appointed a National Commission on Law Observance and Enforcement in 1929 to study crime and law enforcement in the United States. Also known as the Wickersham Commission, after its chairman George W. Wickersham, the National Commission produced an amazingly detailed and exhaustive study in 1931. The original intent of the study was to look at the proliferation of crime related to prohibition, a flawed policy to start with because enforcing such a law was near impossible. Americans across the nation drank illegally and law enforcement selectively enforced the law. Moreover, the dramatic increase in gang-related bootlegging produced sensational murders and crimes that grabbed the public's attention. Hollywood had more or less made a hero out of the gangster, whereas the exploits of Dillinger, Nelson, and others made for excellent press.

The FBI often took credit for nabbing these bandits and busting up illegal booze rings when it was often the hard work of local police that brought success. Hoover tended to place his FBI at the pinnacle of law enforcement professionalism, usually at the expense of police departments, many of which were leading the way in professional development. Police Chiefs O. W. Wilson in Chicago and William H. Parker in Los Angeles, in particular, took Hoover to task for failing to recognize the vital role played by local law enforcement in enforcing the Volstead Act and professionalism.

To the credit of Hoover and the National Commission, both recognized the deeply complicated nature of crime during the 1920s and that no quick fixes would solve the problem. As far as police issues were concerned, the National Commission confirmed the same problems that Bruce Smith had found and would continue to find in major city police departments throughout the United States: poor training, low morale, lack of coordinated planning and implementation, and most of all, the presence of hamstrung chiefs of police who held their positions at the whim of corrupt political machines, mayors, and commissioners. Like Smith and others, the National Commission believed that only a professional, independent police executive could effectively do something about the growing crime problem in American cities. August Vollmer wrote most of the report and not surprisingly took the opportunity to promote the successes of and the need for police professionalism.[35]

Enforcing prohibition—A policeman stands guard over a wrecked car and several cases of moonshine, 1922. (Library of Congress)

These recommendations, however, did not have the impact that the National Commission report volume titled *Lawlessness in Law Enforcement* had on the public. This report further exposed the extent of police brutality and the so-called "third degree." Public outrage at police brutality, much of which was already common knowledge, followed the release of the report. To get information and confessions, police frequently used beatings, pressurized questioning, threats, and other unacceptable practices. Police were riding a fine line between upholding constitutional obligations and doing their jobs. The balance depended on how much the public would tolerate abuses such as the third degree. Not surprisingly, the report found that minorities, especially Blacks, were more often than not on the receiving end of these tactics.[36]

Public awareness proved to be the great benefit of the National Commission reports. As a federally sponsored entity, the National Commission set the stage for further federal involvement in policing. Unfortunately, the reports overshadowed much of the progress police had made in professionalization. Departments in Cincinnati and Milwaukee, not to mention Vollmer's Berkeley police department, had made great strides in many of the areas mentioned in these commission reports and were setting the example for others to follow. The era of the crime commission provided consistent examination of police by "experts" in public and police administrations who offered viable solutions to common problems found in departments across the country.

THE FEDERAL GOVERNMENT AND POLICE DURING THE GREAT DEPRESSION AND WORLD WAR II

Hoover's National Commission represented the hesitant introduction of federal interference into local law enforcement, something that had been resisted on a variety of levels since the formation of the United States. Under Franklin D. Roosevelt, the federal government would lose its hesitancy. An alleged crime wave gave J. Edgar Hoover's FBI the green light to bring the power of the federal government to the front door of local law enforcement. This was a big change, and one that set a trend in law enforcement relations for the rest of the twentieth century.

Quite the opposite of what one might expect, the Great Depression improved policing. The lack of funds forced departments to adopt the efficient consolidation plans proposed by crime commissions and surveys. Because of high unemployment, the pool of recruits was much larger than ever before, which also increased the quantity and quality of the cream at the top of the pool. The quality of police recruits increased dramatically through the 1930s. Likewise, once on the police force, the new recruit wanted job security, which fed the growing trend toward treating police work as a professional career, not as a job of the moment. Although police salaries dipped and then rose again to pre-Depression levels in many cities, the decrease in the cost of living meant that police were making more money by the end of the 1930s, even though their salaries did not reflect it. On the whole, police came out of the Great Depression unscathed compared to many others.[37]

The nature of crime helped bring the federal government into the police picture. Under J. Edgar Hoover's leadership, the small but increasingly professional FBI grew into a large and effective law enforcement organization. Its growth can be

"Bonus" veterans clash with police in Washington, D.C. (Library of Congress)

attributed to the growing number of criminal acts that became federal crimes. Federal crimes, according to Hoover, required federal enforcement, and his FBI was just the agency to do it. It had already been busy fighting the losing battle of enforcing federal prohibition laws, but lacked the manpower and resources. Congress made robbing banks a federal offense, as well as kidnapping (the famous Lindbergh Law). By 1941, Hoover's FBI had grown from just 772 total employees in 1934 to 4,370 in 1940. World War II would, of course, almost double the total staff of the FBI for homeland security.

This federal intervention was part of Roosevelt's "law and order" emphasis, which became popular among local police agencies. The extreme disorder and the uncertainties in the American public during the post-World War I period and the Great Depression demanded a return to normalcy or "order." The method behind the rhetoric of "law and order" was the old military analogy in policing—the "war on crime." Hoover was its greatest advocate, promoting the war on crime constantly through the 1930s and 1940s. Crime was increasing and becoming more dangerous, according to Hoover, and threatened *all* Americans. His speeches sounded more like anti-Nazi or anti-Soviet propaganda for World War II or the

Cold War rather than pep rallies to fight crime: "This army of crime is larger than any unified force in history. If this tremendous body of evil doers could be welded into a unit of conquest, America would fall before it not in a month, not in a day, but in a few hours."[38]

Although Hoover led the charge in the war on crime, he symbolized the pinnacle of police professionalism. More than any single individual during the 1930s through World War II, Hoover did more to professionalize police. Hoover promoted the image of law enforcement officers as highly trained, skilled, and ethical defenders of the public good. He announced a zero-toleration policy against using the third degree. He decried police abuse of any sort, believing that the public should trust police completely and any incidents would do lasting harm to that trust. In fighting crime, Hoover believed in criminalistics and using science to every advantage and benefit. National fingerprint catalogs, crime labs, and educated field officers were only a few of the programs and ideas Hoover built to fight the war on crime during this period.

His prize accomplishment during the 1930s was probably the establishment of the National Police Academy in 1935. This national training school proved a brilliant tool for law enforcement. A select few local police officers across the nation received extended training in the latest crime fighting techniques from the best instructors in the country, whereas the FBI used the academy to widen federal influence into local police practices and affairs. Hoover's program for professionalization fit hand in hand with the recommendations of the various crime commissions. The FBI helped train and improve crime-fighting techniques, whereas the commissions focused on improving administrative and organizational capabilities. Both approaches were aimed at the common goal of efficient policing through professionalism.[39]

Under the FBI's influence as well as that of Vollmer and other reformers, police academies, state-run regional training facilities, and college-level police education programs grew dramatically. By 1940, all cities with populations of over five hundred thousand had police academies in place for new recruit training. Admittedly, the quality and length of sessions of these schools varied widely, but considering the status of academies in the United States before 1920, the advancement had been nothing short of spectacular. State training programs and so-called zone schools taught by already established police departments such as New York City's, helped train police of small-city and village departments that had neither the resources nor in some cases the inclination to offer training for recruits or veteran officers. Partial federal financial support of these programs came in 1936 under the George–Deen Act, again showing the growth of federal involvement in local policing. Postsecondary education also grew during the 1930s. Programs at Michigan State University, San Jose State University, Yale, and the City College of New York, among others, complemented Vollmer's program at Berkeley. Additionally, the number of college-educated recruits increased in part because of the Great Depression but also because of higher recruiting standards and the positive perception of police work as a professional career.[40]

World War II ended many reform attempts and programs. As the nation made its way into war in 1940 to 1941, governments at all levels turned their attention toward the national emergency. Funding had to be rerouted elsewhere for obvious reasons. The mission of police as crime fighters expanded as police took on additional duties such as organizing civil defense, looking out for spies and saboteurs, enforcing rationing laws, and regulating the transport of restricted goods. Although duties increased, manpower during the first year of the war decreased, as many police officers enlisted or were drafted into military service. Auxiliary police units eased the burden somewhat, but overall the war put a great strain on police capabilities.[41]

An interesting development, however, occurred as a result of one of the sad moments of the American war experience. Japanese Americans were rounded up by the War Relocation Authority (WRA) and interred for the duration of the war in ten camps, most of which were located in the western United States. These camps operated like small cities, complete with city services, medical and recreational facilities, schools, and limited shopping conveniences. Under WRA administration, internees, or evacuees as they were called by the WRA, were allowed to govern themselves under strict WRA regulations.

This self-government included law enforcement. Each camp set up a police force, again under WRA guidelines, to enforce infractions of camp codes, which included over thirty-five offenses not listed as felonies under state or federal law. A noninternee security officer headed each camp police force, and police were recruited directly from the camp. Camp councils appointed a police chief from the camp as well. The security officer was responsible for training the police force and making sure it functioned fairly, just as a police commissioner or board did. In fact, some camps ultimately created camp police boards. Arrest procedures were very strict, and officers could only arrest without a warrant when they caught the person in the act of committing a crime. WRA regulations did not allow camp police to have investigative units. The FBI would investigate serious crime and any subversive acts in the camps.

Gambling seems to have been the biggest problem faced by camp police. The Poston, Arizona, camp in particular had a serious problem with gambling. Organized gangs managed to run gambling dens inside the camp, involving tens of thousands of dollars. Various gangs bribed the Poston internee police chief, Mr. Shimada, to look the other way, which he did. One block even managed to build a basement gambling room complete with electric light. Police apparently gambled for high stakes (their government paychecks) inside the police station. Things came to a head in March and April 1943, when the Poston camp council responded to angry complaints about the gambling gangs, which now had brought young teenagers into the dens where they quickly lost what little money they had. Some resorted to stealing paychecks from their parents to pay gambling debts. Threats, even beatings, grew too common for camp leaders to ignore.

Poston camp police did nothing, at first. They were part of the problem. They might as well have been police in New York or Chicago during the late nineteenth century—they would have fit well. After the April meeting of the camp council, however, police went into action, closing down the gambling dens and making several arrests. It was not enough, as Shimada was forced to resign at the end of April. The new police chief, a Mr. Ota, and the camp director, W. Wade Head, reorganized the police force (many of whom had quit after Shimada's resignation) and created a six-member police commission that was representative of the various ethnic and political factions within the camp. They also issued proclamations declaring an end to illegal gambling in the camp. From that point on gambling and the gangs disappeared.

Interred Japanese Americans learn how to handle a knife attack as part of their training to create a camp police force, Granada Relocation Center, Amache, Colorado, 1942. (National Archives)

On the whole, these police forces functioned effectively and dealt with minor issues. Only three murders took place in the ten camps during their existence, and the overall crime rate was much lower than the national crime rate during the war. Japanese Americans, interred by their government, successfully recreated that government's function, including that of the police, in the camps. It was truly a remarkable achievement considering the circumstances.[42]

CONCLUSION

Professionalization and bureaucratization often meant the same thing—reforms of the 1920s and 1930s centered on control, training, and administrative efficiency. The drive for bureaucratic efficiency, however, eroded the link between the patrol officers on the street and the neighborhoods they served. Racial problems continued to flare up and would not be fully addressed until the end of the twentieth century. Some will argue that these problems remain unresolved.

Still, police experts and administrators had made progress toward professionalism and were beginning to see themselves and their patrol officers as professional, career-oriented crime fighters, protecting the public. What remained to be added to the equation was a balance between protecting the public and serving the public—"to protect and to serve."

CHAPTER 7

POLICE AND TECHNOLOGY

INTRODUCTION

Police have at the same time been both fascinated by and horrified of technology. Since the Industrial Revolution in America, technology has been both a benefit and a curse for police. Although technology made patrolling easier and more efficient, for example, the impact of that efficiency came at the cost of police relations with the community. This love affair with technology continues at the beginning of the twenty-first century, as rapid advances in DNA testing, greater computer use, and the Internet have been major influences on police work and crime prevention. But what about the cost? That has yet to be determined.

The technological advances of the industrial period were extraordinary. Spurred by industrialization and progressivism from the 1870s through the 1910s, science and technology enjoyed a pinnacle of prominence that would not return until World War II. Technology during this time was seen as a means to make life easier and more efficient and to increase production of an already productive America. It embodied the "can do" spirit of American capitalism and republicanism. Through the trend of professionalism during the Progressive movement, police across the United States adapted and utilized the amazing technological tools that enabled them to better protect and serve their communities. Progressives also brought vigorous enthusiasm for what was already a tradition in America—the belief in technology as an advantage for American society. Police would embrace technology more readily than they would embrace Progressive reform and they would use technology to better fight the "war on crime."

The Progressive movement initiated the police love affair with technology, and like any love affair, highs and lows in the relationship characterize the experience. Technology was not the panacea that many thought it was, but it did move the odds more in favor of the police rather than of the criminal. Technology also changed the relationship between the police and the communities they served, as the new, more mobile patrol officers became more isolated from the people they once knew as foot-patrol officers.[1]

Funding often limited or delayed the adaptation of available technology, and police on the beat usually resisted it, feeling that gadgets and new machines undermined their hard-won authority with citizens and criminals in their patrol areas. Others resisted technology believing that their police departments were already doing a fine job, so why "muck it up" with gadgets and expensive apparatus that had little proof of effectiveness? For the promoters of technology in policing, the answer was simple: using the latest technology kept police "abreast of the march of progress" and thus showed citizens that police were leading the way in making safer communities.[2]

The major developments in police technology from the mid-nineteenth century through the twentieth century centered around communication, transportation, weapons, criminalistics, the use of science, and computer technology. Like most bureaucratic organizations, police departments tended to resist new technology because of cost, job security, and just because it was "new." Incorporating the new advances of the industrial age forced police departments to accept a paradigm shift. Gone were the days of block bosses and foot patrolmen. For the first time, the federal government provided funding for technology for local police. The new police would be armed, informed, mobile, and more knowledgeable than ever before, partially because of science and technology. The same can be said of the current information age.

COMMUNICATION

The advances in communication technology greatly improved the ability of police to respond to calls of distress and the effectiveness of police as a deterrent. The telegraph, telephone, and radio each had a profound impact on policing.

As far back as the 1600s, night watches used the rattle as an alarm to alert citizens and other watchmen to trouble. The whistle had yet to be invented. Rattles stayed in use until the advent of the whistle and telegraph. With the decline of the regular watch and the organization of modern patrols, rattles were retired from police service.[3]

Whistles came into use in the early 1850s. Carved wooden whistles allowed an officer in need to clearly signal for help. In 1860, the "pea" whistle improved the high-pitched sound even more. Whistles remained in use even after the advent of telegraph and electric alarm technology. In 1883, the London Metropolitan Police adopted Joseph Hudson's distinctive "police whistle," which is still used today by London bobbies. New York City police began using the tubular whistle in 1889. Its shrill sound could be heard up to a mile away![4]

Beginning in the 1850s, police departments started using the telegraph as a means to share information on fugitives and other issues with neighboring law enforcement authorities. The telegraph had actually been around since the 1770s, but up to the 1840s cumbersome wiring made the system impractical for widespread use. In the late 1830s, American Samuel Morse and his partners improved the idea of the telegraph to a two-wire, dots-and-dashes system that was easy to use. By the early 1850s, Western Union had linked much of the nation, even before railroads did. Enterprising capitalists easily adapted the simplified telegraph for telegraphic alarms and signal devices.[5]

Private security systems using telegraph technology also developed during this time. The Edwin Holmes Company developed the first centralized burglar alarm system for private use in 1858. The American District Telegraph Company vastly improved these nascent systems in 1874. By 1889, many New York City businesses and homes had alarms through private alarm companies.[6]

Police quickly found the usefulness of the telegraph as well. Boston installed a telegraph alarm system in all of its watch houses and new stations beginning in 1855, giving Boston police the ability to send its reserve force anywhere in the city at a "moment's" notice (compared to what it was like before the telegraph!) and respond to neighborhood alerts.[7]

New York City police began using the telegraph in the 1850s. The New York police telegraph, a simple inefficient system compared to later improvements, ran from the chief's office to each precinct, but not between precincts. Although this system obviously gave the chief control over the precincts, it put precinct captains in tight spots when they urgently needed reinforcements from a nearby precinct. All communication went through the chief's office, which wasted valuable time and penalized initiative on the street. Yet, despite this direct communication link with each precinct captain, the chief remained weak in relation to the whole. Too many precincts with headstrong captains and an oversight system that placed real power in the hands of police commissioners gave precinct commanders some latitude.

The New York police telegraph system proved its worth during the bloody Civil War draft riots of July 1863. Irish immigrants feared that a war to free slaves would result in an influx of Blacks to New York. Once there, the freed slaves would accept lower wages and thus undercut Irish wage labor. Combined with what the Irish perceived as upper-class Protestant exploitation and minor incidents throughout the summer, the city seemed on the edge of explosive violence. As a new round of drawings for the draft began on July 11, the Irish anger exploded into several days of unbelievably violent riots. Mobs attacked military offices and businesses that employed or were owned by Blacks. Others took the disorder as an opportunity to loot and destroy property. In the end, at least 105 people were killed, including 11 Blacks, 8 soldiers, and 2 policemen. Rioters, many of whom were killed by police, made up the remaining dead.[8]

Telegraph operators at police headquarters sent and received over five thousand messages during the four days of the riot. Most were between headquarters and precincts. Rioters even noted the role of the telegraph, as they ripped down lines across the city to impede police response. Police commanders centered reserve forces at headquarters and then dispatched them as needed to the widespread locations of violence. The telegraph helped commanders decide where to send police en masse to resist the mob, but transportation problems often delayed their arrival. Although police commandeered carriages and wagons, most ended up getting to the scene on foot, often too tired and bedraggled from the trek to be much use against the mob. Still, communication and centralized command allowed police to eventually overpower the mob at several locations, thus preventing an already deadly riot from becoming even more horrific. Battle-weary troops from Gettysburg arrived on the scene late after a long forced march but had little impact on the end result, as Army commanders could not agree on what action to take.[9] The incident proved the value of telegraph communication for police and that police could coordinate an effective response to mob violence.

The telegraph became even more usable as an alarm and signal device by the end of the 1870s. Because of industrialization, wire was cheaper, as were the devices themselves. The big development, however, was that of the telephone. Alexander Graham Bell's telephone could transmit voice instead of dots and dashes. First demonstrated publicly at the Centennial Exposition in Philadelphia in June 1876, Bell created the Bell Telephone Company to market his device the following year. With telegraph and telephone, the possibilities abounded for police, especially for departments in large cities.[10]

Chicago took advantage of these developments to experiment with a new Police Patrol and Signal Service in 1880. The mayor and secretary of the police department hatched the idea over drinks at a social engagement. Their conversation turned toward quicker police reaction to crime and the impact of instant communication between officers on patrol and their station. The secretary later that evening ran into the superintendent of the Fire Alarm Telegraph Service and shared his conversation with the mayor. Both quickly concluded that a system similar to the fire telegraph would work just as well for police purposes. The superintendent presented a plan to the secretary and the mayor the following day. From this plan was born the Chicago signal box system.

The plan was simple. Throughout Chicago weatherproof call boxes with electrical links to local police stations would be placed in strategic but accessible and visible locations. Each box would be enclosed in a sentrylike structure and also contain a telephone with a direct wire to the operator at the area station. The sentry houses containing the call boxes would remain locked, with the patrolman on duty and area residents having keys to the sentry house. This would achieve two things. First, citizens would have almost instant access to police protection. Second, the security citizens would feel by the mere possession of a key would greatly calm neighborhood concerns about crime. The result: once criminals learned of the boxes, the very existence of the boxes would act as an effective deterrent. Each station would keep a manned wagon on constant alert to respond to signal box alarms.

An early multiple-signal box, with both telegraph and telephone. (George W. Hale, *Police and Prison Cyclopaedia* [Boston: W. L. Richardson Co., 1893], p. 795)

Surprisingly, Chicago patrolmen opposed the system as rumors of its introduction spread throughout the department. Many believed that this was simply a modern way of checking up on beat patrolmen to make sure they were not slacking off while on duty. Moreover, city leaders at first resisted because of the cost of the initial outlay of such a system. Through some creative budget rearranging, the Chicago Police Department installed some boxes to test the system. It proved a great success, and before long signal boxes and their increasingly familiar sentry box enclosures dotted the entire city.

The boxes worked rather simply. Upon opening the sentry box door, the citizen only had to pull down the lever on the signal box, which set off a signal unique to that box's location at the local police station. Within minutes, theoretically, police would arrive on the scene. The signal box success extended to the private sector as well. By 1881, private signal boxes were available at the cost of twenty five dollars for businesses and even for private residences. Four hundred signal boxes were installed in Chicago that year.

Some initial problems resulted in practical solutions that improved the system. For example, the question arose about the cost of having an ambulance service and manned-response wagons. Why not combine the two? A wagon designed with fold-down stretchers allowed the vehicle to be used as a transport for police or as an ambulance for the injured when needed. The maintenance of the signal boxes and wires constantly made budgets bulge. Over time, efficient beats and strategically placed stations made the signal system even more effective. Of course, one problem remained unsolved—how to stop criminals from cutting the wires from the sentry house.[11]

Boston was slow in learning from Chicago's successful experience with signal boxes. Commissioners in 1883 recommended installing a signal box system, but the cost caused aldermen to pause. Installing the system would cost over one hundred thousand dollars, and yearly maintenance was estimated at over ten thousand dollars. Moreover, the Boston alarm firm that had put in the first bid for the system had yet to prove its system successful. Perhaps more significantly, commissioners and aldermen alike agreed that Boston had the best police force in the nation—mass disturbances had not occurred since the bloody Civil War draft riots, theft had decreased as had homicide, and streets throughout the city could be safely traveled by day or night, at least according to the assessment of this eminent body. This over-confident feeling convinced city fathers that "if it ain't broke, don't fix it." Infamous Boston politics clouded the issue as well, as Democrats and Republicans debated not only the viability of the signal system but also which Republican or Democrat distributor should get the contract (Gamewell or Wilson). The issue was finally resolved in 1885, when Boston began installing Gamewell signal box devices.[12]

By the early 1890s, departments across the United States had installed signal box systems and applauded the results. Gamewell and other alarm companies now had signal boxes that combined telegraph alarm and telephone technology. Dallas put in telephone boxes in 1908, and Phoenix installed boxes in 1912. W. J. McKevley, superintendent of the Brooklyn police department, lauded the advantages of the call box to the International Association of Chiefs of Police annual meeting in 1896. Before the advent of the telegraph, the telephone, and the call box, a patrol officer might have to escort an unruly prisoner for many blocks to a station house, wasting valuable time and effort and leaving his beat unprotected for a long period of time. With the patrol box, the beat officer simply had to get the prisoner to the nearest box, which was normally only a few blocks away at most, and "in a jiffy" a wagon with two patrol officers arrived to take the prisoner to the local station. William P. Rutledge of the Detroit Police Department claimed that the advent of the telephone patrol box was an "epoch-making improvement" in policing.

The next step was wireless communication. Guglielmo Marconi's radio experiments and inventions during the early 1900s made radio for police use possible. Spurred by the Titanic disaster and World War I, radio evolved into a usable communication medium by the 1920s. August Vollmer of the Berkeley Police Department put two-way radios in police cars for the first time in 1921. However, as was the case with most new technology, other police departments were slow to catch on and accept the radio's usefulness. Not until the 1930s did police departments across the country begin to utilize two-way radios in their patrol cars. Part of this hesitancy lay in practical problems with the technology. The first radios were bulky and temperamental. By the 1930s, the equipment had been modernized to a more practical size. With this improvement came better reception and reliability. Primitive frequencies caused problems as well. Early radio bands were all open to public ears. The Federal Radio

Pasadena, California, police inspect newly installed Transitone radio receivers in a patrol car, ca. 1910s. (Library of Congress)

Commission at first did not see the benefit of police frequencies, thus forcing departments to use public airwaves to, in effect, broadcast their activities.

Detroit's William P. Rutledge commented on the frequency problem and on other radio issues in 1929. Detroit experimented with radios for police work in 1921, putting receiving sets in its patrol cars and using radio to broadcast license numbers of stolen cars throughout the state of Michigan. Because of infantile federal regulations on radio use, the Detroit Police Department had to basically open its own station to broadcast to its patrol cars and to share other information with other local departments. Under federal regulations, all radio broadcasts had to include entertainment. Thus, "if we wished to broadcast an alarm of a murder or a holdup, we must first play a tune on a fiddle." Detroit gave up on the public station but a few years later obtained an amateur license, which did not require fiddle playing.

These early receivers in patrol cars could also pick up commercial broadcasts, but in so doing had to be tuned to a frequency different from that of the police station. Patrols were often caught listening to music instead of to the police band. Supervisors then rebuilt car receivers with locked cabinets so the band could not be changed. Rutledge predicted that "before long" all patrol officers and patrol cars would have personal radio receivers, and radio orders would direct all police patrols twenty-four hours a day, seven days a week. Radio, in his opinion, would cut crime in half and be a "powerful deterrent."[13]

By the mid-1930s, police departments around the nation had adapted two-way radio communication for patrol cars and motorcycles. Radios certainly helped police respond to calls quicker and also allowed stations to keep an eye, or ear, on their units patrolling the streets. The next great shift in police communication came with the creation of the 911 emergency telephone system, which would once again alter how police did their work.

TRANSPORTATION

Hand in hand with communication advancements, the development of better transportation also changed the way police did their job. The automobile, another product of industrialization and urbanization, had a huge impact on American society. Foot patrols were often inefficient, and even as late as the 1920s, many cities operated patrols under plans that had not changed in over fifty years, failing to take into account the dramatic changes urbanized growth had wrought on cities across the United States.

Walking a beat of several square blocks meant that the single foot patrolman could not be everywhere at once. This system had been in place since the colonial watches, using the rattle as their only means of alarm. Under this system, superiors had no way of contacting a patrolman, nor did the patrolman realize when his services were needed blocks away. As urban areas expanded and population in inner-city areas became denser, the foot patrol could not adequately cover beats and provide effective deterrence, protection, and response. To do it properly would break a department's budget because of the large number of officers on patrol needed to do the job. Criminals adapted to the new conditions. Foot patrolmen were predictable and regular in their beat. All the criminal needed to do was wait for the officer to pass and then commit the crime. Crime in the new suburban neighborhoods tended to be committed by criminals from other parts of the city, thus turning the foot patrolman into a mere "signal and warning" to the criminal, but no longer into an effective deterrent.[14]

Using horse and wagon to transport officers to patrol different areas eased the burden on police departments somewhat. Patrol wagons became more advantageous as cities grew in size and as fewer foot patrolmen were available to cover the larger patrol areas. Along with improved communication, wagons enabled police to concentrate large numbers of men at a central point to respond to larger emergency situations, such as manhunts and riots. In 1881 in Chicago, where the wagon served as transport for both police and ambulance, officers in command of the wagons began to receive basic medical training as the number of alarms for accidents increased as people became aware that the alarm could also be used for first aid.[15] Boston put into service three police ambulances in the 1870s, and many other cities utilized wagons as well. Wagons and mounted patrols increased the amount of ground a patrol could cover, but the basic problem remained: Those who made budgets figured that fewer men in wagons covering more ground was more efficient than fewer foot patrolmen covering more ground.[16] Relative coverage did not change.

Some departments would turn to bicycles, which actually proved quite effective. New York police introduced a bicycle squad in the mid-1890s. With only twenty-nine officers, the New York Bicycle Squad made over thirteen hundred arrests in its first year of operation. Ultimately, the squad would grow to over one hundred officers who did everything from arresting drunks to chasing down runaway carriages, all on bicycles.[17]

The automobile went furthest in solving the patrol problem. With the car, a patrol could cover more ground faster than ever before. This solution pleased the accountants as well as the police. Both private security companies and public law enforcement agencies saw the benefit of the automobile.

For private security companies, the automobile greatly improved guarded transport. Perry Brink's payroll transport company, which started in 1891 with a contract with Western Electric Company, used horse and buggy to move cash boxes from one place to another until a shipment was attacked (drivers murdered) in 1917. Brink made the shift to trucks, which he would develop into armored cars by the mid-1920s. His first trucks had few modifications, mainly steel sheets bolted over the wooden sides of the vehicle. A clever bomb attack on a Brink's truck in 1926, which blew out the unprotected undercarriage and allowed the robber to get away with $104,000 in cash, forced Brink to redesign the trucks into what is more familiar to us today. Wells Fargo and American Express, along with Brink's transport company, dominated private secure transport and provided businesses and banks with secure means to move cash and other valuables without relying on police for protection.[18]

Kansas City and Berkeley were the first large cities to try automobiles as replacements for foot patrols. In Kansas City, budget cuts and fewer officers made the switch to automobiles a viable alternative. August Vollmer's Berkeley Police Department made a successful switch to cars, finding that a patrol officer in a small Ford could cover one thousand street miles per month. Moreover, patrol officers in cars could respond to calls faster, not be tired out when they arrived to the scene of the crime, and overall could perform much more effectively and efficiently. Statistics proved Vollmer's case for car patrols. From 1908 to 1915, Berkeley's population grew from thirty-seven thousand to sixty-four thousand people. In response to this growth, Vollmer only added five officers to his force. His now-mobile patrol officers increased their response time by 14 percent against a 78 percent increase in population. The value of stolen property actually decreased by 28 percent due in part to car patrols and better police training—another Vollmer innovation.[19]

An early-1900s traffic stop by the bicycle patrol. (National Archives)

In 1908, Louisville Police Chief J. H. Haagar ordered three automobiles to replace the department's horse and buggy teams. Haagar praised the automobile for its economy and faster response time. The automobile could make a long trip much faster than a horse and buggy. Arriving at a scene several minutes earlier than usual often made a difference of several hours, even days, in apprehending criminals and, in some cases, saving lives. Combined with the gradual installation of residential telephones and call boxes on the streets, the automobile enabled police to get the crooks as they left the house instead of missing them completely. Haagar boasted that now his police could respond to four calls compared to one on horse or on foot.

The new cars cost Louisville nineteen hundred dollars each, compared to eighteen hundred dollars apiece for horse and wagon. The longevity and maintenance expenses of the automobile compared to those of the horse-drawn wagon made it even more of a bargain. Citizens decried this initial expensive outlay as "extravagant" but after seeing the results gladly accepted the new machines as an integral part of their protection. Said Haagar, "The horse as a means of locomotion is restricted in strength, speed, and endurance, but the automobile never tires, and in my opinion it will only be a short time when it will be universally adopted for patrol service in all of the police departments of the county."[20] His prediction was right.

In 1909, the Omaha Police Department purchased automobiles out of necessity. The police stable burned to the ground one night, destroying all of the department's wagons and tragically killing most of the horses. Omaha Police Chief J. J. Donnohue decided the time was right to try the automobile.[21]

Detroit put 150 Fords (no surprise) on former foot-patrol beats in 1918. Each car carried a uniformed patrol officer and a plainclothes officer and added a very visible deterrent to the streets of Detroit, so much so in fact that responses decreased by 125 during the first month of operation. Detroit found the cost of cars appealing, as did many other cities that turned to automobiles. The initial hesitancy because of start-up costs and maintenance was overcome by the salary savings of what two patrol officers in a car could do compared to six or eight officers on foot. Dallas put its first patrol car on the streets in 1912; Orlando, in 1920; Portland, in 1911; Phoenix, in 1920; and Yonkers had one car on patrol in 1912. Cars did not completely replace the beat officer, however, as heavily congested inner city streets still favored the patrol officer on foot. Moreover, the car isolated patrol officers from the people they once knew well as they walked their neighborhood beats.[22]

GUNS

Firearms are also technology, and of all the apparently obvious things that police should have adopted earliest and without question, sidearms come immediately to mind. This was not the case, however. The fear of a standing army and centralized authority had not died away just yet, and armed, even uniformed, police represented just that. Moreover, the uncertain role of police in city politics and conflict among urban groups made an armed police force rather daunting to many urbanites of the industrial period. Replacing the traditional club with revolvers and other firearms was a reluctant, reactionary move on the part of citizens and police in many American cities.[23]

In Boston, for example, watchmen and patrolmen had only carried rattles for alarm and rarely had to use these as weapons to defend themselves, or, as occasionally happened, the person they were apprehending would take the rattle and use it against the officer. In 1855, the Boston General Court gave police permission to carry an eighteen-inch club. Other than clubs, however, guns had not been previously considered for police use. Sheriffs and constables had been armed for decades, but these officers of the court also performed civil duties. Arming the watch was never an option because of the very nature of the men who often manned it!

Consider that before signal boxes and patrol wagons the patrolman walked his beat alone and unarmed in a world where criminals increasingly armed themselves with pistols and revolvers. In Boston, before the Civil War, escaping criminals gunned down three policemen and watchmen in one year. The Massachusetts assembly had never listed guns as outlawed weapons, which makes some sense when the constitutional right to bear arms, as it was then interpreted, is taken into account. Guns, however, were extremely deadly in the hands of the criminal element, yet, the Massachusetts assembly had banned slingshots, brass knuckles, "billy" clubs, and other dangerous weapons, leaving guns unregulated. By the end of the 1850s, many officers began carrying revolvers, even though they had no official authority to do so.[24] What grew out of unauthorized habit became accepted practice, mainly because there was simply no other way to deal with rowdy, armed criminals.[25]

The Boston draft riot of 1863, indicative of draft riots across the North, the most violent of which took place in New York City, changed the gun policy. Boston police were not armed when the riot began on July 14. As usual, the riot began small enough, but quickly expanded as mob mentality took over. Irate women started the event by attacking a couple of marshals serving official papers in a working-class neighborhood. Bystanders jumped in and nearly killed a patrolman who tried to intervene. The telegraph spread the alarm as the mob grew and moved toward the armory. Soldiers there repulsed the mob's advance. Police reserves blocked the mob's route to the Dock Square gun shops. Here, mostly unarmed police stopped the crowd with clubs.

In response to the police disadvantage during the riot, the Massachusetts assembly granted police the authority to carry firearms later in 1863. Another significant result of the incident was that police became seen as heroic for the first time in Boston. From this point on, the image of Boston police as drunken, lazy watchmen disappeared. It was not until 1884, however, that Boston armed each member of the patrol force. Eight hundred Smith and Wesson .38-caliber revolvers were purchased and kept at stations to be checked out when on patrol.[26]

New York City police carried twenty-two-inch clubs, which became standard issue in 1853. These could be used only for self-defense. As was the case in Boston, New York criminals tended to be better armed than police. Throughout the 1850s, crime in New York remained constant and violent, becoming so critical that citizens' groups threatened to form vigilance committees. Newspapers decried that the streets of New York were more dangerous than any place out West! Bars and other houses of ill repute overflowed with gun- and knife-carrying young men. Fights in these places normally resulted in injury or death. Six were killed in one night alone in November 1857. Police found themselves at risk in these situations because they were unarmed.

Police Superintendent Frederick Tallmadge suggested arming New York officers in the late 1850s but was refused. (As in Boston, many officers carried small revolvers anyway.) New York police had not authorized a standard revolver until the Roosevelt Board adopted the .32-caliber Colt in the 1890s. Other cities finally came around to adopting sidearms as standard issue for police officers. Philadelphia gave police sidearms in 1892. Phoenix, still a somewhat wild and wooly place in the early 1900s, did not adopt a standard-issue sidearm until 1911.[27]

The 1920s and 1930s represent the full "coming over" of police to the use of firearms. Revolvers remained the weapon of economic if not practical choice. "Firearms expertise" became a symbol of professionalism in police departments across the nation. Chicago, New York, and Los Angeles in particular boasted extensive training and competitions, primarily with revolvers. Los Angeles police even claimed that revolver training and practice had helped reduce robberies by 44 percent and automobile theft by 24 percent. More bandits, rather than escaping, were finding their way into the morgue because of gunfights with police. Competitive police shooting leagues began to develop, such as the New England Police Revolver League and the American Police Revolver League. The National Rifle Association sponsored police marksmanship competitions with teams representing police departments from all over the United States.[28]

One of the most intriguing developments during the 1920s and 1930s was police use of the machine gun. Not until the last year of World War I did a hand-held machine gun become available for public use. J. T. Thompson's submachine gun was the most famous, but U.S. Army tests deemed it impractical for use in the military. Thompson modified the weapon for police tests, using cartridges with birdshot instead of with solid slugs. Although Thompson promoted the machine gun as an effective weapon against criminals, his idea of using less-than-lethal force anticipated police concerns about using force against large crowds. Considering the race and labor riots of the then recent past, Thompson should have promoted the weapon for crowd control. Less than lethal force was, however, a police concern and would remain so: tear gas became popular in the late 1930s, whereas rubber bullets were used beginning in the 1960s to disperse riotous crowds.

Thompson demonstrated his weapon in New Jersey in 1922, convincing police departments in New York, Boston, and San Francisco that the weapon had some potential. Ironically, police seldom used the Thompson gun against criminals, preferring to use it instead to frighten striking workers. Mobsters took to the gun as if it were the greatest thing since gunpowder itself. The gangster could drive by and spray his intended target without regard for killing or wounding innocent bystanders. Police, on the other hand, could not afford such luxury. The potentially uncontrollable spray of the machine gun could kill or maim dozens of innocents in the attempt to get a few bad guys.

The most famous incident involving machine guns was, of course, the St. Valentine's Day Massacre of 1929 in Chicago. Dressed as police, two Capone thugs machine-gunned seven of Bugsy Moran's men in systematic cold blood. From this point on, Hollywood immortalized the machine gun-toting gangsters in film after film. The machine gun would play a prominent role again in the 1930s as the weapon of choice for bank robbers like John Dillinger, Pretty Boy Floyd, Baby Face Nelson, and Machine Gun Kelly.

Women police receiving marksmanship training, ca. 1910s–1920s. (Library of Congress)

Police, however, could not risk widespread use of the machine gun to fight crime or crowds. They continued to rely upon shotguns and revolvers for everyday use and only rarely turned to automatic weapons to chase down criminals. Gradually, as the repeal of Prohibition in 1933 decreased mobster activity in the big cities, the Thompson machine gun fell out of use.[29]

CRIMINALISTICS

The modern science of criminalistics developed in the 1880s. A European innovation adopted by American police departments, this new approach to crime fighting involved using science and scientific methods to detect and analyze clues and solve crimes. The movement began with the use of commercially available technology and scientific methods and then moved on to utilize tools specifically developed for police.

Photography was one of the earliest technological developments to impact police work. By the Civil War, daguerreotype photography enabled police to create "rogues'" galleries. New York created a rogues' gallery in 1857—within eight months the collection had grown to over seven hundred photographs. Boston police took up the practice in 1862. Other police departments using photographs during this time included those of Philadelphia and Chicago.[30] Kansas City did not create a rogues' gallery until 1893, but the collection of wanted scoundrels was by all accounts quite extensive.

Galleries of known criminals were helpful but limited. What was needed was a system of recognizing criminals *before* they committed the crime. Science and technology made crime prevention theoretically possible. French criminologist Alphonse Bertillon made the first great advancement in the new field of criminalistics. Bertillon developed a system whereby criminals could be identified through unique physical characteristics. Using body measurements, distinguishing characteristics such as scars, photographs, and upon its development, fingerprint technology, Bertillon created a standardized system for identifying criminals and repeat offenders. Bertillon also developed the modern "mug shot," the idea of photographing crime scenes, and the use of handwriting analysis as an investigative tool. In essence, Bertillon began what would become the modern police crime laboratory.

Typical of the medical and psychological vogue of the time, the Bertillon system became widely popular in both Europe and the United States. The Chicago Police Department was the first to use the Bertillon identification system in 1888. The Kansas City Police Department adopted the system in 1895. New York police began using the Bertillon identification system under the Roosevelt Board but quickly turned to new fingerprint technology as a means to identify people.

Fingerprint technology proved much more reliable than the increasing fallible Bertillon system. Bertillon failed because not all physical characteristics are unique. Many people exhibit the same arm, head, and finger measurements, and may have scars or other body marks in similar places. A new, more reliable identification method was needed. It came with the perfection of dactyloscopy, or fingerprinting, which was developed separately by amateur English scientists Dr. Henry Faulds and Sir William J. Herschel, who both used what they at first considered a novelty to successfully identify criminals in the 1870s and early 1880s. Sir Francis Galton, a famous English scientist, built upon Faulds and Herschel's work and established

The New York City Police Department's rogues' gallery, 1909. (Library of Congress)

the principle that fingerprints are unique and do not change over a person's life-time. Based on Galton's work, Scotland Yard added fingerprinting to the Bertillon identification method in 1894.

Police in the United States hesitated to latch on to European success with finger-printing. St. Louis became the first city to have its own fingerprint agency after police leaders there witnessed a demonstration of the technology at the 1904 St. Louis World's Fair. New York began using fingerprinting as standard procedure in 1906. Still, politics, money, and reluctance among police to learn new scientific methods kept fingerprinting from gaining widespread acceptance in the United States until the 1930s, when over half of the states and the FBI had fingerprint bureaus and labs.[31]

Microscopes (used to identify hair and blood) were commercially available in the 1860s but were scarcely used by police and detectives.[32] By the early 1900s, however, police began to see the light and utilized microscopes and other scientific instruments in their investigations. Los Angeles established the first police crime laboratory in the United States in 1923, modeled after Edmund Locard's crime lab-oratory in Lyon, France, built in 1910.[33] This significant development centralized evidence analysis and other tasks under one roof with trained criminologists. The first involvement of an institution of higher education in crime laboratories came in

1929 when Northwestern University established a crime lab as a result of the St. Valentine's Day Massacre investigation. The FBI crime lab opened in 1931 and would become the best facility of its type in the world.[34]

POLICE STATIONS

The physical buildings housing police also had to change with all the new technological developments and police reorganization of the late nineteenth and early twentieth centuries. For practical reasons as well as for their image, police began to build what would evolve into the modern police station.

In 1855, Boston began converting its watch houses into police stations. The reorganization of the department promoted this change in physical structure to house the police. First and foremost, Boston replaced the old watch with paid, uniformed patrolmen. Additionally, investigative officers (sergeants, captains, etc.) now needed work space. This switch to a more military-like organizational structure made police work more efficient, instilled discipline, and gave cause for permanent quarters beyond what the old watch required. Stations had to have office space, detention cells, sleeping quarters for policemen, and a reception area in which the public could lodge their complaints. A station completed in 1857 included the following: a jail in the basement with twelve separated cells (four for female prisoners, eight for male), a public reception office, captain's office, muster room, equipment room, sleeping quarters for lieutenants plus four more for patrolmen. Boston police considered it one of the most modern in the nation.[35]

New York stations in the 1850s suffered from overcrowding, poor ventilation, and overall foul conditions. Part of this problem came from the homeless, who often slept in stations, a condition that remained until 1896 when police stations no longer had to keep vagrants overnight. Architects redesigned over twenty stations over a twenty-year period, but urban growth combined with budget limitations kept the stations from keeping pace with growth. New York police consistently found themselves behind the times instead of ahead of the game. Currently, however, New York police stations maintain their past heritage by continuing to display a green lamp outside station entrances, just as the old watch houses did more than a century before, as a reminder to citizens that the NYPD is on the job.

By 1896, Brooklyn had over thirty stations for almost two thousand policemen. Each station boasted "spacious, clean, and well ventilated" bunk rooms, built to health department specifications. Jails attached to the stations had lavatories and showers and "other conveniences of first-class hotels." Spaciousness and cleanliness apparently resulted in a decrease of 60 percent in sick leave among policemen.[36] Cities like Pittsburgh, Philadelphia, Boston, and Brooklyn also reacted efficiently and swiftly to urban population and geographic growth, building stations and detention facilities accordingly.[37]

COMPUTERS AND "911"

The boom of technological growth for police waned in the late 1930s and continued to decline through World War II. The Great Depression, the war, and resulting strains on manpower prevented technological developments during this time, such as radar and computers, from trickling down to local police. Although reform again revolutionized police departments in the 1950s and 1960s, technology was slow to catch on.

President Lyndon Johnson's 1967 Crime Commission report criticized police agencies for failing to keep pace with the remarkable advances in science and technology since World War II. The advent of the telephone, the radio, and the automobile brought huge benefits to policing, but that change stagnated after the 1930s. Crime labs of the 1960s looked much like the labs of the 1920s. Police fell into the habit of calling on science and technology to help solve specific crimes rather than to contribute to overall community policing and crime prevention. Many factors influenced this stalemate, including funding, uncertain markets for police-related technology, and lack of technology-literate personnel in law enforcement. The commission's report recommended that the federal government assist local law enforcement in advancing the use of science and technology by supporting research and development for the 911 emergency telephone system and the use of computers.

The idea of a single telephone number that could be used nationwide to report emergencies had been around since the early 1960s. The problem had been, of course, funding to research and develop the system. American Telephone and Telegraph (AT&T) at first hesitated researching the idea because of problems with overlapping jurisdictions, dialing areas, and other similar issues. Cost savings, however, eventually persuaded AT&T that the idea was feasible. The traditional operator "0" system that usually handled emergency calls to police and fire stations was expensive and not solely dedicated to emergency service, and operators were not trained for emergency service. By placing the burden of training and employing emergency operators on local law enforcement agencies, AT&T could now see the financial benefit of creating a nationwide system.

AT&T unveiled the new "911" system in January 1968, and after several successful pilot programs, many urban areas adapted the system. The first ten years of the system proved invaluable, perhaps too much so for some police departments, as the number of calls and the tendency among citizens to use the system for non-emergency calls increased dramatically because of the convenience of the system. Still, the system performed beyond expectations. By the 1990s, over 95 percent of police departments in the United States used the 911 system. By providing trained personnel to handle emergency calls, police departments have greatly improved their response efficiency, and citizen confidence in policing has also increased.[38]

Computers came to police roughly the same time as did the 911 system and, in fact, made the 911 system possible. Developed during and after World War II for code breaking, computer technology advanced rapidly in the 1960s through private enterprise (IBM) and federal programs (mainly from the Defense Department and NASA). Like the telegraph more than a century before, the computer at first was used for only everyday tasks, such as word processing and record keeping. Lack of funds, little or no training, and "fear of Big Brother" made many departments and city governments reluctant to fully embrace computer potential. Another hindrance was the computer industry itself: why spend valuable research and development money on police computer technology when much more money could be made in developing business machines and technology for defense contracts? With only seventeen thousand law enforcement agencies around the country in the early 1970s, computer companies found the needs of half a million hotels, thousands of hospitals, and thousands more businesses much more appealing to their profit margins. Only federally subsidized research and development could make it work. Federal support for purchasing computer technology for police was vital from the 1970s on. Few departments had the money to buy new technology, much less research and develop it.

With the development of an economical personal computer in the mid-1980s, more police departments began investing in computer technology. Easier programming meant more adaptable software programs to specifically help police. Improved spreadsheet programs allowed police to keep track of crime and other statistics, allocate manpower more efficiently, and analyze effectiveness. Computers have enhanced mapping, communication, and criminal investigation. By 1993, two-thirds of police departments across the United States made use of computers, up from only one-half three years before. The National Crime Information Center, the Automated Fingerprint Identification System, and the 911 system were all possible because of police adapting to computer technology.

In addition to computer technology, 911, and other tools, the National Institute of Justice led the way in developing "less than lethal" weapons (pepper spray and stun guns) and observation devices. Perhaps the most useful developments from this agency were advances in DNA analysis and the successful testing of the lightweight body armor known as Kevlar. The influx of federal funding for police technology research and development has created the necessary market for meaningful technological advancement, much like increased defense spending during the early years of the Cold War made the defense industry possible and economically important.

Although the benefits of technology for policing have been great, there are potential drawbacks as the technology advances. First, because of disparity in local funding for police departments, neighboring police jurisdictions can have a limited amount of technology available to them: in other words, not everyone has the advantage of the latest stuff. Second, no nationwide specification and testing standards exist for police technology. Finally, the "Big Brother" specter and civil rights issues judicially and publicly cloud how far police technology can go in fighting crime and protecting the public.[39]

CONCLUSION

Police and technology now go hand in hand, but history shows that this was not always a smooth relationship. Technological advances in communication, transportation, criminalistics, and other areas combined with the police's use of science and scientific methods for the first time gave the public an image of the police as leaders of progress. Police were not only involved in fighting crime and crime prevention but also were now one of the great examples of progressivism through science and technology. Only after the 1960s, when federal funding became available, could police departments afford to continue their love affair with technology.

This image has returned to police at the beginning of the twenty-first century. Police are no longer hesitant to use the latest technology and science to assist them in investigations and community policing. Although money and civil rights issues occasionally hinder progress in the use of science and technology in policing, historically police have managed to solve these problems and utilize the benefits of science and technology for their work.

CHAPTER 8

LEADERS IN AMERICAN POLICING

INTRODUCTION

Every profession or discipline has a special group of leaders that profoundly influence the direction and growth of that particular profession. Policing as a profession is no different. Police in America have been fortunate to have people who dared to think "outside the box" and challenge the accepted paradigm of police practice and purpose. Philip John Stead called these individuals "pioneers in policing."[1]

The people who have influenced the development and direction of American policing are a unique and exceptional group. Many were concerned citizens. Some actually came from the ranks. Others made lateral moves into police leadership positions as chiefs or commissioners. Still more came from the academic world. One became president of the United States. Regardless of their background, these leaders took creative risks to address what they saw as severe weaknesses in the way police in America did their job. Leaders in American policing have consistently been those who have had the foresight to recognize that current police practices did not meet current community needs. Like most professions, policing requires a high degree of standardization to function effectively and efficiently. The downside of this process is that organizational standardization and rigidity tends to frown on imaginative individual leadership. Organizations resist change, and it requires bold thinking to shift the massive momentum inherent in organizational behavior. As leaders in policing faced new problems, their innovative thinking, political insight, determination, and timing proved invaluable elements to forcing beneficial change in American police doctrine and practice.

One model of American police history is the transformation of independent police development to rather standardized, consistent police methods. This process has already been outlined, suggesting that what began as good practice in a few cities gradually became standard practice across the country. Faced with this uniform, quasi-military, politicized structure, the basic nature of police institutions is to resist creative approaches to law enforcement problems. Despite this, however, leaders have emerged to profoundly influence policing in the United States. Often they were in positions that required them to make decisions based on the exigent circumstances of the moment. Crime waves and riots, training and organizational efficiency, and political corruption, among many other issues, have on occasion given an innovative police leader the stage to present new ideas and different ways to think about police work.

Recall that the Introduction of this work suggests that the terms "law enforcement" and "sustaining tradition" are basically synonymous. The paradox of this argument is that leaders in policing have the responsibility to improve the police department by changing the very organization responsible for sustaining the status quo in support of community traditions. Change in any organization is difficult, but change in an organization that has been formed and designed to sustain tradition creates unique problems beyond those experienced by leaders in other organizations. The stakes are indeed higher. Developing an idea that leads to change in a police organization requires courage as well as creative leadership.

With these ideas in mind, this chapter explores the careers and impact of leaders in American policing since the nineteenth century. This is not an exhaustive list, nor is it intended to be authoritative. Others would certainly and justifiably add or delete from this group. The purpose here is simply to offer several vignettes that are representative of the creativity and influence that police leaders have exhibited in over two hundred years of American policing.

LEADERS IN EARLY POLICE ORGANIZATION

Josiah Quincy and Stephen Girard

In the early nineteenth century, police in American cities had no real organization in the modern sense. In 1823, Boston Mayor Josiah Quincy was one of the first to incorporate police duty with municipal government in an effective way that approached modern police organization. Mayor Quincy consolidated responsibility and authority for several elements of public safety under one department of city government. In the early years of policing in America, governmental control over police authority sometimes rested with the state rather than with the city. Quincy was able to gain political support of both the city council and the state legislature for the development of a city department with broad police authority. This seemingly minor adjustment placed direct law enforcement authority in the hands of a local municipal government rather than in those of the state. This was a unique change in local government and a major step in the formulation of modern-day municipal police departments. Through Quincy's leadership, police authority was developed as an organized local community responsibility. Although this new department brought together a broad range of city services under one roof, police authority for the first time was placed under the jurisdiction of the mayor. Quincy made this possible.[2]

The posthumous leadership of Philadelphian Stephen Girard is unique in American policing. Philadelphia faced many of the problems that challenged Boston. Through the benevolent use of his estate, Girard set in motion the development of a new police structure in Philadelphia. Girard, a wealthy citizen with a sense of civic duty, provided funding for a nascent police force in his will:

> To enable the corporation of the city of Philadelphia to provide more effectually than
> they now do for the security of the persons and property of the inhabitants of the said

city by a competent police, including a sufficient number of watchmen really suited to the purpose; and to this end I recommend a division of the city into watch districts of four parts, each under a proper head; and that at least two watchmen shall in each round or station patrol together.[3]

Girard had both the sense of civic responsibility and the financial ability to support the implementation of his ideas for a more organized and thus effective watch. Upon his death in 1833, and with financial support in place, Philadelphia passed an ordinance that provided for 24 day policemen and 120 night patrolmen, dramatically increasing the size of both forces. Combined with the reorganization of Philadelphia's wards, this enabled Girard to set in motion what would become one of the first municipal police departments with both a day patrol force and a night patrol force under the same leadership. Philadelphia implemented this organizational change five years before New York City put in place a similar realignment. Girard was the first to see the need for a unified day and night force of competent police, working together around the clock. This concept became part of the model for modern police function.[4]

LEADERS IN REFINING AMERICAN POLICE ORGANIZATION

Sir Robert Peel

The name Sir Robert Peel is synonymous with police innovation. Although British, Peel profoundly influenced American police development. He in fact is often cited as the "father of modern policing." Although that moniker is an exaggeration, Peel is certainly among the most influential police leaders. As Home Secretary of Great Britain in the late 1820s, Peel introduced a bill into Parliament called "An Act for Improving the Police in and Near the Metropolis," better known as the Metropolitan Police Act, that would organize a central, government-administered police force. Initially, the bill ran into stiff opposition. Placing the enforcement power for over two hundred capital crimes into one, a centralized police organization raised serious concerns. The crisis of London's unruly streets, however, overrode such concerns about possible abuses of centralized authority. Something had to be done to stem the problems of public disorder and rising crime.[5]

Peel's plan for a metropolitan police force revolved around four central ideas. First, he developed the concept of crime prevention as a primary goal for police. Second, he outlined an organizational structure for policing that placed competent police officers in uniform both to serve and protect the public. Third, he proposed the revolutionary idea that the best assessment of effective policing was the absence of crime, not the measurement of police reaction to crimes already committed. Last, Peel developed the notion of a professional police service. By hiring well-educated, honest, and disciplined officers to a dedicated, professional force, the community's respect for the law and for those responsible for enforcing the law would improve public safety. He outlined his ideas in a list of principles that have become the basis of municipal policing:

1. The basic mission for which the police exist is to prevent crime and disorder as an alternative to the repression of crime and disorder by military force and severity of legal punishment.

2. The ability of the police to perform their duties is dependent upon public approval of police existence, actions, behavior, and the ability of the police to secure and maintain public respect.
3. The police must secure the willing cooperation of the public in voluntary observance of the law to be able to secure and maintain public respect.
4. The degree of cooperation of the public that can be secured diminishes, proportionately, the necessity for the use of physical force and compulsion in achieving police objectives.
5. The police seek and preserve public favor, not by catering to public opinion, but by constantly demonstrating absolutely impartial service to the law, in complete independence of policy, and without regard to the justice or injustice of the substance of individual laws; by ready offering of individual service and friendship to all members of the society without regard to their race or social standing; by ready exercise of courtesy and friendly good humor; and by ready offering of individual sacrifice in protecting and preserving life.
6. The police should use physical force to the extent necessary to secure observance of the law or to restore order only when the exercise of persuasion, advice, and warning is found to be insufficient to achieve police objectives; and police should use only the minimum degree of physical force which is necessary on any particular occasion for achieving a police objective.
7. The police at all times should maintain a relationship with the public that gives reality to the historic tradition that the police are the public and that the public are the police; the police are the only members of the public who are paid to give full-time attention to duties which are incumbent on every citizen in the interest of the community welfare.
8. The police should always direct their actions toward their functions and never appear to usurp the powers of the judiciary by avenging individuals or the state, or authoritatively judging guilt or punishing the guilty.
9. The test of police efficiency is the absence of crime and disorder, not the visible evidence of police action in dealing with them.[6]

This expansion of police authority was not well received by Londoners, particularly among the working class. The passage of the Metropolitan Police Act gave formal approval to organize a metropolitan police force administrated by the national government, but the enabling legislation did not ensure that the public would immediately accept such a force. Peel faced a daunting challenge to develop a new police force that could effectively control crime and social disorder while at the same time win the respect and support of the citizens of London. Skeptics and critics attacked the new force, noting the dangerous precedent of the potentially intrusive role of the national government. Experiencing the ill effects of industrialization, the established social order certainly felt threatened by the new labor movement. Critics among the working class claimed the new police were actually really intended as a centralized means to control labor, prevent strikes, and deal with other civic unrest.

Undaunted, Peel appointed Colonel Charles Rowan and Irish Barrister Richard Mayne as the first police commissioners of the London Metropolitan Police. Their first priority was to hire over three thousand policemen, "bobbies" as they came to be called, of sound mind and character who met Peel's strict and demanding service standards. This was no small task: recruits had to be at least five feet, eleven inches in height; no more than thirty-five years of age; capable of reading and writing; and willing and able to take orders. Of course, criminals need not apply, which suggests this had been a problem on the old force. The pay was modest, but this assured that the men who sought the job "would not adopt a superior air toward the public and that they would speak the same social language as most of the people with whom they would have to deal." In the first ten years of the new police force, nearly five thousand police officers were fired and another six thousand officers resigned for failing to meet the rigid standards.

Peel was convinced that the police must be highly visible to the public and be seen as public servants, not as uniformed henchmen of centralized authority. As long as the police were easily recognizable, citizens would have little reason to fear being watched by government spies or harassed by uniformed thugs. This was one of the reasons that there were no plainclothes detectives in the early years of the British police force. Citizens could also easily spot an officer when in need of assistance. This meant that officers had to wear an identifiable, distinctive uniform, so citizens would know who they were, where they were, and what they were doing. Furthermore, because the police force was a civilian organization separate from the military, Peel wanted to be sure his police officers did not resemble British soldiers.

Peel's Metropolitan Police gradually took positive effect and became accepted by London citizens as a legitimate police authority. The popularity of Peel's model partially influenced the organization of police departments in America. For example, with an upsurge of crime and violence in the 1840s, New York City used Peel's model of police organization as reference material for organizational changes in the New York Police Department.[7]

Although many of Peel's policing concepts received support in the United States, it is important to recognize that some of his ideas raised objections. A national police force, with fully uniformed police officers, given the power and authority to arrest and search citizens was unacceptable. The very idea of a federal police force was unfathomable to a people who valued local, decentralized control of just about everything. Even organized municipal police forces ran into some opposition.

The primary contribution of Peel to American policing lies in the formulation of a clear police mission. His "Policing Principles" are easily discernable in the mission statements of many American police departments. The idea that the police should prevent crime and work with the community is the cornerstone of contemporary community policing. Yet, some of Peel's most valid principles have not found fruition in American policing. For example, measuring the success of a police organization by the absence of crime rather than measuring the number of reactions to crime is still elusive, yet, this is an accurate barometer for police effectiveness.

Webber Seavey

A veteran of the Civil War who escaped from the dreaded Confederate prisoner-of-war camp in Andersonville, Georgia, Omaha Police Chief Webber Seavey is largely responsible for planting the seed for a nationally organized police movement in the United States. Each year, the International Association of Police Chiefs, which Seavey helped create, awards police organizations for the development of creative new policing programs. The award that bears the name "Webber Seavey Award for

Quality Law Enforcement" is among the most prestigious in the American law enforcement community.

After the Civil War, Seavey traveled the world, developing business interests along the way. Seavey returned to Omaha around 1886 with a tidy sum in hand and invested it in the local real estate market. The tidy sum became a large fortune, which planted Seavey at the forefront of civic affairs in the growing city of Omaha. With a wide range of experience, and a growing reputation as a leader, Seavey was appointed chief of police in 1887. Under his leadership, the Omaha Police Department became known as "one of the best drilled, disciplined, and most efficient police departments of any of our Western cities."[8] Seavey served as chief of police in Omaha until 1895, building one of the earliest national reputations for a police chief west of the Mississippi River.

During his tenure as police chief, Seavey developed publicly funded benefit programs for police officers and patrol strategies that dramatically increased the effectiveness of Omaha police. Some of these concepts, particularly in patrolling, became the foundation for modern police strategies. For police officers injured or killed in the line of duty, he initiated a program to provide financial assistance for officers and their families. Publicly funded, the program was ahead of its time, as most early police benevolent societies relied on private donations and police dues for financial support.

Seavey also instituted patrol techniques that improved placing police officers in areas of need. With a larger population than that of Kansas City and Denver, but with fewer police officers, he developed patrol strategies that ensured a police patrol that used certain tactics to best combat crime in Omaha. Utilizing projected population increases in 1893, Seavey developed patrol strategies, personnel assignments, and a budget to meet the demands of projected city growth. Through these planning techniques, he was able to sustain community security and maintain a professional approach to police management. He stated, "Whenever I undertake to guard the resident portions of the city with my present force, the business localities are not properly protected, and none of our citizens understand this so well and so readily as the criminal class."[9]

Seavey's greatest impact, however, came in establishing a national organization for chiefs of police. Knowing that other cities across the United States faced similar issues to those that he had in Omaha, Seavey invited police chiefs from around the nation to meet in Chicago at the 1893 World's Fair to discuss mutual problems and new methods to solve them. This meeting, as discussed in Chapter 5, helped put in motion the establishment of the International Association of Chiefs of Police. Fifty-two police chiefs attended the meeting, enjoyed the World's Fair, and discussed problems of common concern, from "vagrancy" to police uniforms to sharing information on criminals. Seavey was elected the first president of the National Chiefs of Police Union, which became the International Association of Chiefs of Police. Several leaders in American policing, including August Vollmer, later served as presidents of the association and used the group as a platform for national debate on police reform.[10]

Theodore Roosevelt

Theodore Roosevelt entered American policing in 1895 at thirty-seven years of age as a member of the newly created board of commissioners for the New York City Police Department. The future president of the United States served as police commissioner only two years, until 1897, but managed to turn the corruption-ridden department inside out in that short time. Challenging an intransigent political environment, Roosevelt aggressively pushed for police reform in the face of political corruption. Utilizing a military model, he developed and initiated uniform discipline. From close-order drill and parades to military-style commendations, Roosevelt defined the police mission in military terms. Although the military analogy in policing is under fire at the beginning of the twenty-first century, it was all the rage at the beginning of the twentieth century. Roosevelt, a military and history enthusiast of the most intense sort, is credited with first using the phrase "fighting the war on crime."[11]

Roosevelt supported the development of civil service and strongly advocated that police promotions be based on merit. Although he opposed the political spoils system, he did not support written testing for police officer promotion. His opinion was based on a strong commitment to the value placed on a police officer's experience. He advocated the idea that police officers should be evaluated in the field or on the street by superiors—not from a written examination. He justified his position this way: "In the police department I found these [written] examinations a serious handicap in the way of getting the best men promoted. . . . But once in office the best way to test any man's ability is by long experience in seeing him actually at work. His promotion should depend upon the judgment formed of him by his superiors."[12] Often during the evening hours, Roosevelt would travel the neighborhoods of New York City spot-checking police officers on duty. As a firm disciplinarian, he consistently brought charges against officers who were drunk on duty, asleep on patrol, or involved in some sort of corruption. Try as he might, Roosevelt could not completely overcome the corrupt system, and his lack of authoritative disciplinary power irked him to no end.

George Coffin cartoon depicting New York Police Commissioner Theodore Roosevelt, "A Roosevelt to the Rescue!" *Washington Post,* May 3, 1895. (Library of Congress)

Roosevelt was fascinated by technology, even by the simplest of machines. As mentioned in Chapter 7, he helped institute the first bicycle squad, the patrol strategies of which form the basis for the use of bicycles for police operations today. Roosevelt continued his belief in effective police organization and purpose as president of the United States. With Attorney General Charles Bonaparte, Roosevelt established the Bureau of Investigation in 1908 to investigate crimes for the Department of the Treasury. This federal-level law enforcement agency later became the Federal Bureau of Investigation.

Although many of Roosevelt's police reforms failed to survive subsequent administrations, several of his ideas are still functional in contemporary police departments. From the use of bicycles to police officer promotion, Roosevelt's concepts continue to influence American policing. When Robert Fogelson lists the individuals responsible for the "professional model" of policing, he points out that the first generation of police leaders in America must include Theodore Roosevelt.[13]

LEADERS IN POLICE PROFESSIONALISM

August Vollmer

August Vollmer, like Peel, was strongly committed to the concept of crime prevention. He pointed out to a new police recruit, "I'll admire you more if in the first year you don't make a single arrest. I'm not judging you on arrests. I'm judging you on how many people you keep from doing something wrong."[14] He was opposed to the "crime fighter" image that often attracted public attention to police work and supported cooperation with community members and university professors in an effort to understand the causes of crime. His writings and actions reflected a commitment to finding factors that caused a person to commit crime and to isolating these factors so that criminals could be rehabilitated. As a practitioner in policing, he attempted to organize his police department in a manner that would deal effectively with the theories found in criminology rather than have police officers respond to crimes that had already been committed.

Vollmer first experienced law enforcement as a young Army policeman in the Philippines during and just after the Spanish-American War of 1898. After the war, Vollmer returned to California and became a mail carrier in Berkeley. As an outgoing person, he became politically involved in city government and in 1905 was selected to be the town marshal. In 1909, Berkeley moved to a "mayor-council" form of government and as a consequence created the office of chief of police. The city of Berkeley chose Vollmer, who quickly experimented with innovative ideas to make the small Berkeley Police Department one of the most progressive in the nation.

Vollmer served as police chief of Berkeley for twenty-three years. During his tenure as chief, he conducted one of the earliest "scientific" investigations of a crime scene, became the first to utilize motorcycles and then automobiles for patrolling, and instituted "I.Q." tests and psychiatric examinations for police officers and recruits. He reorganized the chain of command by reducing the number of higher ranking officers within the department, used fingerprinting and handwriting analyses in criminal investigation and identification, and made use of one of the earliest lie-detector systems.

August Vollmer, Police Chief, Berkeley Police Department. (Berkeley Police Department, Historic Preservation Society.)

Vollmer put in place a criminal records system based on the concept of "modus operandi" (M.O.). This record-keeping system was based on the idea that criminals would continue to use successful criminal techniques, and if those techniques can be identified through criminal investigation, identifying the criminal would become much easier. Developing the M.O. of a criminal suspect is a universally accepted concept in modern policing and can be found in profiling and other investigative practices. When Vollmer initiated a record-keeping system based on the methods of operation criminals used, he was indeed plowing new ground.

Vollmer's greatest contribution came in police education and training. He revolutionized education, particularly in criminology, bringing police officers into university classrooms for college-level instruction. Vollmer had a great resource for this revolution right in his own town of Berkeley—the University of California. He viewed the University of California at Berkeley as an untapped resource for new ideas in policing. A first in the United States, Vollmer worked closely with the university, developing police training and education programs that incorporated courses in the sciences and sociology to help officers solve and prevent crime. These early university-taught courses helped promote the idea of forensic science on both national and international levels. Vollmer recruited teachers from the fields of parasitology, law, and photography, as well as from other fields. He himself taught classes and coordinated teaching schedules to ensure that Berkeley police officers could easily participate in the program during off-duty hours. It is significant that

Berkeley police were not paid while in the classroom; thus, course work and field training occurred after work hours or on days off. Vollmer encouraged other police leaders to work closely with colleges and universities in their own areas for the benefit of their police departments.

Vollmer's other influence came as a member of crime commissions and as an author. His work on the famous Wickersham Commission, as mentioned in Chapter 6, generally praised police departments that had utilized his ideas on professionalization and administration, while heavily criticizing those departments that continued to do things the old way.

His seminal book *The Police and Modern Society* outlined how police departments evolved and functioned. From initial concern and enforcement of "major crimes" to the development of traffic enforcement responsibilities, Vollmer identified five major areas of police responsibility—major crimes, vice, traffic, general services, and crime prevention. Vollmer recognized the importance and value of crime prevention over reacting to crimes that had already been committed. His insights foreshadowed community-policing ideas of the late twentieth century: "The character of the community is but a reflection of the character of its residents, and no matter how many laws are on the books, enforcement can go no farther than the citizens will permit."[15]

Vollmer was both praised and criticized for being too theoretical, but police departments in Chicago, Los Angeles, and numerous other cities found practical use for ideas in police administration and practice. As his reputation grew, Vollmer was elected as the first president of the California Police Chiefs Association and was later chosen as president of the International Association of Chiefs of Police. Vollmer's foresight and ability to communicate his ideas effectively earned him the title "father of modern police administration," which he richly and justly deserved. At a time in America when the national reputation of municipal policing was still one of corruption and ignorance, Vollmer encouraged the notion that police work was more than a job—it was a profession. He worked with police leadership from around the country to improve the professionalism of police departments. As a nationwide mentor for police leaders, Vollmer's most enduring legacy was his disciples. Influential police leaders like O. W. Wilson, who briefly worked with Vollmer in the Berkeley Police Department, Los Angeles Police Chief William Parker, and FBI Director J. Edgar Hoover willingly accepted his ideas and leadership. As a consequence, Vollmer left a lasting and indelible imprint on American policing.[16]

THE DISCIPLES OF AUGUST VOLLMER

O. W. Wilson

While a student at the University of California, O. W. Wilson joined Vollmer's Berkeley Police Department in 1921. Wilson's ability to work as a patrolman while attending college was facilitated by Vollmer's desire to bring college-educated people into the Berkeley Police Department. As a protégé of Vollmer, Wilson completed his degree at the University of California while working full time as a police officer. With Vollmer's assistance, Wilson became the chief of police of Fullerton, California, in 1925. As the nation's youngest police chief, Wilson was unprepared for the overbearing political interference and pressure and wanted to quit police work. He resigned after only a few months to look for work in other fields of criminal justice, but Vollmer urged him to consider police administration. Wilson followed the advice of his mentor and at twenty-eight years of age became the chief of police for Wichita, Kansas, in 1928.

During his tenure as chief of police in Wichita, Wilson relied on Vollmer's police principles, adapting Vollmer's ideas of police professionalism for a municipal police department somewhat larger than Berkeley's. Wilson's success demonstrated that Vollmer's concepts could be universally applied.

Serving as Wichita police chief from 1928 to 1939, Wilson began to expand his reputation beyond the shadow of his mentor Vollmer. World War II interrupted Wilson's police experience in the United States, but he was able to put that experience to good use as the chief public safety officer for the Army in Italy. After the war, Wilson bypassed a return to Wichita to instead take a position at the University of California as an instructor in the police administration program. It was in this capacity that Wilson made his most significant contributions to police professionalism and administration. He authored two major textbooks on strategies for police administration. *Police Administration* (1950) and *Police Planning* (1952) were widely read and accepted as the best guidelines for professionalized police administration in the United States.[17]

Before long, *Police Administration* became known as the "bible of police professionalism." Wilson refined Vollmer's ideas and developed police department organizational structures and strategies that supported the concepts that Vollmer developed. O. W. Wilson blended contemporary public administration ideas with Vollmer's professional model of policing to give police chiefs a guide for police organization and function in the late 1950s and early 1960s. With America's military success in World War II a recent memory, Wilson's writings and recommendation of a pragmatic, quasi-military approach to policing were accepted, strongly supported, and unquestioned at the time.

National acclaim opened other doors for Wilson. He was recruited by the city of Chicago to reform its problem-ridden police department. During his seven years as superintendent of Chicago police, Wilson employed many of the concepts and ideas he had implemented as a police chief in Wichita and refined in his writings. With a history of entrenched corruption and political interference, the Chicago Police Department was a perfect laboratory to test Vollmer and Wilson's administrative concepts. Stead points out that several of Wilson's reforms had lasting effect in Chicago, particularly his reorganization that placed the vice division directly under the command control of the chief. Wilson's legacy to American policing has been the continuous refinement over the course of sixty years of his and Vollmer's police concepts.[18]

William H. Parker

William H. Parker's police career began and ended in the Los Angeles Police Department. Starting as a patrolman in 1927, he died in office as chief of police in 1966. As a police officer with a law degree (earned while on the force), Parker quickly moved up the ranks. In 1934, he became the Los Angeles Police Department's trial lawyer and was assigned as an assistant to the chief of police. During World War II, Parker joined the U.S. Army, gaining valuable administrative experience while serving in North Africa and Europe.[19] Returning to Los Angeles after the war, he had developed a professional reputation for leadership grounded in his education and experience. Parker served as chief of police for the Los Angeles Police Department from 1950 to his death in 1966.

Parker was not a direct protégé of Vollmer but was greatly influenced by Vollmer's work through a close professional relationship with Wilson. Like Wilson, Parker was committed to police professionalism, a dedication that was tested in the early years of his tenure as police chief. The Los Angeles Police Department suffered from widespread police brutality and corruption, placing Parker at the center of a very high profile and potentially explosive situation. After conducting a thorough investigation, Parker fired or disciplined over forty police officers. On the heels of this investigation, Parker discovered corruption in vice division and again took swift and firm action, bringing charges against the officers involved. In both situations, he handled the problems in a manner that gained public trust and confidence in his leadership, thus restoring public faith in the Los Angeles Police Department.

Once his leadership was securely established and the political influences were held at bay, Parker advanced police professionalism by instituting organizational changes and expanding the concepts developed by Vollmer and Wilson. Parker's commitment to professionalism can be seen clearly in the standards he required for recruiting new employees. He felt that the recruitment of qualified police officers was key to the future success of the Los Angeles Police Department. Physical fitness, psychological testing, and scholastic attainment were utilized to identify and select new officers. Once hired, recruit officers faced a rigorous police academy regime with demanding standards in both physical fitness and scholarship. Continuing education and training meant that officers would always be up to date on the latest policing methods and concepts throughout their careers. Parker created the image of the tough, disciplined, but courteous, police officer that became the model for police across the country.

The 1965 Watts riot brought negative attention to Parker's policing methods. His military-style police force was riddled with institutionalized racism and had a long history of police brutality. The professional model of policing had shown some serious cracks. Watts brought national attention to the glaring gap between the community and the police. Although the professional model did not suggest a lack of community involvement, it did not highlight community support or recommend community programs for policing.

Parker, like Vollmer and Wilson, also put his ideas in writing. His book *Parker on Police*, which was edited by Wilson, was a "how to do it" plan for city managers and police administrators. Having the experience of working in a political environment, Parker outlined the benefits and pitfalls of police administration and how to implement his version of the professional police model.[20]

During Parker's tenure as chief of police, he pushed other law enforcement organizations to meet responsibilities more effectively. In developing strategies that forced the Los Angeles County Sheriff's Office to assume more responsibility for Los Angeles police prisoners and convincing the California Highway Patrol to assume responsibility for the state highways in Los Angeles, Parker was able to free up over two hundred police officers for patrol duty. These strategies improved police effectiveness within Los Angeles without increasing in the police department's budget and more importantly established cooperative links with area law enforcement agencies. As a strong leader and firm disciplinarian, Parker became professionally and politically influential. Hollywood even borrowed his police models for popular television programs in the 1950s and 1960s, such as *Dragnet*.[21]

For approximately twenty-five years, from the late 1930s to the Watt's riot of 1965, municipal police departments in California were considered to be the most professional and effective police departments in America. The work of Vollmer and Wilson, combined with their practical application of professional policing ideas, pushed California police departments into the national limelight and allowed the concepts of these police leaders to become models for American policing.

LEADERS IN ESTABLISHING CONTEMPORARY VALUES IN AMERICAN POLICING

Patrick V. Murphy

Patrick V. Murphy, the son of a New York police sergeant, joined the New York police force along with his brother after serving in World War II as a Navy bomber pilot. He rose quickly through the ranks of the New York Police Department and was promoted to lieutenant in 1950. Working as a precinct supervisor for several years, he was assigned to the Police Academy in 1961. He lectured on police science at the City College of New York, and through night and weekend classes earned a bachelor's degree from St. John's College. Shortly after receiving his master's degree in public administration, he was promoted to captain and then became a deputy inspector in 1963.

In January of 1963, Murphy was asked by New York Governor Nelson Rockefeller's special counsel on law enforcement to head the reorganization of the Syracuse Police Department. Murphy became the chief of police of Syracuse, employing administration improvements he had developed. He established an organized crime division, an intelligence department, and a community-relations office. One of the innovative ideas Murphy initiated was the establishment of a scholarship fund for Syracuse police officers to continue their college education.[22] In June of 1964 he returned to the New York Police Department at the rank of deputy chief inspector. Assigned as the commanding officer of the police academy, his interest in improving the education level of police officers continued. He was also appointed Dean of the School of Public Administration and Police Science at the City College of New York.

In 1967, Murphy became the first public safety director of Washington, D.C., and was then tapped by President Lyndon Johnson to head the Law Enforcement Assistance Administration. He served in this position until the end of the Johnson presidency and then became chief of police for Detroit. In 1970, Murphy became commissioner of the New York Police Department.

Having gained a wealth of experience as the chief of police in Syracuse, Detroit, and Washington, D.C., and as New York police commissioner, Murphy was in a position to strongly promote the administrative ideas and policing concepts he had both developed and used over the previous twenty years. He set in motion programs designed to enhance community involvement in police activities. He augmented police presence in high-crime neighborhoods and increased the number of minority police officers. Committed to improved community relations, Murphy

Patrick V. Murphy. Former Commissioner of the New York City Police Department; Detroit, Michigan Chief of Police and Administrator of the Law Enforcement Assistance Administration. (Reprinted with permission.)

pushed for community involvement in police decision making long before the advent of "community policing." His early positions in support of heroin maintenance programs, gun control, and a complete overhaul of courts and prisons were considered provocative in the 1960s. Today, many of Murphy's ideas are considered to be mainstream policing. Using his national reputation effectively, Murphy helped make community policing the standard practice in most American cities.

In 1970, Murphy became the first president of the Police Foundation, an organization founded by the Ford Foundation to promote and support police improvement on a national scale. The thirty years of renowned work by the Police Foundation are a direct result of Murphy's foresight and leadership. Under his leadership, the Police Foundation intensively studied the concept of community policing, institutional racism in policing, and other issues to improve American police practices.

Hubert Williams

Hubert Williams is a thirty-year veteran of policing. One of the youngest major-city police chiefs in America, he served as director of the Newark Police Department from 1974 to 1985. Training at the John Jay College of Criminal Justice and earning

Hubert Williams. President
of the Police Foundation
and former Newark, New
Jersey, Director of Police.
(Reprinted with permission.)

a law degree from Rutgers gave Williams a solid background for police administration. Following in the footsteps of Murphy, Williams was appointed president of the Police Foundation in 1985. The Police Foundation has grown dramatically under his leadership, conducting studies and developing programs on civil disorder, police use of force, efficient foot patrol, community policing, and professional police standards. Williams directed these studies toward the development of positive community- relations strategies. In the aftermath of the Rodney King incident in Los Angeles, it became clear that the police in America needed new direction. Williams has worked to this end.

As Newark's chief of police, Hubert Williams was in the vanguard of police leaders during the civil unrest of the 1970s. With a law degree from Rutgers and practical police leadership experience, he developed a national reputation for creative ideas. Newark, New Jersey, suffered one of the country's most notorious riots. Williams, working closely with the community and the police department, established programs for both citizens and police officers to find success.

CHAPTER 9

POLICING TO THE TWENTY-FIRST CENTURY

INTRODUCTION

By the end of World War II, police departments had become a universal component of American society. As a result of the Great Depression, police service had gained in value and prestige created by the stability and security of civil service employment. The immediate post-World War II environment only enhanced this feeling, as former G.I.'s now filled the ranks of American police departments. The ambiguous relationship involving police responsibility for crime problems had been resolved and institutionalized by the 1950s. Police objectives and department mission statements outlined responsibilities for crime detection, control, and prevention, using patrol, investigation, and administration as the guiding principles. The nationwide acceptance of August Vollmer's idea of professional police models and the organizational goals and structures outlined by O. W. Wilson had on the surface transformed police departments into professional crime fighting organizations. Police officers patrolled the city looking for crime and, by their very presence, expected to prevent crime. For serious crimes, such as murder, the responding patrol officer would call the department's detectives for a complete, formal investigation. In clearly marked four-door Fords, Chevrolets, and Dodges, uniformed police officers patrolled the streets of American cities following guidelines that supported the professional model of policing.[1]

Problems, however, continued to surface. During the postwar years, an elitist esprit de corps developed among American police departments. Police not only accepted full responsibility for crime prevention and control but also jealously guarded these responsibilities from other law enforcement agencies as well as from citizens' groups. Police officers came to view private security guards, traffic officers, and other "unsworn" law enforcement personnel as "rent-a-cops" and "wanna be's." Many states limited the authority of private security agencies in order to keep the responsibility for crime control within municipal police departments. The adherence to the professional model of policing maintained that only sworn police officers had the training, authority, and public trust to properly handle community crime problems. Nonsworn civilian staff within police departments fell into the same second-rate category as private security guards, forcing them to work in a tense, demeaning environment among arrogant, elitist police officers. All critical assignments were given to "sworn" police department personnel, whereas civilian employees were relegated to menial administrative tasks. This elitist attitude permeated police departments across the country and helped create a distinct barrier between sworn police officers and other citizens. This elitism placed police on the path leading to civil unrest in the years ahead.[2]

The often-cited myth that "police and politics don't mix" became the standard for American police forces. Fearing that civilian meddling into professional police affairs would only set back decades of professional progress in crime fighting, police resisted efforts to subjugate police authority to external, civilian review. In fact, the more professional police became, the more they opposed external control of police functions.[3]

From the 1950s through the 1990s, police continued the rough evolution that had characterized police development since colonial times. Old problems resurfaced, whereas new issues challenged police to look again at what they do and how they do it—to protect and serve the local public citizenry. The last half of the twentieth century was ripe for a paradigm shift in policing.

THE 1950s

The decade following World War II was one of great change in American society. The postwar years brought relative peace, but only under the increasingly dark clouds of the new Cold War. Prosperity found many, mostly white middle-class professionals, but failed to reach everyone, including many inner-city and rural Blacks and Hispanics. Technological advances heralded a new age but still did not provide all of the answers to solve society's ills. A nation that had just defeated the sick, racist regimes of Nazi Germany and Imperial Japan and now battled the twisted social ideas of Soviet communism suffered dreadful racial division in its own backyard.

Prosperity brought suburban growth, but at the price of dilapidated inner-city neighborhoods. Inner-city ghettos created by two African American migrations from the rural South and the abandonment of inner-city neighborhoods by new middle-class Blacks for the more prosperous suburbs intensified segregation in both northern and southern cities. With the absence of a black middle-class center of leadership, stability, and guidance, poor Blacks found themselves stuck in the city ghettos without an effective political voice to address the problems of poverty, limited educational opportunity, single-parent families, unemployment, and crime.[4]

As inner cities deteriorated amidst suburban prosperity, the "crime-fighting" battle lines became clear and inflexible. Police departments assigned police officers in ever-increasing numbers to inner-city neighborhoods. Most of the officers, almost exclusively Whites, now lived in the suburbs and came to resent having to patrol inner-city streets. Following public administration practices of the day, however, police resources were placed to fight crime in the most "efficient and effective" manner. This was right in line with the old military model of policing originally supported by Theodore Roosevelt and transformed by Vollmer and Wilson. The military idea had returned in the form of an evolved military-style organizational strategy for police departments. With a rampart of World War II and Korean War veterans now in police uniform, police departments almost naturally followed a military-like structure, and the terminology of a "war on crime" returned to the police vernacular.[5]

As though a military operation was underway, police followed military-like procedures to fight a war on crime. Police departments expected their sworn officers to follow a chain of command. Adopting military organizational charts and rules of supervision and administration, police chiefs expected police officers to be disciplined, trained, and honor-bound to duty. Police departments held military-style inspections of uniforms and firearms to provide basic discipline, which helped instill "high morale" and a "mutual respect between officers and men." The principles of "unity of command" and "span of control" added to the "delegation of responsibility with commensurate authority" made the police efficient and effective warriors in the war on crime.[6]

As with the American military's infatuation with technology to fight the Cold War, police also turned to technological advances to help them in the war on crime. Advancements in communication and scientific investigation techniques dramatically improved a police department's ability to conduct criminal investigations and to present evidence in court. Enhanced fingerprinting capabilities, the chemical analyses of blood samples, and better crime scene investigation practices benefited from better equipped crime labs and more thorough training programs.[7]

These technological advancements became an integral part of the professional model of policing. Officers on patrol responded quickly by utilizing the latest technology in communications, whereas detectives handled criminal investigations more effectively with the latest advancements in scientific technology. The more effectively and efficiently police departments responded to crime, the more they were viewed as being "professional." American police departments in the 1950s took great pride in using the latest techniques and practices and sought superior statistical assessment ratings against other departments as a measure of their professionalism.[8]

With this strong commitment to professionalism and growing elitism, police began to lose touch with the citizens they were charged to protect and serve. The desire for cost-efficient effective police service overshadowed the immeasurable value of police–community interaction.[9] Military-style police organizations gave the public a perception that police were closed, secretive, and unreceptive to public discourse about policing. Police viewed community problems unrelated to crime as issues outside their purview. Speeding with sirens blaring from call to call, shielded from public contact inside clearly marked patrol cars, police officers isolated themselves from the communities they served.

It was in the ideas and concepts designed to improve public administration, however, that attempts to redirect police administration toward a more community-friendly approach to crime fighting came to the forefront. Among other public administration frameworks, Luther Gulick's POSDCORB (Planning, Organizing, Staffing, Directing, Coordinating, Reporting, and Budgeting) seemed to offer some solution to police department problems. The International Association of City Managers (IACM) altered Gulick's public administration principles to better reflect city functions, including police. Police administrators should instead follow the POST–BECPIRD formula for administrative success (Planning, Organization, Staffing, Training—Budgeting, Equipment, Coordination, Public Information, Reporting, and Directing). This holistic approach to public and police administration, it was thought, would improve community–police relations and also make police more effective in the war on crime. Departments that tried these formulas experienced some success, but as with most models, problems occurred in trying to fit square pegs into round holes. There was no right way or wrong way to do things for each city across the United States. What worked in one place was not guaranteed to work elsewhere.[10]

Patrol and staffing patterns of the 1950s contributed to the inconsistent effectiveness of these police administration concepts. More often than not, white male police officers patrolled predominantly black inner-city neighborhoods. The racial tension of the 1950s ensured that no matter the formula, if white policemen patrolled black neighborhoods, there would be mistrust if not conflict. Staffing patterns also contributed to the problem. Municipal police employment was only available at the bottom rank as a patrol officer or at the top as a chief of police. Sergeants, lieutenants, captains, and so forth were restricted to sworn members of a department who had risen through the ranks. There was no lateral movement from the outside. These staffing and patrol patterns limited the development of creative ideas within the department and restricted the level of police understanding regarding community issues. Simply put, police inbreeding stifled progress.[11]

The police problems of the American South rivaled those of the inner-city areas of the rest of the country. Untold incidents of police brutality and neglect took place involving black citizens and white police officers in southern towns and cities. In the most blatant cases, police stood idly by while white mobs attacked black individuals.

Many of these incidents were ignited over the issue of integration. As a result of the Supreme Court's *Brown v. Board of Education* decision in 1954, federal courts began ordering the integration of public schools. Many states and local municipalities across the South were reluctant, sometimes violently so, to enforce the court orders. One of the most famous and historically significant incidents was the integration of Little Rock High School in Arkansas in September 1957. Nine black students tried to enter the campus against the jeers and taunts of a large and angry white mob. Arkansas Governor Orval Faubus refused President Dwight Eisenhower's request to mobilize units of the Arkansas National Guard to protect the black students. Faubus ordered the Guard onto the Little Rock High School grounds but then had them withdrawn at the last minute, leaving Little Rock police to deal with the unruly mob. Using billy clubs, Little Rock police tried to keep the mob behind barricades, not so much to protect the nine black students but rather to prevent property damage to the school and any harm to the white students inside. Livid Whites badgered police, questioning their "whiteness" and calling them just about every racial slur in the book. In the police line, patrolman Thomas Dunaway gave in to the taunts. He threw down his club, ripped off his badge, then joined the mob, which hailed him as a white hero. The mob passed an ad hoc collection plate for Dunaway, giving two hundred dollars to the officer who had forsaken his sworn oath as a policeman and would certainly lose his job. The nine students made it into the building but had to later be whisked away in a patrol car to avoid what police feared would be a lynching.[12]

Police were indeed challenged by civil rights protests. Martin Luther King's Montgomery bus boycott, school integration, Klan violence, and other events and incidents forced police to sometimes choose between their personal beliefs and their duty to the public. Police in the South had to choose sides, as white mobs attacked and lynched Blacks, for as little as whistling at a white woman in one Mississippi county. Brutal beatings of protest marchers by uniformed police officers seemed a constant feature on the nightly news in 1955 and 1956. History seemed to repeat itself, as those charged with enforcing the law and keeping the peace terrorized those they were supposed to protect and serve. The same dichotomy could be said of McCarthyism and the anticommunist campaign. Police were caught in an unenviable situation. There was a fine line between abuse of authority and real threats to the public security. Yet, the history of police in America has shown this to be the norm rather than the exception, and at no time was this more true than during the 1950s and 1960s.[13]

THE 1960s

No other decade in American history proved so turbulent than that of the 1960s. The civil rights movement, Vietnam, public disorder and riots, political assassinations, and the counterculture/antiauthority movement threatened the very fabric of the nation. Police in America should have been accustomed to these challenges, which characterized in varying degrees almost every decade since the 1830s. They had learned little from history, however, and the scale of civic disorder in the 1960s was indeed exceptional. By the end of the decade, problems in policing became a national issue, drawing once again the attention of the federal government. Commissions, reports, and administrative laws forced police departments to finally go the extra distance to resolve conflicts in police–community relations and better serve the public good.

Police continued to have problems with the community. Striving for the administrative perfection modeled by public administration trends in the early 1960s, police departments still did not focus on community problems or on understanding the culture of the community. No instant solution presented itself. Change took time, especially in highly bureaucratized organizations such as police departments. Instead, professionalism had led police down a path to unintended consequences. For example, police succumbed to a misguided dependency on statistical data as a measure of efficiency. Typical of the social science trends of the time (body counts in Vietnam were among the more famous of these statistical measures of "success"), police claimed that statistical analysis could prove their capability to protect and serve the public.

Police departments identified quantifiable results for police employees that measured their crime-fighting skills. In measuring effectiveness, police used numbers of arrests, responses to calls, crime reports, and other quantifiable data as assessment tools. Reaction rates became the end all and be all for crime fighting effectiveness. From keeping track of the number of miles driven while on patrol to the number of radio calls answered, police departments depended on measurable criteria to rate efficiency and effectiveness. A daily activity report was created for each officer, noting radio calls, making arrests, writing traffic warnings and citations, conducting field interrogations, and the like. Each task or work product was given a hierarchical value in a rating system. A police officer initiating a felony arrest based on the officer's familiarity with his beat was highly valued. A misdemeanor arrest generated by responding to a radio call was of less value. A traffic citation for speeding was highly valued compared to "nonmoving" citations like a parking ticket. Highly productive officers were the ones who generated the most felony arrests while on patrol and had a representative balance in all other department work activity measurements such as field interrogations, traffic citations, and so forth. All of these things had been police duties and responsibilities since the turn of the century, but now they mattered to an individual patrol officer's performance rating and the overall rating of a department, both of which influenced promotion boards and budget decisions made by city managers and elected municipal officials. The root causes or crime and the possible impact that improved community–police relations could have on fighting crime continued to escape serious attention amidst this trendy emphasis on statistical analysis.

Recruiting practices also did little to improve community relations. Police officers continued to be recruited from two basic sources in the 1960s, just as they had since the turn of the century. Recruits tended to come from families with a strong tradition of police service or from military backgrounds. Recruiters aggressively went after those with military service, which provided discipline and an understanding of the rigors of a military-style organization. If an individual's father, brother, or close relative was a police officer, police recruiters assumed that the individual would understand the demands of police work and adhere to long-held police traditions. This institutionalized recruitment process was locked in a pattern of organizational behavior that was difficult to change. The recruitment patterns of the 1960s basically filled America's police departments with fairly well-disciplined white males, which left minorities and women on the outer edges of police service. At the same time, these individuals often lacked the educational background and the cultural understanding of critical issues affecting neighborhoods that they were assigned to patrol. Although some college education was preferable, most police officers across America were, and still are, required to have only a high school education.

Other problems were patrol patterns and personnel management. Police had yet to learn how to best use their most effective people. It was common practice in the 1960s to shift patrol officers from one beat to another on a regular basis. As a consequence, police seldom patrolled an area long enough to really get to know it and understand the issues affecting the neighborhoods. Assignments to vice squads or narcotics divisions usually lasted a brief time, because police administrators feared the temptation of corruption would be too great for officers to resist. With unpleasant memories of graft and corruption still in mind, police leadership followed the advice of Wilson and others to use frequent transfers as a means to prevent corruption.[14] The dilemma again was that officers did not get a chance to gain the knowledge necessary to be effective in these very specific jobs.

By the end of the 1960s, police had basically become an occupation force for high-crime, inner-city neighborhoods. Larger police departments developed shift schedules that consistently transferred police officers in and out of these areas, prohibiting the time necessary to develop close neighborhood relationships that might help resolve some of the inner-city problems. To meet the demands of efficiency and effectiveness, departments arranged patrol shifts that ensured that most officers were on duty during high-call-load times patrolling neighborhoods with high crime rates. Evening shifts had a higher concentration of police officers than day beats did. Often based on seniority, older more experienced officers "earned" the day shift to patrol low-crime neighborhoods or were assigned to investigations. New officers and recruits, with limited experience and low seniority, were placed on night shifts in high-crime areas, usually on Friday and Saturday nights. This set of circumstances virtually guaranteed failure. With the least experienced patrol officers supervised by the least experienced officers at the peak of crime calls on the highest crime days, it is no wonder that the civil disorder of the 1960s caught American police departments unprepared.

Professionalization had worked too well. Police now believed they no longer needed John Q. Citizen to assist them in their work. Deploying resources according to whichever model still did not guarantee a decrease in crime. Rapid response did not drastically increase the number of criminals caught. Moreover, police needed citizens to cooperate as witnesses. Police could not do their jobs without the help of the community; yet, police were headed in such a direction that autonomy from the community had become the norm of police professionalization. People did not feel safe in their neighborhoods because a cop could respond to a crime scene in three to five minutes. What would make them feel safe was the frequent sight of a uniformed officer walking a beat, talking with people, and getting to know what people thought about the neighborhood they lived in. The realization of this relatively simple idea, which had been common before the twentieth century, was slow in coming.[15]

The hostility between police and inner-city neighborhoods erupted several times during the 1960s. A whole myriad of factors contributed to these events, but they are worth examining to get a sense of police issues during this critical period. The Civil Rights movement, Vietnam, the youth counterculture, a strong undercurrent of anti-authoritism, and economic distress all contributed to a boiling pot waiting to spill over into violence. Traditional police methods based on concepts of professionalism had only irritated community relations. Moreover, the aggressiveness of what amounted to racial profiling by police only aggravated the situation. From Watts to Newark, inner-city riots broke out with frightening intensity—often as a result of inappropriate or questionable police action such as a poorly handled arrest. Racial tension between the police and black neighborhoods reached unprecedented levels across the nation, even in comparison to that in the early twentieth century. Riots, looting, and the destruction of property were common, as civil society broke down.[16]

One of the most notorious incidents erupted in 1962, when James Meredith attempted to enter, as the first black student, the University of Mississippi in Oxford. Mississippi in the 1960s was much like it was during the previous eighty years—poor, corrupt, saddled with a White-dominated government, media, and police, and not very much interested in the civil rights of its large black population. The small police force in the tiny town of Oxford was in no way prepared for or capable of dealing with the battle that exploded between white mobs and Mississippi highway patrolmen protesting integration against federal marshals and Army troops sent in to restore order and enforce a federal court ruling to allow Meredith to exercise his right to register for classes. The institutionalized racism of southern law enforcement showed its uglier side over several days of pitched battles in the streets around the university. Oxford police, to their credit, tried to minimize the violence, as did students and faculty at Ole Miss, but had a difficult time facing off against the Mississippi highway patrol. In the end, heavily armed forces from the U.S. Army had to be called in to gain control of the town.[17]

Other race-related riots and incidents took place across the South. Police fell on both sides. The year 1964 was one of the most violent and tense for the Civil Rights movement. In St. Augustine, Florida, tense stand-offs and minor violence lasted throughout the summer. At one point police tried to protect black and white civil rights supporters as they staged a protest on a local beach reserved for Whites only. As a white mob gathered to attack the protesters as they waded along the shore, police staved off the attack with clubs. The police used an interesting tactic that day. Instead of arresting only protestors, which had been the norm, they arrested pairs of protestors and attackers. White segregationists were appalled that police had apparently taken sides, the wrong side in this case. Similar scenes played out in violent acts in Hattiesburg and Meridian, Mississippi; Mansfield, Texas; and in other locations around the South.

Police were caught in a social revolution and were indeed part of its causes. The following year brought the famous marches, including the Selma, Alabama, march led by Martin Luther King, Jr. Selma proved a great victory for King's non-violent approach to protest. Selma and Alabama police authorities wanted a violent confrontation and allowed themselves to be easily goaded into attacking the peaceful demonstrators. Using dogs, tear gas, whips, and clubs, police moved in on the demonstrators with extreme fury. Over seventy marchers were hospitalized with severe injuries, some caused by police clubs wrapped with barbed wire, which were more reminiscent of the barbarous trench clubs of World War I than modern police equipment. Police again proved unable to handle the protests and stop acts of murder, violent assault, and destruction of property. It took federal intervention in the form of congressional legislation to finally bring order in the South.[18]

As serious as the riots of 1964 and 1965 were, the 1965 Watts riot in Los Angeles was perhaps the most shocking in its level of violence and destruction and in its impact on police. The worst was that it foreshadowed even greater violence to come. Just five days after President Lyndon Johnson signed the Voting Rights Act, widespread violent riots erupted in the predominantly black neighborhoods of the Watts community in Los Angeles. Watts epitomized the worst of inner-city problems: low unemployment, substandard schools, high crime rates, and an increasingly serious drug problem. The Los Angeles Police Department, under the leadership of the influential William Parker, was also part of the problem and was caught completely unprepared for widespread urban violence. Parker had created a highly professionalized, technology dependent, paramilitary police force, which looked amazingly efficient on paper and somewhat efficient in practice. "Negro-phobia" infected the Los Angeles Police Department, however, and serious racial conflict within the department and between white cops and black and Hispanic citizens lay just beneath the surface of the thin veneer that things in Los Angeles were in good order.[19]

From August 11 through August 16, Watts became a war zone. Like the race riots of the early twentieth century, the riot began with a relatively minor incident. In the case of Watts, a patrolman arrested a black man for drunk driving, which somehow got twisted through the rumor mill that a police officer beat a black taxi driver and a black pregnant woman without provocation. Gangs of roving young Blacks began throwing rocks and bottles at police cars and other vehicles driven by Whites. Police failed to respond. When night fell, looting and arson took over. Watts quickly became an insurrection against years of what Blacks saw as White abuse and racially selective law enforcement. In the end, it took sixteen thousand police, highway patrol officers, and National Guard troops to stop the violence. Over four thousand rioters were arrested in five days. One thousand were injured, and thirty-four people were killed. The millions of dollars in property damage included 250 buildings that were completely destroyed.[20]

Governor Edmund G. Brown appointed a commission to study the cause, conduct, and consequences of the Watts riot in August 1965. Chaired by former CIA director John A. McCone, the McCone Commission identified police misconduct and brutality among the causes of the riot. The commission recommended a stronger board of police commissioners and that an independent inspector general be named to investigate citizen complaints. The commission's report failed, however, to address how to resolve racism among police officers and offered little of substance to improve police–community relations in the Watts area. Critics of the commission called the whole process nothing more than window-dressing.[21]

It got much worse before things dared to improve. In 1966, at least thirty-eight major riots occurred across the United States—not just in the South. The most violent happened in Chicago, San Francisco, and Cleveland; not in Atlanta, Memphis, or Dallas. Fortunately, only seven people lost their lives, but close to four hundred were injured in these riots. In 1967, Detroit and Newark exploded in deadly mayhem. Forty-three people were killed in the Detroit riot alone, and Newark suffered over one million dollars in property damage. Thirty-nine cities experienced forty-one major or serious instances of civil disorder that year. Again, these riots were mostly eruptions of long-standing grievances between Whites and Blacks, and were often touched off by confrontations with police. Unfortunately, none of these incidents resulted in any long-term improvements for rioters or police.[22] The remaining two years of the decade saw Martin Luther King and Robert Kennedy gunned down, the massive riots and demonstrations at the 1968 Democratic National Convention in Chicago, and a moderating shift from race-based riots to massive protests against the American war in Vietnam.

Police take cover from sniper fire during the Watts riot. (Library of Congress)

Citizens and police leaders tried, however, to glean some lessons from police behavior. As it did in the case of the race riots of the early twentieth century, government at all levels turned to commissions to examine the violence that had erupted on their streets in the 1960s. In addition to police difficulties was the fact that crime rates for homicide, assault, theft, and domestic violence increased dramatically over the course of the decade. President Johnson appointed two commissions to study the growing violence in American society: the National Advisory Commission in Civil Disorders and the National Commission on Law Enforcement and Administration of Justice. In addition to exploring the root causes of crime and social disorder, both commissions had recommendations for police to better deal with these problems.

The 1967 National Advisory Commission on Civil Disorders was extremely critical of police and not just of police behavior during the riots, but more so of police failings in general. Also known as the Kerner Commission, named after its chairman, Illinois Governor Otto Kerner, the commission's final report was released to the public just weeks before the murder of Martin Luther King in Memphis, which set off days of riots around the country. The study found that police had instigated over half the riots in 1967 alone. To Blacks, police symbolized the power of white racism and oppression. Despite statistics to the contrary, Blacks perceived a double standard of justice—one form of justice for Whites, another for Blacks. The study recommended more black patrol officers to patrol black neighborhoods and that departments look hard at policing practices in ghetto neighborhoods. The major recommendations of the commission centered on community–police relations. As the most critical aspect of law enforcement, according to the study, relations with the community were imperative to effective policing and could prevent not only riots and insurrections but also general crime. Police now needed to lead the way in establishing solid, productive relations with the community they served. Moreover, departments needed to instill a new attitude among officers: that their primary function is one of public service. The report advised that it would take federal support to make these recommendations happen and police should be made part of the solution rather than part of the problem.[23]

The National Commission on Law Enforcement and Administration of Justice report of 1968 was one of the most in-depth and thorough evaluations of criminal justice in American history. Among many other areas, the report made numerous recommendations to improve police and police—community relations. It cited long-standing shortcomings in American policing, namely, the inefficiency of overlapping local, state, and federal jurisdictions; poor training and education; and the prevalence of white male-dominated police forces across the country. Before any improvements could be made, the commission sagely pointed out that both the police and the community had to understand the scope and complexity of the urban problems police faced on a daily basis. Moreover, police themselves had to become more adept at recognizing and responding to social change in the communities they served. One way to achieve this was for police to be subject to external review and perhaps even to control. Beginning at the turn of the century, police control had been taken away from most elected officials because of corruption. Now that policy had worked too well, as police had no accountability. Police autonomy, once seen as a solution, was now a problem. External control and review needed to be reestablished, which would get citizens involved with policing, and hopefully better police–community relations would ensue.

The commission also saw the individual patrol officer as a solution to the police problem. The patrol officer, since the days of the night watch, was almost exclusively the first contact with a criminal or with citizens in need of assistance. Considering the commission's findings that the average patrol officer was poorly trained, overworked, and not well motivated, and that promotion to detective, and so forth, comes only from the ranks, there was little mystery that this first contact could easily, as it often had, go wrong. Some suggested that more patrol officers would help, but the commission concluded that this would only add to the problem. Before adding patrol officers, cities had to first take a look at their manpower strategies to get the best use out of the officers they already had. More important, police departments needed to recruit more minorities onto their forces and come up with screening programs to weed out white recruits with strong racial or ethnic prejudices. Surveys of departments that patrolled large black neighborhoods and inner-city areas found that black police officers consistently did a better job of patrolling those neighborhoods. Using only white officers to work these beats produced a range of problems. In some cities, black police officers could not arrest a white citizen, and in others black officers could not make felony arrests. Discrimination, ineffective management, and inadequate training contributed to the crisis in police–community relations.

The commission declared that police would have to take the initiative in community outreach. Large departments should have a community relations division or at least a community officer. In smaller departments, the police chief should take the lead in the community relations effort. Innovative, new concepts like team policing and neighborhood crime-watch programs should be organized and promoted by local police. Surveys found that the average patrol officer spent one-third of his/her day on crime, which meant the remaining two-thirds could be better used in improving community relations and serving individual citizens. Relatively simple things, like speaking engagements with local service clubs and neighborhood groups, programs with area schools, and police interest in the well-being of neighborhoods could, according to the report, make a huge difference in the long term.[24]

Once again the federal government had stepped in to help address issues of local law enforcement. The idea of police review boards was abhorrent to police officers, but congressional and local support of the commission's work pushed the concept forward. The International Association of Chiefs of Police (IACP) came out against external review, claiming that police should and could police themselves. Recruitment of Blacks by police forces also hit resistance in the IACP, although Washington increased the number of Blacks in its 1969 recruiting class from one-third to one-half of total recruits, and Detroit hired twice as many black officers in 1968 than it had the previous year. New York City, with the financial support of the Ford Foundation, started a program in 1969 to recruit Blacks and Hispanics returning from Vietnam.

Federal commissions represented only part of the response to the increase in crime and the widespread disorder. City and police leaders also held national conferences to address crime- and riot-related issues. During the winter of 1967–1968, over four hundred mayors, city managers, and police leaders representing 136 cities across the United States gathered in Washington to share ideas on riot control and prevention. Sponsored jointly by the Department of Justice and the IACP, the group concluded that to really understand effective riot control and prevention, they had to learn more than just riot control tactics. Community relations, command supervision, and quick response to disorder, would lead them to better strategies to avoid the tumult of the previous years. Other studies by the International City Managers Association and the IACP found that despite the level of violence and the questionable police response to rioting, many cities and their police were satisfied with their policies regarding riot control and use of fatal force. Rapid response was key, but in several instances response was slow. Police had to learn to recognize the embryonic stages of a mass riot.[25]

Improving community–police relations proved difficult. Many police officers saw programs directed at bettering police relations with the local community as more public relations campaigns than programs of substance. The return of unionism among police did not help their image with the public. For police to go on strike, as they did in 1968 in Detroit, Kansas City, and New York City during years of riots and increasing crime rates, risked further alienating Blacks and even Whites.[26] Nothing easily resolved any of these problems, and each of the issues varied from city to city, police department to police department, and sometimes from precinct to precinct.

Federal intervention in police issues set the trend for the rest of the century. Congressional legislation in a series of crime bills and the establishment of the Law Enforcement Assistance Administration to coordinate federal grants to local police departments firmly established the federal role in local community policing. Federal courts also had a direct impact on police, none more lasting and influential than the now-familiar Miranda warning. In 1963, Phoenix police arrested Ernesto Miranda for robbery and questioned him about the kidnapping and rape of an eighteen-year-old girl. In the process of interrogation, Miranda signed a confession to the crimes. Police did not advise Miranda that he had the right to an attorney or that any evidence he gave could be used against him at trial. Constitutionally, Miranda had the right to representation and could not be forced to incriminate himself. Claiming that Miranda's constitutional rights had been violated, his defense counsel tried to have the confession withdrawn, but the court denied the petition. Miranda was convicted. His appeal reached the Supreme Court in 1966. In *Miranda v. Arizona* (1966), the high court held that Miranda's conviction be thrown out and that police must advise people of their rights to remain silent, to legal counsel, and to not incriminate themselves. Since the *Miranda v. Arizona* decision, police have had to use the now-standard Miranda warning when making an arrest or questioning a suspect. Congress in 1968 attempted to overrule *Miranda v. Arizona* by passing legislation that allowed judges to decide whether or not a confession was voluntary on a case-by-case basis, with or without a Miranda warning. Police and prosecutors, on the other hand, wanted to be safe rather than sorry, and before long Mirandizing a suspect became standard police practice. The Supreme Court upheld *Miranda v. Arizona* in *Dickerson v. United States* (2000), ruling further that Congress could not effect through legislation the admissibility of evidence in court, thus nullifying the 1968 law.[27]

The face of American policing was deeply affected by the 1960s. Dramatic changes in the way police approached community and crime problems began a forced transformation that would take most of the 1970s to institutionally impress American policing. Police placed themselves in a real dilemma with the community they served. They needed strong public support to do their job, but they could not get that support because many of the public felt so threatened by the police.[28]

Still, American society survived the 1960s, and police remained, as always, the primary enforcers of laws and social order.

THE 1970s

The 1970s are generally treated as a period of malaise in American history, as the Vietnam War ended without a sense of closure, the Watergate scandal intensified general distrust in government, the Cold War entered a period of détente, and the energy crisis racked American perceptions of invincibility. As the turbulence of the 1960s passed into memory, police began to return to crime fighting and in some ways lose sight of the community relations issues that had caused so much trouble during that decade. It was a classic "out of sight, out of mind" situation. Yet, the 1970s brought attempts by police to do their job better. Innovation and forced change best describe the police experience of the 1970s, as police, like the American military, tried to recover from the unpleasant experiences of the 1960s.

Federal programs spurred by the 1967 commission report made some headway in providing long-term solutions to some police problems. In 1968, the federal Law Enforcement Assistance Administration began awarding fully funded educational opportunities to police officers and giving large grants to police departments to enhance crime fighting technology at the local level. Although disbanded in 1982 under charges of wasted tax dollars and poor results, the Law Enforcement Assistance Administration gave out millions of dollars during the 1970s to help fight crime. Other federal incentive programs encouraged recruitment of minority police officers. Most important, federal support provided opportunities for community leaders, and police leaders finally began to discuss the issues and problems that had contributed to community unrest for so long. Private organizations, namely, the Police Foundation, provided money to study policing issues under the leadership of Patrick Murphy, Hubert Williams, and others. The studies were damning and forced police to consider new, alternative strategies.

By the mid 1970s, however, the crises of the 1960s had disappeared, and for a while so too did attention to police issues. Downturns in the economy and high interest rates forced municipalities to tighten their budgetary belts, thus limiting the ability of police to experiment with new strategies. The new emphasis on police responsiveness to emerging community social concerns waned, as the political insulation of traditional police professionalism made it difficult for the community to influence police actions and priorities. Moreover, scholars, community leaders, and others studying the police problem began to recognize that current police strategies had little impact on preventing or even on controlling crime.[29]

A major problem involved police theory versus actual practice. What the leaders in police and public administration outlined as effective police strategies was one thing; its practice in the field was quite another. Discretion continued to be a major factor in actual field procedures. A considerable gulf existed between the formal definition of a particular function on the one hand and actual practice on the other; from the 1960s it was apparent that the police did not enforce the law with distant objectivity. In many communities, citizens developed a not-inaccurate perception that police selectively enforced the law according to the racial, ethnic, or economic composition of a neighborhood.[30] The professional concept that the police treated everyone equally and objectively was still highly valued, but actual practice invited challenge to this time-honored police principle. Citizens felt that they had limited channels through which to voice their concerns about police practices and the problems in their neighborhoods. In many instances, the police were practically an independent agency operating under few governmental controls. It was often unclear exactly who was accountable for specific police practices.

Police finally got the message. The much talked about concept of community policing finally became a realization. By implementing police–community relations programs, police hoped to provide a direct and open link with the community that had more substance than the window-dressing of the past. Although some of these programs were admittedly motivated by public relations, many of these initiatives concentrated on providing the opportunity for concerned citizens to have input with police administration authorities. However, these programs sometimes bypassed local government political structure and often failed to address police accountability. In many ways, community relations became a fashionable strategy for police departments. Much attention lauded these programs, but within inner-city neighborhoods they often ran into suspicious opposition. Community relations offices did not equate to police review boards that could hold police accountable for their actions. Citizens remained on the fringe of the police system, attempting to influence police actions from an insulated distance.[31]

Professionally, police efforts in the 1970s focused on management, control of corruption, and police effectiveness. Through the support of the Police Foundation and the Law Enforcement Assistance Administration, several studies and initiatives attempted to address these issues. In a number of cities, community groups pressed for the establishment of formal mechanisms to provide influence over police procedures and conduct. By the end of the decade, Rochester, New York City, and Philadelphia, among many other cities, revived or established independent civilian review boards to monitor police conduct and provide formal avenues for civilian complaints. Kansas City's preventive patrol experiment, Rochester's criminal investigation management experiment, and several response-time studies were indicative of this trend to study police effectiveness and professionalism.[32]

The Kansas City study was perhaps the most telling about the failure of the time-honored tradition of police patrol as an effective method of crime prevention. Using three different levels of car patrols (reactive, proactive, and control), the study looked at the impact of criminal activity, community perceptions, and police behavior in fifteen beats of the South Patrol Division in Kansas City. It was the biggest, broadest, and most encompassing study of police patrolling attempted under scientific conditions. It ran for twelve months from 1972 to 1973, collecting data on response time, arrest procedures, use of time by officers, and officer attitudes. Statistics, interviews, surveys, and other methods measured just how effective patrolling really was in fighting crime.

The results challenged every accepted notion about the effectiveness of patrols. The study found that the varying levels of patrol had little to no effect on how citizens felt about safety, much less on criminal activity. Attitudes toward police changed little regardless of the type of patrol used in a neighborhood. More or fewer patrols did not equal more or less crime in a given beat. A study in Newark examining the impact of foot patrols had similar findings, except that people in Newark were significantly more aware of increased foot patrols in their neighborhood than people were aware of increases in car patrols in Kansas City. The Newark study offered a vital lesson: citizens feel safer if they have a more positive attitude toward police, and feeling more secure about one's neighborhood helped prevent crime. Other studies found that one- or two-officer car patrols made no difference in preventing crime and that police rarely, if ever, made arrests for major crimes by arriving on the scene quickly. Such damning evidence forced police to reexamine how they protected and served the community.[33]

To their credit, by the late 1970s, police departments also began to look outside their own profession for information and guidance. Police had not been open to independent assessment or research, much less to other government agencies looking to collect data on police procedures or strategies before the 1970s.

A resurgence in criminal justice programs at universities, the growth of sociology and social work as professions, and advances in criminal psychology brought police practitioners into increasing contact with people interested in police issues, who were outside the traditional professional field of policing. Sociologists William Westley and Jerome Skolnick studied police subculture and working environments, focusing on the effects of police organization and the culture of violence that made it easier if not desirable for police to occasionally exercise authority outside the law. Criminal justice Professor Samuel Walker offered an intriguing study of police reform since the nineteenth century, pointing to the difficulties in reforming police in a democratic society. Urban historian Robert Fogelson studied police development from the historical perspective of large-city police forces and cited the stagnation of police innovation in the late 1970s. Even the Rand Corporation studied police, producing in 1975 an extremely critical assessment of the effectiveness of police detectives and follow-up investigations.[34]

Still, problems continued, as new threats to civic security surfaced to challenge police and citizens. One of these threats was drug abuse. The 1970s could be called the decade of drug enforcement, as the war on crime spawned the war on drugs. A clearly recognizable problem in the 1960s, drug abuse reached epidemic levels in the early 1970s. Metropolitan Enforcement Groups were among many community efforts to utilize resources at all levels of government to fight the new war on drugs. Again, inner-city neighborhoods were the primary battlegrounds and often included community residents in active support of police efforts to enforce drug laws. The problems of drug abuse hit all levels of American society but especially saturated inner-city areas. Congressional hearings brought national attention, along with federal money, to the problem. The correlation between drug abuse and other crime was both a subject of study and a reality. Although the drug war was not won, several important changes occurred to America's police departments during the battles. In the aftermath of the civil unrest of the 1960s, the police were quick to realize the importance of citizen involvement in fighting illegal drug violations as a means to control drug use and fight related crime. If police could stop drug sales, they could also reduce crime, so the thinking went.

In addition to drugs, gangs and domestic violence also skyrocketed in the 1970s, again drawing the attention of research institutions and other government agencies. Police practice in dealing with these issues improved as a result of the assistance of social workers and sociologists. This had the positive effect of boosting police confidence in outside researchers, thus paving the way for outside assessment of police effectiveness and opening the minds of police to different methods of dealing with these problems.

TO THE TWENTY-FIRST CENTURY

The last two decades of the twentieth century brought little relief for American police. Despite monumental efforts to win the wars on crime and drugs and build community relations, the problems continued. New criminal categories, such as hate crimes and carjacking, and increased media attention to police brutality through some very high-profile incidents made policing and improving community relations all the more difficult.

In the realization that past police practice was not solving crime problems and was contributing to community mistrust, concepts of community and problem-oriented policing gained popularity among police departments across the country. Community policing was put in place in three phases: First, when crime occurred, police officers continued to respond as quickly as possible. Second, when a specific criminal problem was identified, police initiated multiple forces to stop this sort of crime, including neighborhood watches, information campaigns, and variations in patrol. The third phase of the community policing model was designed to identify the factors that contribute to crime in the neighborhood. With this information in hand, community members, working closely with the police took steps to create a healthy neighborhood. Herman Goldstein's problem-oriented policing concept centered on this last phase, looking at crime and neighborhood blight as specific problems with solutions such as renovating a housing project or demolishing dilapidated homes that were being used as drug dens. Community policing of the 1980s was all about the development of positive working relationships between the police and the neighborhood members with the purpose of identifying community crime problems.

James Q. Wilson and George L. Kelling brought this new strategy to broad public attention through a concept known as "broken windows." It was not a complex notion, and the idea had been around since the late 1960s. Leaving an unrepaired broken window in a building would result in all the windows being broken before long. Broken windows left broken was a sign that no one cared about the building and thus the neighborhood. Untended property fed vandalism, provided places to hide drug use, and at the extreme could promote violent crime. Long before violent crime actually occurs in "untended" areas, local people sense that the area is dangerous and stop walking by it or letting their children play around it. In no time, the area deteriorates with overgrowth, litter, homeless people, drug users, drunks, and gangs. The local people had now lost their neighborhood and live in fear.

The solution was to fix the first "broken window." According to Wilson and Kelling, police could do the repairs. Police had traditionally helped to maintain the informal social controls of a community. With "broken windows," the community lost its informal social control. Since the 1920s, police had moved toward professionalization, which meant less contact with the community and thus less support from those informal social control mechanisms. The eruptions of the 1960s were indicative of this trend. Cops could also help by enforcing the relatively small stuff, like public intoxication and loitering. By enforcing small violations, larger crimes such as assault and rape would in turn decrease, so the thinking went.

In the 1980s, police began to see the value of informal social control and the role citizens could play in helping to maintain it. Newport News, Virginia, was one of the first to put such a program into action, with the interesting finding that local government had failed in its obligations to keep city streets clean and enforce building codes. Through threats of hearings and investigations, local citizens basically coerced city departments to do their jobs more effectively. This alone resulted in improvements. Once again, police found a valuable asset in local citizens.[35]

Realizing that they could not win the war on crime alone, police renewed their interest in community relations. Much of the more effective progress in this area came with an increased role in police accountability, reorganization of departments, improving police recruiting, and finding creative ways to involve citizens in protecting their own neighborhoods. In the 1970s, Santa Ana, California, Police Chief Raymond Davis managed to turn a troubled police department into a "tightly run, technologically advanced" police force that was "unusually sensitive to the local community." Davis civilianized nearly half of the department's employees, took advantage of affirmative action programs to recruit officers and employees from all over California, and reorganized his department to give creative, dedicated officers the opportunity to test their ideas and advance. Community relations with the Santa Ana police soared, as people reclaimed their neighborhoods, banks invested in properties once considered too risky for loans, and crime decreased in relation to projected increases.[36]

Detroit found success as well. By the early 1980s, Detroit was indeed the murder capital of the United States. Serious crime was rampant in downtown areas. Of course Detroit police made radical changes to attack the problem. Instead of the usual reactive style of policing that had been used for decades, Detroit police turned to community-based "self-defense" programs. A new Crime Prevention Section coordinated crime prevention activities with local neighborhoods, organizing Neighborhood Watch committees and establishing programs for schools, private security officers, community service organizations, and others who might be in contact with street crime. Fifty-two "mini" stations, reporting directly to the chief of police, were established across the city. Each station had only a few officers who did not respond to radio calls or walk beats. Instead, they provided a place for area citizens to walk in and report crimes and disturbances, or to alert police of some neighborhood problem. Other officers were placed in roving task force units, assisting neighborhoods in establishing self-defense, conducting undercover surveillance on suspected criminals, and patrolling area streets by car. Both the task forces and the ministations were disconnected from the Detroit 911 system. The Detroit program required a massive reallocation of manpower at a time when the Detroit police force suffered severe cutbacks in personnel.

The Detroit program was the brainchild of Detroit's first black mayor, Coleman Young, and was strengthened by the hard work of Detroit's first black police chief, William Hart. After some initial growing pains, Hart turned the ministation concept into a workable "bridge to the community." The Detroit program, on the whole, could not be declared a success statistically, because crime actually increased, whereas the number of arrests fell. On the positive side, citizens felt safer in their neighborhoods than they did before the program was instituted. What is significant about the Detroit experience is the radical course of action taken to deal with the crime problem. Shifting from such a traditional policing approach to an extreme community-oriented program was expensive, risky, and filled with possible pitfalls. Nonetheless, Detroit police made the effort with the support of the community. Considering Detroit's history of mass disorder and racial violence, the program was indeed, at the very least, a step in the right direction.[37]

Other cities instituted community policing in innovative ways. Houston, New York City, Denver, Oakland, and Newark, among dozens of others, all gave community policing a chance. Los Angeles Police Chief Daryl Gates was perhaps the leader in police reform in the 1980s, creating such successful programs as the Community Mobilization Project and the Drug Abuse Resistance Education program (DARE). Gates prided the Los Angeles police on their discipline and lack of corruption. Unfortunately, events in the early 1990s would shatter that perception.[38]

Newark in particular was a glowing example of what could be accomplished with community help. Like Detroit, Newark's immediate past was one of violence and racial conflict. Moreover, Newark police had a long history of brutality, abuse, and extralegal practices. Both the police department and the community needed attention. Under the leadership of Hubert Williams, Newark police overcame limited staffing and budgetary resources to modernize its police force, make it more diverse, increase its effectiveness, and instill an ethic of accountability. An internal affairs division was created to investigate complaints against officers. A truancy task force helped get kids off the streets and back into school. Newark police used "sweeps" to clear street corners and storefronts of milling youths, drunks, and drug dealers. Roadblocks were used to check for drunk drivers and to check identification through a new computer network for warrants. Buses and subways were inspected regularly. Police supported and participated in community-watch programs. Although each of these programs had an impact, Newark police still faced a mountain of challenges in trying both to reduce crime and to restore public confidence in police in a city that continued to suffer from economic distress as well as from a dreadful public-image problem. Williams and Newark police strongly supported downtown and river-front renewal initiatives, some of which began to have a positive impact by the mid-1980s.[39]

Community policing, with a problem-oriented police focus, seemed to provide a hopeful model for successful crime prevention and improved police–community relations. By the 1990s, these ideas had become the rage among police departments of all sizes across the country. Studies continued to tinker with the concept, showing that police were not afraid of innovation and new ideas. The idea of "community wellness" was just one of these alterations. Supported by a grant from the Police Executive Research Forum, Robert C. Wadman and Robert K. Olson introduced the concept in 1990. Basically, the community wellness approach treated police–community relations and crime prevention holistically as a community problem, not just as a police issue. Taking the analogy from the medical concept of wellness as preventive against disease and other ailments, police and citizens could do the same by being preventive against crime through building prosperity in their communities.[40]

Old problems, however, came back with a haunting vengeance in the 1990s. The institutionalized racism of American policing reared its ugly head, and police corruption reached troubling levels. No matter what progress had been made by police in their communities, for each step forward police seemed to take two steps backward. The savage and brutal beating of Rodney King by Los Angeles police officers in 1991 again pointed to serious problems police still had with race, abuse of authority, and accountability. Videotaped by a bystander, the incredible scene of white officers beating a black man brought back the horrific images of the 1950s and 1960s. Community policing, it appeared, was failing as a policing concept. When the California state court acquitted the officers in question, Los Angeles erupted in massive, violent riots reminiscent of the Watts riots. In just five days, all covered live on CNN, the nation watched as Whites, Blacks, Koreans, and Hispanics fought each other in the streets of Los Angeles. Lesser riots developed in other cities, but paled in comparison to what was happening in Los Angeles. Police seemed powerless to get the situation under control. In the end, over one billion dollars in property was either destroyed or damaged, and forty people lost their lives. In 1993, two of the four officers were convicted in federal court for violating King's civil rights, both receiving relatively short prison sentences.[41]

In response to the outburst of mass violence and the apparently racially motivated beating of King, several government and private organizations investigated the incident through hearings and commissions. The National Association for the Advancement of Colored People (NAACP) took the opportunity to go beyond Los Angeles and look at police–race problems across the United States. Working with the Criminal Justice Institute at Harvard Law School, the report was released in 1995. Once again, the findings found police rife with age-old problems. Racism had become institutionalized and now motivated suspicion, investigation, even stops and searches. Racial profiling had become a national problem according to the report. Excessive use of force, physical abuse, and verbal harassment were the rule rather than the exception. Although many departments had procedures in place to hear citizen complaints against police officers, officers were rarely found at fault. In some cities, people feared police retaliation for even filing a complaint. The "code of silence" among police officers had helped renew the "us versus them" relationship between police and community.

The report recommended little that differed from previous commissions and reports on police effectiveness and community–police relations. It suggested change in attitude, a greater emphasis on police work as social work, and improved hiring practices to ensure that police had well-educated, diverse, and socially responsible officer candidates. Training and education needed continued attention, especially in teaching officers about cultural diversity and sensitivity. Finally, in somewhat of a catch-all recommendation, the report recommended that all police departments institute civilian review boards and adopt community-policing methods as the primary police strategy. The irony was, of course, that it was community policing that did not seem to be solving the problem.[42]

The Criminal Justice Institute/NAACP report read much the same as the commission reports from 1919, the 1940s, and the 1960s: similar causes, same results.[43] Unfortunately, the King incident was not the last. New York City police brutally sodomized a Haitian immigrant in 1997. Racial profiling continued to be a central divisive issue between the police and the community. Los Angeles police again found the front page with the Rampart scandal of 1999. Conflict between minorities and police remained on edge throughout the decade.

Still, police and those that studied the police saw hope in the community-policing concept. One approach that many departments experimented with was the zero-tolerance concept of community policing. Former New York City Police Commissioner William Bratton, with the support of Hubert Williams and the Police Foundation, made the zero-tolerance concept a national initiative. Bratton started his program as the head of the New York City Transit Police in 1990. Zero-tolerance policing centers on the "vigorous" enforcement of all violations, even on the most "trifling."

Also known as "quality of life" policing, Bratton used the program to refocus the New York City Police Department after it ended its community-policing program in 1993. In many ways, zero tolerance was a throwback to the old statistically based efficiency ratings of the 1960s. Success with the transit police convinced Bratton that success could also be had with the New York City police. Bureaucracy was decentralized, as were precinct command structures. Precinct captains had to submit weekly crime statistics. Computer technology in the form of mapping and spreadsheet analysis approached real-time views of crime and police effectiveness in New York City. In the tradition of Los Angeles Police Chief William Parker, Bratton brought back a paramilitary attitude to New York police with new uniforms, high-tech weapons, and "results." Again, body counts from Vietnam come to mind, as Bratton's new New York City police racked up arrest after arrest. From 1994 to 1998, the overall crime rate in the huge city dropped by 43 percent. Murder rates declined by 60 percent.

The apparent success of zero tolerance in New York City came with a price. From 1994 to 1998, complaints of police brutality by New York police officers rose by 62 percent. The city settled several lawsuits involving police brutality to the tune of one hundred million dollars during the same time period. The American Civil Liberties Union and other watchdog groups claimed the zero-tolerance program as the root cause of widespread civil rights abuses by New York police.

Other cities adopted zero tolerance as their principal police strategy. New Orleans, San Francisco, Baltimore, Indianapolis, Miami, and Minneapolis were among many cities that tried out this new program. Most experienced similar results to those in New York. Crime rates declined quickly and sharply, arrests increased, and citizen complaints against police for brutality and harassment increased as well. Critics charged that programs like zero tolerance had little to do with the "quality of life" and only harmed community–police relations.[44]

In reality, zero tolerance was nothing new in American police history. Even President Bill Clinton's initiative, through the 1994 Crime Bill, to put one hundred thousand more cops on the street was misguided according to earlier studies about patrol effectiveness. Still, despite these problems, police in the 1990s had once again shown a remarkable openness to experimentation and innovation. The jury is still out on community policing at the beginning of the twenty-first century. Paradigm shifts do not take hold overnight, and it may take years of patience to properly assess whether or not such policing strategies are really effective.

THE LEGACY OF AMERICAN POLICE HISTORY

September 11, 2001, completely reversed the downward trend police had been riding since the 1980s. The heroic sacrifices of New York police and firefighters and the immediate and effective response of police all over the country to safeguard airports, hospitals, national landmarks, and the like placed police in the most favorable public position they have ever experienced. Old barriers among local, state, and federal agencies have become more permeable, as law enforcement of all shapes and sizes has had to cooperatively unify to fight the domestic war on terrorism.[45] The question remains as to how long this upward ride will last. In August 2002, white police officers in suburban Los Angeles were caught on videotape beating a black youth that they had apprehended at a local gas station. Yet, police have achieved amazing success during the summer of 2002 in recovering abducted children through community-based alert programs such as California's Amber Alert System, which became a national program in April 2003.

New successes, old problems—this has been the constant of American police history. Police in America are caught in a true dilemma. They are charged with maintaining law and order in an open society that values personal liberty above all. Can police effectively fight crime under such constraints? The question continues to beg an answer. American police history has been influenced by the constant violence between individuals and groups within the rubric of a free, open, and democratic society. The forces of change continue to force police to reexamine the way they approach policing. In the end, police have been placed in the most delicate social balance to protect and serve American citizens, and the United States remains the most free and open society in the world.

NOTES

INTRODUCTION

1. David R. Johnson, *American Law Enforcement: A History* (Wheeling, Ill.: Forum Press, 1981). See also Johnson, *Policing the Urban Underworld: The Impact of Crime on the Development of American Police, 1800–1887* (Philadelphia: Temple University Press, 1979); Bryan Vila and Cynthia Morris, eds., *The Role of Police in American Society: A Documentary History* (Westport, Conn.: Greenwood Press, 1999); Samuel Walker, *A Critical History of Police Reform: The Emergence of Professionalization* (Lexington, Mass.: D. C. Heath, 1977); Robert M. Fogelson, *Big City Police* (Cambridge: Harvard University Press, 1977).

2. Frank R. Prassell, *The Western Peace Officer: A Legacy of Law and Order in the American West* (Norman: University of Oklahoma Press, 1972); Roger McGrath, *Gunfighters, Highwaymen, and Vigilantes: Violence on the Frontier* (Los Angeles: University of California Press, 1984); and Larry D. Ball, *Desert Lawmen: The High Sheriffs of New Mexico and Arizona, 1846–1912* (Albuquerque: University of New Mexico Press, 1992); Sally E. Hadden, *Slave Patrols: Law and Violence in Virginia and the Carolinas* (Cambridge: Harvard University Press, 2001).

3. Roger Lane, *Policing the City: Boston, 1822–1885* (Cambridge: Harvard University Press, 1967); Douglas Greenberg, *Crime and Law Enforcement in the Colony of New York, 1691–1776* (Ithaca, N.Y.: Cornell University Press, 1974); James F. Richardson, *The New York Police: Colonial Times to 1901* (New York: Oxford University Press, 1970); and Joseph Laythe, "'Trouble on the Outside, Trouble on the Inside': Growing Pains, Social Change, and Small Town Policing—The Eugene Police Department, 1862–1932," *Police Quarterly* 5, no. 1 (March 2002): 96–112. These studies are representative of a growing body of scholarly work on regional and local law enforcement.

4. Robert A. Harris, *Keeping the Peace: Police Reform in Montana, 1889–1918* (Helena: Montana Historical Society Press, 1994); Charles M. Robinson II, *The Men Who Wear the Star: The Story of the Texas Rangers* (New York: Random House, 2000).

5. Raymond B. Fosdick, *American Police Systems* (New York: Century Co., 1920; reprint Montclair, N.J.: Patterson Smith, 1969); August Vollmer, *Police and Modern Society* (Los Angeles: University of California Press, 1936; reprint Montclair, N.J.: Patterson Smith, 1971); Bruce Smith, *Police Systems in the United States*, rev. ed. (New York: Harper Brothers, 1949); O. W. Wilson, *Police Administration* (New York: McGraw-Hill, 1950); and James Q. Wilson, *Varieties of Police Behavior* (Cambridge: Harvard University Press, 1968).

6. See, for example, Randy L. LaGrange, *Policing American Society* (Chicago: Nelson-Hall Publishers, 1993), 33; Frank Schmalleger, *Criminal Justice Today: An Introductory Text for the 21st Century* (Upper Saddle River, N.J.: Prentice Hall, 1999), 180; Joseph Senna and Larry Siegel, *Introduction to Criminal Justice*, 7th ed. (Minneapolis/St. Paul: West Publishing Company, 1996), 230.

7. See Thomas S. Kuhn, *The Structure of Scientific Revolutions* 3d ed. (Chicago: University of Chicago Press, 1996).

8. See Wilson, *Varieties of Police Behavior;* George L. Kelling, *Fixing "Broken Windows": Restoring Order in American Cities,* with a chapter by Catherine M. Coles and foreword by James Q. Wilson (Westport, Conn.: Praeger, 1995); Herman Goldstein, *Police Corruption: A Perspective on Its Nature and Control* (Washington, D.C.: Police Foundation, 1975); and Goldstein, *Policing a Free Society* (Cambridge: Ballinger, 1977).

9. Robert C. Wadman and Robert K. Olson, *Community Wellness: A New Theory of Policing* (Washington, D.C.: Police Executive Research Forum, 1990), 1–2.

CHAPTER 1—POLICE IN EARLY AMERICA

1. David R. Johnson, *American Law Enforcement: A History* (Wheeling, Ill.: Forum Press, 1981), 1.

2. Bryan Vila and Cynthia Morris, eds., *The Role of Police in American Society: A Documentary History* (Westport, Conn.: Greenwood Press, 1999), 3.

3. Douglas Greenberg, *Crime and Law Enforcement in the Colony of New York, 1691–1776* (Ithaca, N.Y.: Cornell University Press, 1974), 155.

4. Howard P. Chudacoff and Judith E. Smith, *The Evolution of American Urban Society* (Upper Saddle River, N.J.: Prentice Hall, 2000), 13–14.

5. Carl Bridenbaugh, *Cities in the Wilderness: The First Century of Urban Life in America, 1625–1742* (New York: The Ronald Press Company, 1938), 63.

6. Allan R. Millett and Peter Maslowski, *For the Common Defense: A Military History of the United States of America*, rev. and exp. ed. (New York: Free Press, 1994), 6–8.

7. A Commission to the Privy Council, January 24, 1615, quoted in Abbot Emerson Smith, "The Transportation of Convicts to the American Colonies in the Seventeenth Century," *American Historical Review* 39, no. 2 (January 1934): 233–34.

8. Smith, "The Transportation of Convicts to the American Colonies in the Seventeenth Century," 243–44.

9. A. Roger Ekrich, "Bound for America: A Profile of British Convicts Transported to the Colonies, 1718–1775," *William and Mary Quarterly* 3, no. 42 (1985), 184–200.

10. Michael Zuckerman, "The Social Context of Democracy in Massachusetts," *William and Mary Quarterly* 25 (1968): 538.

11. David H. Flaherty, "Crime and Social Control in Provincial Massachusetts," *Historical Journal* 24, no. 2 (1981): 339–60.

12. Quoted in David Freeman Hawke, *Everyday Life in Early America* (New York: Harper and Row, 1988), 105, and in Robert F. Oaks, "Things Too Fearful to Name": Sodomy and Buggery in Seventeenth-Century New England," *Journal of Social History* 12 (1978): 275.

13. Hawke, *Everyday Life in Early America*, 106–107.

14. Hawke, *Everyday Life in Early America*, 108, Bridenbaugh, *Cities in the Wilderness*, 77; idem., *Cities in Revolt: Urban Life in America, 1743–1776* (New York: Knopf, 1955), 120–21.

15. Greenberg, *Crime and Law Enforcement in the Colony of New York*, 155.

16. Andrew Cocker, *N.Y.P.D.: An Illustrated History* (New York: James Brown House, 2001), 1–2.

17. Greenberg, *Crime and Law Enforcement in the Colony of New York*, 180–82.

18. Greenberg, *Crime and Law Enforcement in the Colony of New York*, 89, 108–11, 118–19.

19. Greenberg, *Crime and Law Enforcement in the Colony of New York*, 91–98.

20. Donna J. Spindel and Stuart W. Thomas, Jr., "Crime and Society in North Carolina, 1663–1740," *Journal of Southern History* 49, no. 2 (1983): 223–44; Spindel, "The Administration of Criminal Justice in North Carolina, 1720–1740," *American Journal of Legal History* 25 (April 1981): 141–62.

21. Quoted in Bridenbaugh, *Cities in the Wilderness*, 63–64.

22. Bridenbaugh, *Cities in the Wilderness*, 64; Howard E. Mitchell, Jr., *Law Enforcement in Early Boston, 1660–1736: Controlling the Social Order in Pre-Industrial Society* (Philadelphia: University of Pennsylvania Institute for Environmental Studies, 1969), 15; Spindel, "The Administration of Criminal Justice in North Carolina, 1720–1740," 151.

23. Bridenbaugh, *Cities in the Wilderness*, 64; Spindel, "The Administration of Criminal Justice in North Carolina, 1720–1740," 152.

24. Bridenbaugh, *Cities in the Wilderness*, 64, 215–16.

25. Vila and Morris, *The Role of Police in American Society*, 6.

26. Bridenbaugh, *Cities in the Wilderness*, 65.

27. Bridenbaugh, *Cities in the Wilderness*, 375–76.

28. Bridenbaugh, *Cities in Revolt*, 298.

29. James F. Richardson, *The New York Police: Colonial Times to 1901* (New York: Oxford University Press, 1970), 8.

30. Bridenbaugh, *Cities in the Wilderness*, 65.

31. Quoted in *N.Y.P.D.: An Illustrated History*, 4.

32. *N.Y.P.D.: An Illustrated History*, 4–5.

33. Bridenbaugh, *Cities in Revolt*, 113.

34. Greenberg, *Crime and Law Enforcement in the Colony of New York*, 167.

35. Bridenbaugh, *Cities in the Wilderness*, 66, 218–21.

36. Bridenbaugh, *Cities in Revolt*, 298–99.

37. See City of Philadelphia, "Police Department History" (September 2001).

38. Louis Bernard Cei, "Law Enforcement in Richmond: A History of Police–Community Relations, 1737–1974" (Ph.D. diss., Florida State University, 1975), 1–21.

39. See Bridenbaugh, *Cities in the Wilderness* and *Cities in Revolt*.

40. Bridenbaugh, *Cities in Revolt*, 299–300.

41. Michael Stephen Hindus, *Prison and Plantation: Crime, Justice, and Authority in Massachusetts and South Carolina, 1767–1878* (Chapel Hill: University of North Carolina Press, 1980), 1–32.

CHAPTER 2—THE DEVELOPMENT OF MUNICIPAL POLICING IN THE NORTHEAST

1. See Daniel Feller, *The Jacksonian Promise: America, 1815–1840* (Baltimore: Johns Hopkins University Press, 1995); and Howard P. Chudacoff and Judith E. Smith, *The Evolution of American Urban Society*, 5th ed. (Upper Saddle River, N.J.: Prentice Hall, 2000), 38–117.

2. See Dwight Waldo, *The Administrative State: A Study of the Political Theory of American Public Administration* (New York: Ronald Press Co., 1948), and Max Weber, *The City,* trans. and ed. Don Martindale and Gertrud Neuwirth (Glencoe, Ill.: Free Press, 1958).

3. Ferrel Heady, *Public Administration: A Comparative Perspective* (Upper Saddle River, N.J.: Prentice Hall, 1966), 11.

4. William A. Geller, ed., *Local Government Police Management* (Washington, D.C.: The International City Managers Association, 1991), 3.

5. Randy L. LaGrange, *Policing American Society* (Chicago: Nelson Hall, Inc., 1993), 33; David R. Johnson, *Policing the Urban Underworld* (Philadelphia: Temple University Press, 1979), 22–23.

6. Wilbur R. Miller, *Cops and Bobbies: Police Authority in New York and London, 1830–1870,* 2d ed. (Columbus: Ohio State University Press, 1999), 22.

7. Johnson, *Policing the Urban Underworld*, 36–39.

8. James F. Richardson, *Urban Police in the United States* (Port Washington, N.Y.: National University Press, 1974), 41.

9. David R. Johnson, *American Law Enforcement: A History* (Wheeling, Ill.: Forum Press, 1981), 41.

10. Leonard V. Harrison, *Police Administration in Boston* (Cambridge: Harvard University Press, 1934, reprint New York: Arno Press & *The New York Times,* 1971), 6.

11. Jay S. Albanese, *Criminal Justice* (Boston: Allyn & Bacon, 1999), 160–61.

12. Raymond B. Fosdick, *American Police Systems* (New York: The Century Co., 1920, reprint Montclair, N.J.: Patterson Smith, 1969), 61.

13. Roger Lane, *Policing the City: Boston 1822–1885* (Cambridge: Harvard University Press, 1967), 15–19.

14. James A. Conser and Gregory D. Russell, *Law Enforcement in the United States* (Gaithersburg, Md.: Aspen Publishers, 2000), 54.

15. Harrison, *Police Administration in Boston*, 21; Fosdick, *American Police Systems*, 65–67.

16. James F. Richardson, *The New York Police: Colonial Times to 1901* (New York: Oxford University Press, 1970), 13.

17. Miller, *Cops and Bobbies*, 5–8.

18. LaGrange, *Policing American Society*, 34.

19. Richardson, *The New York Police*, 36.

20. Miller, *Cops and Bobbies*, 8.

21. Richardson, *The New York Police*, 36–37.

22. Miller, *Cops and Bobbies*, 8.

23. Richardson, *The New York Police*, 37–45; Fosdick, *American Police Systems*, 66.

24. LaGrange, *Policing American Society*, 37

25. Miller, *Cops and Bobbies*, 43.

26. Elmer D. Graper, *American Police Administration* (New York: Macmillan, 1934; reprint Montclair, N.J.: Patterson Smith, 1969), 4.

27. Richardson, *The New York Police*, 64–65.

28. Fosdick, *American Police Systems*, 122.

29. Philadelphia Police Department, *A Brief History of the Philadelphia Police Department* [accessed April 23, 2002]: available from http://www.ppdonline.org/ppd_history.htm.

30. Johnson, *Policing the Urban Underworld*, 20.

31. See, for example, ed. Allan Nevins and Milton H. Thomas, eds., *The Diary of George Templeton Strong* (New York: Macmillan, 1952), 403–404.

32. Fosdick, *American Police Systems*, 63–64; Johnson, *Policing the Urban Underworld*, 16–19.

33. Philadelphia Police Department, *A Brief History of the Philadelphia Police Department* [accessed April 23, 2002]: available from http://www.ppdonline.org/ppd_history.htm.

34. Fosdick, *American Police Systems*, 58–117.

CHAPTER 3—POLICING RACE AND VIOLENCE IN THE SOUTH

1. James A. Conser and Gregory D. Russell, *Law Enforcement in the United States* (Gaithersburg, Md.: Aspen Publishers, 2000), 52, 258–59; Carl B. Klockars, *The Idea of Police* (Beverly Hills, Calif.: Sage, 1985), 55–56.

2. Randy L. LaGrange, *Policing American Society* (Chicago: Nelson-Hall Publishers, 1993), 34.

3. Christopher Waldrep, *Roots of Disorder: Race and Criminal Justice in the American South* (Chicago: University of Illinois Press, 1998), 24.

4. Kenneth M. Stampp, *The Peculiar Institution: Slavery in the Ante-Bellum South* (New York: Vintage Books, 1989), 1–33.

5. Bertram Wyatt-Brown, *Honor and Violence in the Old South* (New York: Oxford University Press, 1986), viii–x.

6. Fox Butterfield, *All God's Children: The Bosket Family and the American Tradition of Violence* (New York: Avon Books, 1996), 8–9; Richard Maxwell Brown, "Southern Violence—Regional Problem or National Nemesis?: Legal Attitudes Toward Southern Homicide in Historical Perspective," in *Crime and Justice in American History: The South*, Part 1, ed. Eric H. Monkkonen (Munich: K. G. Saur, 1992), 22, 42; Sheldon Hackney, "Southern Violence," in *Crime and Justice in American History*, ed. Eric H. Monkkonen, 102; Arthur F. Howington, "Violence in Alabama: A Study of Late Ante-bellum Montgomery," in *Crime and Justice in American History*, ed. Eric H. Monkkonen, 196–97; Richard H. Haunton, "Law and Order in Savannah, 1850–1860, in *Crime and Justice in American History*, ed. Eric H. Monkkonen, 168–79.

7. Richard Maxwell Brown, "Southern Violence—Regional Problem or National Nemesis?: Legal Attitudes Toward Southern Homicide in Historical Perspective," in *Crime and Justice in American History*, ed. Eric H. Monkkonen, 18–20.

8. John Hope Franklin, *The Militant South, 1800–1861* (Cambridge: Harvard University Press, 1956), 33–62; Clement Eaton, *A History of the Old South*, 2d ed. (New York: Macmillan, 1966), 110–11; Roger Lane and John J. Turner, *Riot, Rout, and Tumult* (Westport, Conn.: Greenwood Press, 1978), 147–48.

9. United States Department of Justice, Federal Bureau of Investigation, *Crime in the United States: 2000* (Washington, D.C.: Government Printing Office, 2001), 9.

10. David N. Konstantin, "Homicides of American Law Enforcement Officers," *Justice Quarterly* 1, no. 1 (March 1984): 29.

11. See various tables in United States Department of Justice, *Source Book 1998* (Washington, D.C.: Bureau of Justice Statistics, 1999).

12. Brown, *Honor and Violence in the Old South*, 187–89.

13. Brown, *Honor and Violence in the Old South*, 188–213. See also Philip Dray, *At the Hands of Persons Unknown: Lynching in Black America* (New York: Random House, 2002), and Jacqueline Jones Royster, ed., *Southern Horrors and Other Writings: The Anti-Lynching Campaign of Ida B. Wells, 1892–1900* (Boston: Bedford-St. Martin's, 1997).

14. Brown, *Honor and Violence in the Old South*, 190–91.

15. Jay S. Albanese, *Criminal Justice* (Boston: Allyn & Bacon, 1999), 165; Samuel Walker, *The Police in America: An Introduction*, 3d ed. (Boston: McGraw-Hill, 1999), 22.

16. Stampp, *The Peculiar Institution*, 22–24. See also Don E. Fehrenbacher, *The Dred Scott Case: Its Significance in American Law and Politics* (New York: Oxford University Press, 2001).

17. Samuel J. May, *Some Recollections of Our Anti-slavery Conflict* (New York: Arno Press and *The New York Times*, 1968), 345.

18. Roger Lane, *Policing the City of Boston: 1822–1885* (Cambridge, Mass.: Harvard University Press, 1967), 72; Lawrence Lader, *The Bold Brahmins: New England's War Against Slavery: 1831–1865* (Westport, Conn.: Greenwood Press, 1973), 161–67.

19. Stampp, *The Peculiar Institution*, 22–24, 192–209, 210–24.

20. Chase C. Mooney, *Slavery in Tennessee* (Westport, Conn.: Negro Universities Press, 1957), 15; Eugene D. Genovese, *Roll, Jordan, Roll: The World the Slaves Made* (New York: Vintage Books, 1976), 25–31.

21. Robert F. Wintersmith, *Police and the Black Community* (Lexington, Mass.: Lexington Books, 1974), 17; Franklin, *The Militant South*, 72–79.

22. Wintersmith, *Police and the Black Community*, 13–21; Franklin, *The Militant South*, 72–79; Genovese, *Roll, Jordan, Roll*, 22, 619–21; Sally E. Hadden, in "Colonial and Revolutionary Era Slave Patrols of Virginia," in *Lethal Imagination: Violence and Brutality in American History*, ed. Michael A. Bellesiles (New York: New York University Press, 1999), 69–85; Conser and Russell, *Law Enforcement in the United States*, 52; Sally E. Hadden, *Slave Patrols: Law and Violence in Virginia and the Carolinas* (Cambridge: Harvard University Press, 2001), 56, 84, 103.

23. Hadden, *Slave Patrols*, 185, 198; Wintersmith, *Police and the Black Community*, 21–22.

24. Hadden, *Slave Patrols*, 185–87.

25. Paul D. Lack, "Law and Disorder in Confederate Atlanta," in *Crime and Justice in American History: The South*, Part 2, ed. Eric H. Monkkonen (Munich: K. G. Saur, 1992), 249–69.

26. Waldrep, *Roots of Disorder*, p. 104.

27. Wintersmith, *Police and the Black Community*, 37.

28. Haunton, "Law and Order in Savannah," 180–82; Savannah Police Department, "The Historic Savannah Police Department" [accessed June 11, 2002]; http://www.ci.savannah.ga.us/cityweb/SPD.

29. Mobile Police Department History [accessed June 11, 2002]; http://www.cityofmobile.org/html/police/html/dept_info.PDhistory.html.

30. George W. Hales, *Police and Prison Cyclopaedia* (Boston: W. L. Richards Company, 1893), 45.

31. Eugene D. Genovese, *In Red and Black: Marxian Explorations in Southern and Afro-American History* (New York: Pantheon Books, 1971), 139–43; Eric Foner, *Reconstruction: America's Unfinished Revolution, 1863–1877* (New York: Harper and Row, 1988), 412–49, 564–612; John Hope Franklin, *Reconstruction after the Civil War*, 2d ed. (Chicago: University of Chicago Press, 1994), 32–68, 150–69, 189–219; Philip Gerard, *Cape Fear Rising* (Winston-Salem, N.C.: John F. Blair Publisher, 1994), 19; Hadden, *Slave Patrols*, 217–28.

32. Frederic L. Paxson, *The New Nation* (Boston: Houghton Mifflin Company, 1915), 40, 100, 344.

33. Wintersmith, *Police and the Black Community*, 47.

34. Waldrep, *Roots of Disorder*, 23.

35. David R. Johnson, *Policing the Urban Underworld* (Philadelphia: Temple University Press, 1979), 141.

36. Hadden, *Slave Patrols*, 5, 220.

CHAPTER 4—POLICING THE AMERICAN WEST

1. Clyde A. Milner II, Carol A. O'Connor, and Martha Sandweiss, eds., *The Oxford History of the American West* (New York: Oxford University Press, 1994), 33; Frank Richard Prassel, *The Western Peace Officer: A Legacy of Law and Order* (Norman: University of Oklahoma Press, 1972), 180–81.

2. David R. Johnson, *American Law Enforcement History* (Wheeling, Ill.: Forum Press, Inc., 1981), 90.

3. Richard White, *"It's Your Misfortune and None of My Own": A New History of the American West* (Norman, Okla.: University of Oklahoma Press, 1991), 328; Johnson, *American Law Enforcement*, 90–91.

4. Roger McGrath, *Gunfighters, Highwaymen, and Vigilantes: Violence on the Frontier* (Los Angeles: University of California Press, 1984), 268; White, *A New History of the American West*, 330.

5. McGrath, *Violence on the Frontier*, 247–60; Lynn L. Perrigo, "Law and Order in Early Colorado Mining Camps," *Mississippi Valley Historical Review* 28 (June 1941): 41–62.

6. White, *A New History of the American West*, 329.

7. David J. Weber, *The Spanish Frontier in North America* (New Haven, Conn.: Yale University Press, 1992), 325; "Police: The History of the Police Service," 14; Jill Mocho, *Murder and Justice in Frontier New Mexico, 1821–1846* (Albuquerque: University of New Mexico Press, 1997), 4–5, 9–13; Larry D. Ball, *Desert Lawmen: The High Sheriffs of New Mexico and Arizona, 1846–1912* (Albuquerque: University of New Mexico Press, 1992), 4–5.

8. Carol Christensen and Thomas Christensen, *The U.S.-Mexican War* (San Francisco: Bay Books, 1998), 109–11.

9. Ball, *Desert Lawmen*, 2; K. Jack Bauer, *The Mexican War, 1846–1848* (New York: Macmillan, 1974), 134–35.

10. Ball, *Desert Lawmen*, 1–18, 303.

11. Richard Maxwell Brown, in "Legal and Behavioral Perspectives on American Vigilantism," in *Crime and Justice in American History: Historical Articles on the Origins and Evolution of American Criminal Justice: The Frontier,* ed. Eric H. Monkkonen (Westport, Conn.: Meckler, 1991), 62–111.

12. David A. Johnson, "Vigilance and the Law: The Moral Authority of Popular Justice in the Far West," in *Crime and Justice in American History,* ed. Eric H. Monkkonen, 187–215. White, *A New History of the American West*, 332–33; Brown, "American Vigilantism," 62–111.

13. Johnson, "Vigilance and the Law," 187–215; Brown, "American Vigilantism," 62–111; White, *A New History of the American West*, 351.

14. Richard Maxwell Brown, "The American Vigilante Tradition," in *Violence in America: Historical and Comparative Perspectives,* ed. Hugh Davis and Ted R. Gurr (New York: Praeger, 1969), 157–76.

15. Johnson, "Vigilance and the Law," 187–215.

16. Johnson, *American Law Enforcement*, 93–94.

17. Brown, "The American Vigilante Tradition," 166–77; James Willard Hurst, *The Growth of American Law: The Law Makers* (Boston: Little Brown, 1950), 39, 92–93; Johnson, "Vigilance and the Law," 187–215.

18. Robert A. Harris, *Keeping the Peace: Police Reform in Montana, 1889–1918* (Helena, Mont.: Montana Historical Society Press, 1994), 1.

19. White, *A New History of the American West*, 330; Milner, et al., *The Oxford History of the American West*, 415; Johnson, *American Law Enforcement*, 100–102.

20. Harris, *Police Reform*, 1–2.

21. Harris, *Police Reform*, 21–27, 147–48; George W. Hale, *Police and Prison Cyclopaedia* (Cambridge, Mass.: The Riverside Press, 1893), 750. For a biography of Lola Baldwin, see Gloria E. Meyers, *A Municipal Mother: Portland's Lola Greene Baldwin, America's First Policewoman* (Corvallis: Oregon State University Press, 1995).

22. Hale, *Police and Prison Cyclopaedia*, 198–431.

23. Harris, *Police Reform*, 150–55.

24. S. Lyman Tyler, *A History of Indian Policy* (Washington, D.C.: Bureau of Indian Affairs, 1973), 90–94; "A Short History of Indian Law Enforcement," Bureau of Indian Affairs [accessed 08/21/2001]; http://bialaw.fedworld.gov/history/history.htm.

25. Jacqueline Pope, *Bounty Hunters, Marshals, and Sheriffs: Forward to the Past* (Westport, Conn.: Praeger, 1998), 71–74, 119–21; Fredrick S. Calhoun, *The Lawmen: U.S. Marshals and Their Deputies, 1789–1989* (Washington, D.C.: Smithsonian Institution, 1990), 6, 207.

26. Bruce L. Berg, *Law Enforcement: An Introduction to Police in Society* (Boston: Allyn & Bacon, 1992), 36–37.

27. Charles M. Robinson II, *The Men Who Wear the Star: The Story of the Texas Rangers* (New York: Random House, 2000), 7.

28. Robinson, *The Men Who Wear the Star*, 14.

29. Robinson, *The Men Who Wear the Star*, 23–28; Walter Prescott Webb, *The Texas Rangers: A Century of Frontier Defense*, 5th printing, 2d ed. (Austin, Tex.: University for Texas Press, 1996), 19–21.

30. Robinson, *The Men Who Wear the Star*, 87–152; Webb, *The Texas Rangers*, 19–124.

31. See David Paul Smith, *Frontier Defense in the Civil War: Texas' Rangers and Rebels* (College Station: Texas A&M University Press, 1992).

32. Robinson, *The Men Who Wear the Star*, 161–62.

33. Webb, *The Texas Rangers*, 219–29.

34. Robinson, *The Men Who Wear the Star*, 213–21; Webb, *The Texas Rangers*, 233–304.

35. Prassel, *The Western Peace Officer*, 150–78.

CHAPTER 5—URBANIZATION, PROGRESSIVISM, AND POLICE

1. Howard P. Chudacoff and Judith E. Smith, *The Evolution of American Urban Society*, 5th ed. (Upper Saddle River, N.J.: Prentice Hall, 2000), 118–23.

2. James F. Richardson, *Urban Police in the United States* (Port Washington, N.Y.: Kennikat Press, 1974), 51; John C. Schneider, *Detroit and the Problem of Order, 1830–1880: A Geography of Crime, Riot, and Policing* (Lincoln: University of Nebraska Press, 1980), 133–35.

3. Chudacoff and Smith, *The Evolution of American Urban Society*, 157–72.

4. Samuel Walker, *A Critical History of Police Reform: The Emergence of Professionalization* (Lexington, Mass.: D. C. Heath, 1977), 9; Robert M. Fogelson, *Big-City Police* (Cambridge, Mass.: Harvard University Press, 1977), 36.

5. Richardson, *Urban Police in the United States*, 48.

6. Walker, *A Critical History of Police Reform*, 9.

7. Schneider, *Detroit and the Problem of Order*, 119–20; Richardson, *Urban Police in the United States*, 53–55.

8. Walker, *A Critical History of Police Reform*, 11; Fogelson, *Big-City Police*, 36–37.

9. Fogelson, *Big-City Police*, 37.

10. Richardson, *Urban Police in the United States*, 56–59.

11. David R. Johnson, *Policing the Urban Underworld: The Impact of Crime on the Development of American Police, 1800–1887* (Philadelphia: Temple University Press, 1979), 171.

12. David R. Johnson, *American Law Enforcement: A History* (Wheeling, Ill.: Forum Press, 1981), 57–58; Fogelson, *Big-City Police*, 33–34.

13. William L. Riordon, ed., *Plunkitt of Tammany Hall: Series of Very Plain Talks on Very Practical Politics* (New York: Signet Books, 1995), 3.

14. Walker, *A Critical History of Police Reform*, 23–24; Roger Lane, "Urbanization and Criminal Violence in the Nineteenth Century: Massachusetts as a Test Case," *Journal of Social History* 2, no. 2 (Winter 1968), 156–63.

15. Robert H. Weibe, *The Search of Order, 1877–1920* (New York: Hill and Wang, 1967), chapters 5–7.

16. Chudacoff and Smith, *The Evolution of American Urban Society*, chapter 6; Weibe, *The Search of Order*, chapter 7.

17. The term "cop" also originates from "constable on patrol" in England.

18. Johnson, *American Law Enforcement*, 28–29.

19. Roger Lane, *Policing the City: Boston, 1822–1888* (Cambridge, Mass.: Harvard University Press, 1967), 104–105.

20. Ralph D. O'Hara, "Chronological Listing of Significant Events and Dates Relating to Law Enforcement in the Willamette Valley and Portland, Oregon, 1841–2000" (Portland Police Historical Society, 2000), 3.

21. Jennifer Brown and Frances Heidensohm, *Gender and Policing: Comparative Perspectives* (New York: St. Martin's, 2000), 42–51; Deborah Parsons and Paul Jesilow, *In the Same Voice: Women and Men in Law Enforcement* (Santa Ana, Calif.: Seven Locks Press, 2001), 32–42; Chloe Owings, *Women Police: A Study of the Development and Status of the Women Police Movement* (Original published in 1925; reprint Montclair, N.J.: Patterson Smith, 1969), 94–106; Peter Horne, *Women in Law Enforcement*, 2d ed. (Springfield, Ill.: Thomas, 1980), 26–32.

22. Jay Stuart Berman, *Police Administration and Progressive Reform: Theodore Roosevelt as Police Commissioner of New York* (New York: Greenwood Press, 1987), 33–123; Walker, *A Critical History of Police Reform*, 25–26.

23. Walker, *A Critical History of Police Reform*, 26–28.

24. Raymond B. Fosdick, *American Police Systems* (New York: Century Co., 1920; reprint Montclair, N.J.: Patterson Smith, 1969), 269–85. The ten cities without civil service were Birmingham, Indianapolis, Kansas City, Louisville, San Antonio, Salt Lake City, Bridgeport, Camden, Hartford, and Reading.

25. Richardson, *Urban Police in the United States*, 62–63; Walker, *A Critical History of Police Reform*, 45, 67–77.

26. Richardson, *Urban Police in the United States*, 64–76; Berman, *Police Administration and Progressive Reform*, 67–68.

27. Fosdick, *American Police Systems*, 256.

28. Fosdick, *American Police Systems*, 254, 276–85; Richardson, *Urban Police in the United States*, 73–74.

29. Fosdick, *American Police Systems*, 273–74.

30. Fogelson, *Big-City Police*, 54–57.

31. Quoted in Walker, *A Critical History of Police Reform*, 67.

32. Walker, *A Critical History of Police Reform*, 66–67.

33. Fogelson, *Big-City Police*, 61.

34. Weibe, *The Search for Order*, 118–122.

35. Walker, *A Critical History of Police Reform*, 42.

36. Fogelson, *Big-City Police*, 103–104.

37. Fosdick, *American Police Systems*, 298–306.

38. Gene E. Carte and Elaine H. Carte, *Police Reform in the United States: The Era of August Vollmer, 1905–1932* (Berkeley: University of California Press, 1975), 26–30; Walker, *A Critical History of Police Reform*, 72–73.

39. Weibe, *The Search for Order*, 114–32.

40. Walker, *A Critical History of Police Reform*, 38–40, 47–48.

41. Quoted from *Omaha Police Reports* in Walker, *A Critical History of Police Reform*, 48.

42. Carte and Carte, *Police Reform in the United States*, 12–14; Walker, *A Critical History of Police Reform*, 48.

43. Walker, *A Critical History of Police Reform*, 49, 56–59.

CHAPTER 6—THE SHIFT TO POLICE AS PROFESSION

1. See Roderick Nash, *The Nervous Generation: American Thought, 1917–1920* (Chicago: Ivan R. Dee, 1990).

2. Nash, *The Nervous Generation: American Thought*, 12–32; Gerald D. Nash, *The Crucial Era: The Great Depression and World War II, 1929–1945*, 2d ed. (New York: St. Martin's Press, 1992), 10–17.

3. Nash, *The Crucial Era*, 20–108.

4. Michael C.C. Adams, *The Best War Ever* (Baltimore: Johns Hopkins University Press, 1994), 114–35.

5. Howard P. Chudacoff and Judith E. Smith, *The Evolution of American Urban Society*, 5th ed. (Upper Saddle River, N.J.: Prentice Hall, 2000), 212–58.

6. Samuel Walker, *A Critical History of Police Reform: The Emergence of Professionalism* (Lexington, Mass.: Lexington Books, 1977), 111.

7. Sterling Spero, *Government as Employer* (Carbondale, Ill.: Southern Illinois University Press, 1972), 250–52.

8. Walker, *A Critical History of Police Reform*, 112–13.

9. Walker, *A Critical History of Police Reform*, 113–14; Francis Russell, *A City in Terror: 1919, The Boston Police Strike* (New York: Viking Press, 1975), 7–25, 49–53.

10. *Fourteenth Annual Report of the Police Commissioner for the City of Boston, Year Ending November 30, 1919* (Boston: Wright and Potter Printing Co., 1920) in *The Boston Police Strike: Two Reports* (New York: Arno Press and *The New York Times*, 1971), 10–11, 16–20; Russell, *A City in Terror*, 97–170.

11. Walker, *A Critical History of Police Reform*, 117–118.

12. Allen Z. Gammage and Stanley L. Sachs, *Police Unions* (Springfield, Ill.: Thomas, 1972), 37–38; Walker, *A Critical History of Police Reform*, 119–20.

13. Walker, *A Critical History of Police Reform*, 146–47.

14. David M. Kennedy, *Freedom from Fear: The American People in Depression and War, 1929–1945* (New York: Oxford University Press, 1999), 316–19.

15. Robert M. Fogelson, *Big-City Police* (Cambridge, Mass.: Harvard University Press, 1977), 78, 88; United States Senate, "Violations of Free Speech and Rights of Labor: Documents

Relating to Intelligence Bureau or Red Squad of Los Angeles Police Department," *Hearings before a Subcommittee of the Committee on Education and Labor, United States Senate, Seventy-Sixth Congress, Third Session* (Washington, D.C.: Government Printing Office, 1940).

16. International Association of Chiefs of Police, *Police Yearbook, 1938–1939*, pp. 77–119.

17. Gail Williams O'Brien, "Return to Normalcy: Organized Racial Violence in Post-World War II South," in *Violence in America: Volume 2, Protest, Rebellion, Reform*, ed. Ted Robert Gurr, (London: Sage, 1989), 231–37.

18. Fogelson, *Big-City Police*, 121.

19. Arthur Woskow, *From Race Riot to Sit-In: 1919 and the 1960s* (New York: Doubleday, 1966), 209–18.

20. "East St. Louis Riots: Report of the Special Committee Authorized by Congress to Investigate the East St. Louis Riots," in Allen D. Grimshaw, *Racial Violence in the United States* (Chicago: Aldine Publishing Group, 1969), 61–72; Grimshaw, *Racial Violence in the United States*, 111–13.

21. Chicago Commission on Race Relations, "The Negro in Chicago: A Study of Race Relations and a Race Riot," in Grimshaw, *Racial Violence in the United States*, 98.

22. Edgard A. Schuler, "The Houston Race Riot, 1917," in Grimshaw, *Racial Violence in the United States*, 73–87; William M. Tuttle, Jr., *Race Riot: Chicago in the Red Summer of 1919* (New York: Atheneum, 1970), 220–21.

23. Waskow, *From Race Riot to Sit-In*, 4, 21–37.

24. Waskow, *From Race Riot to Sit-In*, 38–104; Grimshaw, *Racial Violence in the United States*, 108–11; The Chicago Commission on Race Relations, "The Negro in Chicago: A Study in Race Relations and Race Riot," in Grimshaw, *Racial Violence in the United States*, 97–105; Walker, *A Critical History of Police Reform*, 122–23; Tuttle, *Race Riot*, 32–207.

25. Grimshaw, *Racial Violence in the United States*, 105–108.

26. Jon C. Teaford, *The Twentieth-Century American City*, 2d ed. (Baltimore: Johns Hopkins University Press, 1993), 94–96; Grimshaw, *Racial Violence in the United States*, 136–52; Howard Sitzkoff, "Racial Militancy and Interracial Violence in the Second World War," in *Riot, Rout, and Tumult: Readings in American Social and Political Violence*, ed. Roger Lane and John J. Turner, Jr. (Westport, Conn.: Greenwood Press, 1978), 307–26; Walker, *A Critical History of Police Reform*, 169–70; Adams, *The Best War Ever*, 118–21.

27. Walker, *A Critical History of Police Reform*, 125.

28. The Cleveland Foundation, "Criminal Justice in Cleveland," in *Urban Police: Selected Surveys* (New York: Arno Press and *The New York Times*, 1971); Walker, *A Critical History of Police Reform*, 126–28.

29. Mark H. Haller, "Civic Reformers and Police Leadership: Chicago, 1905–1935," in *Police in Urban Society*, ed. Harlan Hahn (Beverly Hills: Sage, 1971), 39–56.

30. Bruce Smith, et al., "A Reorganization Plan for the Chicago Police Department, Report No. 4" (Chicago: The Citizens' Police Committee, 1930), in *Urban Police*; Walker, *A Critical History of Police Reform*, 128–29.

31. Bruce Smith, "A Regional Police Plan for Cincinnati and Its Environs" (New York: Institute of Public Administration, 1932), in *Urban Police*.

32. Bruce Smith, "The Baltimore Police Survey" (New York: Institute of Public Administration, 1941), in *Urban Police*.

33. Bruce Smith, "The New Orleans Police Survey" (New Orleans: Bureau of Governmental Research, 1946), in *Urban Police*.

34. August Vollmer, "Annual Report of the Los Angeles Police Department, 1924," reprinted as *Law Enforcement in Los Angeles* (New York: Arno Press and *The New York Times*, 1974); Walker, *A Critical History of Police Reform*, 129–30.

35. National Commission on Law Observance and Enforcement, *Report on Police* (Washington, D.C.: Government Printing Office, 1931; reprint New York: Arno Press and *The New York Times*, 1971); Philip John Snead, ed., *Pioneers in Policing* (Montclair, N.J.: Patterson Smith, 1977), 274; Walker, *A Critical History of Police Reform*, 131–32.

36. National Commission on Law Observance and Enforcement, *Lawlessness in Law Enforcement* (Washington, D.C.: Government Printing Office, 1931; reprint Zechariah Chafee, *The Third Degree*, New York: Arno Press and *The New York Times*, 1969); Walker, *A Critical History of Police Reform*, 133–34.

37. Walker, *A Critical History of Police Reform*, 139–42.

38. Nathan Douthit, "Police Professionalism and the War Against Crime in the United States, 1920s–30s," in *Police Forces in History*, vol. 2, ed. George L. Mosse (London: Sage Publications, 1975), 330–32.

39. J. Edgar Hoover, "The Confession and Third Degree Methods," *Law Enforcement Bulletin* 5 (January 1936): 11–13; J. Edgar Hoover, "Law Enforcement as a Profession," *Law Enforcement Bulletin* 6 (November 1937): 3–4; Walker, *A Critical History of Police Reform*, 159–60; Douthit, "Police Professionalism," in *Police Forces in History*, ed. George L. Mosse, 330–33.

40. Bruce Smith, *Police Systems of the United States*, rev. ed. (New York: Harper and Brothers Publishers, 1949), 150–51, 296–304.

41. Andrew Dirosa, "U.S. Law Enforcement during World War II," *Law Enforcement Bulletin* (December 1991), 1–6.

42. Dillon S. Myer, *Uprooted Americans: The Japanese Americans and the War Relocation Authority during World War II* (Tucson: University of Arizona Press, 1971), 36–38; Richard S. Nishimoto, *Inside an American Concentration Camp: Japanese American Resistance at Poston, Arizona*, ed. Lane Ryo Hirabayashi (Tucson: University of Arizona Press, 1995), 139–59.

CHAPTER 7—POLICE AND TECHNOLOGY

1. Samuel Walker, *A Critical History of Police Reform: The Emergence of Professionalism* (Lexington, Mass.: Lexington Books, 1977), 137.

2. Bryan Vila and Cynthia Morris, eds., *The Role of Police in American Society: A Documentary History* (Westport, Conn.: Greenwood Press, 1999), 60.

3. Bruce L. Berg, *Law Enforcement: An Introduction to Police in Society* (Boston: Allyn & Bacon, 1992), 30.

4. New York City Police Museum, "When did police officers start using whistles?" [accessed November 13, 2001]; http://nycpolicemuseum.org/html/faq/html; "Acme Police Whistles" [accessed February 20, 2002]; http://www.acmewhistles.co.uk/history.html.

5. "Samuel F. B. Morse" [accessed February 20, 2002]; http://web.mit.edu/invent/www/inventorsI-Q/morse.html.

6. Berg, *Law Enforcement*, 39.

7. Roger Lane, *Policing the City: Boston, 1822–1888* (Cambridge, Mass.: Harvard University Press, 1967), 102–103.

8. James M. McPherson, *Battle Cry of Freedom: The Civil War Era* (New York: Oxford University Press, 1988), 609–11.

9. James F. Richardson, *The New York Police: Colonial Times to 1901* (New York: Oxford University Press, 1970), 136–39.

10. "Alexander Graham Bell" [accessed February 20, 2002]; http://web.mit.edu/invent/www/inventorsA-H/graham_bell.html.

11. John J. Flinn and John E. Wilkie, *History of the Chicago Police* (Chicago: Police Book Fund, 1887; reprint, New York: Arno Press and *The New York Times,* 1971), 397–407.

12. Lane, *Policing the City,* 203–204, 210, 224.

13. Vila and Morris, eds., *The Role of Police in American Society,* 60, 122–24.

14. Raymond B. Fosdick, *American Police Systems* (New York: Century Co., 1920; reprint, Montclair, N.J.: Patterson Smith, 1969), 306–309.

15. John J. Flinn and John E. Wilkie, *History of the Chicago Police* (Chicago: Police Book Fund, 1887; reprint, New York: Arno Press and *The New York Times,* 1971), 408, 416.

16. Lane, *Policing the City,* 203.

17. Richardson, *The New York Police,* 263; Jay Stuart Berman, *Police Administration and Progressive Reform: Theodore Roosevelt as Police Commissioner of New York* (New York: Greenwood Press, 1987), 88–89.

18. Berg, *Law Enforcement,* 39–40.

19. Fosdick, *American Police Systems,* 310–11.

20. Vila and Morris, *The Role of Police in American Society,* 83–84.

21. Omaha Police Department, *Annual Report of the Chief of Police, Omaha, Nebraska* (Omaha: Rees Printing Company, 1909), 4.

22. Fosdick, *American Police Systems,* 311–12.

23. Howard P. Chudacoff and Judith E. Smith, *The Evolution of American Urban Society,* 5th ed. (Upper Saddle River, N.J.: Prentice Hall, 2000), 46–49.

24. Lane, *Policing the City: Boston,* 103–104.

25. David R. Johnson, *American Law Enforcement: A History* (Wheeling, Ill.: Forum Press, 1981), 30.

26. Roger Lane, *Policing the City: Boston, 1822–1888* (Cambridge, Mass.: Harvard University Press, 1967), 133–34, 203.

27. Richardson, *The New York Police,* 68, 113, 263.

28. Walker, *A Critical History of Police Reform,* 160–61.

29. John Ellis, *The Social History of the Machine Gun* (Baltimore: Johns Hopkins University Press, 1986), 149–65.

30. Richardson, *The New York Police,* 122.

31. Johnson, *American Law Enforcement,* 106–16.

32. Lane, *Policing the City,* 149.

33. Richardson, *The New York Police,* 263.

34. Johnson, *American Law Enforcement,* 116.

35. Lane, *Policing the City,* 102–103.

36. Vila and Morris, *The Role of Police in American Society,* 60.

37. Richardson, *The New York Police,* 168–69.

38. National Institute of Justice, *The Evolution and Development of Police Technology: A Technical Report Prepared for the National Committee on Criminal Justice Technology* (Washington, D.C., 1998), 3. To ease the burden of the 911 system, a "311" nonemergency number is in the pilot stage. Baltimore first tested the 311 number in 1996 and experienced a 30 percent decrease in 911 calls.

39. National Institute of Justice, *The Evolution and Development of Police Technology,* 3–8.

CHAPTER 8—LEADERS IN AMERICAN POLICING

1. Philip John Stead, ed., *Pioneers in Policing* (Montclair, N.J.: Patterson Smith, 1977).

2. Roger Lane, *Policing the City* (Cambridge, Mass.: Harvard University Press, 1967), 60–65.

3. Quoted in Raymond B. Fosdick, *American Police Systems* (New York: Century Co., 1920; reprint, Montclair, N.J.: Patterson Smith, 1969), 63.

4. Fosdick, *American Police Systems*, 64; Law Enforcement Assistance Administration, *Two Hundred Years of American Criminal Justice* (Washington, D.C.: Government Printing Office, 1976), 17; Howard O. Sprogle, *The Philadelphia Police: Past and Present* (New York: Arno Press and *The New York Times*, 1971), 76.

5. Melville Lee, *A History of Police in England* (London: Methuen, 1901), 227–61; David R. Johnson, *American Law Enforcement: A History* (Wheeling, Ill.: Forum Press, 1981), 18–19.

6. Randy L. LaGrange, *Policing American Society* (Chicago: Nelson-Hall, 1993), 34; Charles Reith, *A Short History of the British Police* (London: Oxford University Press, 1948), 56–57; Lee, *A History of Police in England*, 241–43. Peel's Principles of Policing can still be found prominently displayed in public lobbies in police departments across the United States and the United Kingdom.

7. T. A. Jenkins, *Sir Robert Peel* (New York: St. Martin's, 1999), 30–31; LaGrange, *Policing American Society*, 35; James F. Richardson, *The New York Police: Colonial Times to 1901* (New York: Oxford University Press, 1970), 23.

8. George W. Hale, *Police and Prison Cyclopaedia* (Boston: W. L. Richardson Company, 1893), 361.

9. Hale, *Prison and Police Cyclopaedia*, 350.

10. Law Enforcement Assistance Administration, *Two Hundred Years of American Criminal Justice*, 1; Samuel Walker, *A Critical History of Police Reform* (Lexington, Mass.: D. C. Heath, 1977), 130.

11. Stead, *Pioneers in Policing*, 191; Samuel Walker, *The Police in America*, 3d ed. (Boston: McGraw-Hill, 1999), 11–14.

12. Fosdick, *American Police Systems*, 291.

13. For a solid scholarly assessment of Roosevelt's tenure as police commissioner, see Jay Stuart Berman, *Police Administration and Progressive Reform: Theodore Roosevelt as Police Commissioner of New York* (New York: Greenwood Press, 1987). James F. Richardson, *Urban Police in the United States* (Port Washington, N.Y.: National University Publications, 1974), 60, 116–117, 126; Law Enforcement Assistance Administration, *Two Hundred Years of American Criminal Justice*, 20; Robert M. Fogelson, *Big-City Police* (Cambridge, Mass.: Harvard University Press, 1977), 141.

14. Gene E. Carte and Elaine H. Carte, *Police Reform in the United States: The Era of August Vollmer* (Berkeley: University of California Press, 1975), 45.

15. August Vollmer, *The Police and Modern Society* (Berkeley: University of California Press, 1936), 81.

16. Carte and Carte, *Police Reform in the United States*, 20–24, 55, 112; City of Berkeley Police Department, "Berkeley Police Department—Our History" [accessed August 7, 2002], http://www.ci.berkeley.ca.us/police/history; Johnson, *American Law Enforcement*, 70; Law Enforcement Assistance Administration, *Two Hundred Years of American Criminal Justice*, 22.

17. O. W. Wilson, *Police Administration* (New York: McGraw-Hill, 1950), and *Police Planning* (Springfield, Ill.: Thomas, 1952).

18. Robert B. Denhardt, *Theories of Public Organization*, 2d ed. (Belmont, Calif.: Wadsworth, 1993), 61–63; Stead, *Pioneers in Policing*, 212–18; Law Enforcement Assistance Administration, *Two Hundred Years of American Criminal Justice*, 25.

19. Parker earned the Purple Heart for wounds received during the Normandy invasion, along with the Croix de Guerre with Silver Star by the Free French Government and the Star of Solidarity by the Italian Government. The Parker Los Angeles Police Foundation, "Biography of William H. Parker" [accessed August 8, 2002], http://www.lapdfoundation.com/bio.

20. William H. Parker, *Parker on Police*, ed. O. W. Wilson (Springfield, Ill.: Thomas, 1957).

21. Johnson, *American Law Enforcement*, 119–21.

22. Charles Moritz, ed., *Current Biography Yearbook: 1972* (New York: H. W. Wilson Company, 1972), 328.

CHAPTER 9—POLICING TO THE TWENTY-FIRST CENTURY

1. Elmer D. Graper, *American Police Administration* (Montclair, N.J.: Patterson Smith, 1969), 5, 61; Samuel Walker, *A Critical History of Police Reform* (Lexington, Mass.: Lexington Books, 1977), 19; James A. Conser and Gregory D. Russell, *Law Enforcement in the United States* (Gaithersburg, Md.: Aspen Publishers, 2000), 60; O. W. Wilson and Roy C. McLaren, *Police Administration*, 3d ed. (New York: McGraw-Hill, 1972), 11.

2. James Q. Wilson, *Varieties of Police Behavior* (Cambridge, Mass.: Harvard University Press, 1968), 153–54.

3. Abraham S. Blumberg, "The Police and the Social System: Reflections and Prospects," in *The Ambivalent Force: Perspectives on the Police,* ed. Arthur Niederhoffer and Abraham S. Blumberg (Waltham, Mass.: Ginn and Company, 1970), 9.

4. Oscar Newman, *Defensible Space* (New York: Macmillan, 1972), 187; Nicholas Lemann, "The Origins of the Underclass," *Atlantic Monthly* (July 1986): 54–68.

5. Orin F. Nolting, ed., *Municipal Police Administration* (Chicago: International City Managers Association, 1961), 55; Wilson and McLaren, *Police Administration*, 56, 117.

6. Nolting, *Municipal Police Administration*, 68–69, 167.

7. Paul B. Weston and Kenneth M. Wells, *Criminal Investigation*, 2d ed. (Englewood Cliffs, N.J.: Prentice Hall, 1974), 27.

8. Philip John Stead, *Pioneers in Policing* (Montclair, N.J.: Patterson Smith, 1977), 183; Law Enforcement Assistance Administration, *Two Hundred Years of American Criminal Justice* (Washington, D.C.: Government Printing Office, 1976), 78; Andre A. Moenssens, *Fingerprint Techniques* (Philadelphia: Chilton Book Company, 1971), 158.

9. Robert C. Wadman and Robert K. Olson, *Community Wellness: A New Theory of Policing* (Washington, D.C.: Police Executive Research Forum, 1990), 7.

10. Wilson, *Police Administration*, 52, 77–78.

11. The President's Commission on Law Enforcement and Administration of Justice, *The Challenge of Crime in a Free Society* (Washington, D.C.: Government Printing Office, 1967), 108.

12. James T. Patterson, *Grand Expectations: The United States, 1945–1974* (New York: Oxford University Press, 1996), 411–16; William Doyle, *An American Insurrection: The Battle of Oxford Mississippi, 1962* (New York: Doubleday, 2001), 5–16.

13. Patterson, *Grand Expectations*, 375–406.

14. Wilson, *Police Administration*, 364, 399.

15. Mark H. Moore and George L. Kelling, "To Serve and Protect": Learning from Police History," in *The Ambivalent Force: Perspectives on the Police*, ed. Abraham S. Blumberg and Elaine Niederhoffer, 3d ed. (New York: Holt, Rinehart & Winston, 1985), 40–41.

16. Samuel Walker, *The Police in America*, 2d ed. (New York: McGraw-Hill, 1992), 21–22.

17. See Doyle, *An American Insurrection*.

18. See Taylor Branch, *Pillar of Fire: America in the King Years, 1963-1965* (New York: Simon & Schuster, 1998).

19. Jewell Taylor Gibbs, *Race and Justice: Rodney King and O. J. Simpson in a House Divided* (San Francisco: Jossey-Bass Publishers, 1996), 9–12.

20. Maurice Isserman and Michael Kazin, *America Divided: The Civil War of the 1960s* (New York: Oxford University Press, 2000), 140–41.

21. Gibbs, *Race and Justice*,16–18; United States Commission on Civil Rights, *An Analysis of the McCone Commission Report* (Washington, D.C.: United States Commission on Civil Rights, 1966); Robert M. Fogelson, "White on Black: A Critique of the McCone Commission Report on the Los Angeles Riots," *Political Science Quarterly* 82, no. 3 (September 1967): 337–67.

22. Patterson, *Grand* Expectations, 662–65, 112–16, 206–207. See also Sidney Fine, *Violence in the Model City: The Cavanaugh Administration, Race Relations, and the Detroit Race Riot of 1967* (Ann Arbor: University of Michigan Press, 1989).

23. *Report of the National Advisory Commission on Civil Disorders* (New York: Bantam Books, 1968), 207–480; Urban Coalition and Urban America, *One Year Later: An Assessment of the Nation's Response to the Crisis Described by the National Advisory Commission on Civil Disorders* (New York: Praeger, 1969), 77–79, 117; Dennis E. Gale, *Understanding Urban Unrest: From Reverend King to Rodney King* (Thousand Oaks, Calif.: Sage, 1996), 73–77.

24. The President's Commission on Law Enforcement and Administration of Justice, *The Challenge of Crime in a Free Society, Task Force Report: The Police* (Washington, D.C.: Government Printing Office, 1967), 1–221; Robert W. Winslow, ed., *Crime in a Free Society: Selections from the President's Commission on Law Enforcement and Administration of Justice, the National Advisory Commission on Civil Disorder, the National Commission on the Causes and Prevention of Violence, and the Commission on Obscenity and Pornography*, 3d ed. (Belmont, Calif.: Dickenson Publishing Company, 1977), 322–59.

25. Urban Coalition and Urban America, *One Year Later*, 66–71.

26. Urban Coalition and Urban America, *One Year Later*, 77–83.

27. *Miranda v. Arizona* 384 U.S. 436 (1966); *Dickerson v. United States* No. 99-5525 (2000); See also Richard A. Leo and George C. Thomas, eds., *The Miranda Debate: Law Justice, and Policing* (Boston: Northeastern University Press, 1998).

28. Urban Coalition and Urban America, *One Year Later*, 83.

29. Jerome H. Sklonick and David H. Bayley, *The New Blue Line: Police Innovation on Six American Cities* (New York: The Free Press, 1986), 2–6.

30. Bernard L. Garmire, *Local Government Police Management*, (Washington, D.C.: International City Management Association, 1982), 35.

31. Joanna Kruckenberg and Fred I. Klyman, "Police-Community Relations: An Analysis," *Police Law Quarterly* (Winter 1978): 19.

32. Samuel Walker, *The Police in America: An Introduction*, 3d ed. (New York: McGraw-Hill, 1999), 39; Garmire, *Local Government Police Management*, 35.

33. Samuel Walker, *The Police in America: An Introduction*, 3d ed. (New York: McGraw-Hill, 1999), 85–88; See also George L. Kelling et al., *The Kansas City Preventive Patrol Experiment: A Summary Report* (Washington, D.C.: The Police Foundation, 1974); and The Police Foundation, *The Newark Foot Patrol Experiment* (Washington: The Police Foundation, 1981).

34. See Peter Greenwood, *The Criminal Investigative Process* (Santa Monica, Calif.: Rand, 1975); William A. Westley, *Violence and the Police: A Sociological Study of Law, Custom, and Morality* (Cambridge: Massachusetts Institute of Technology Press, 1971); Jerome Skolnick, *Justice without Trial: Law Enforcement in a Democratic Society*, 2d ed. (New York: Wiley, 1975); Robert M. Fogelson, *Big-City Police* (Cambridge, Mass.: Harvard University Press, 1977); and Walker, *A Critical History of Police Reform.*

35. James Q. Wilson and George L. Kelling, "Broken Windows: The Police and Neighborhood Public Safety," *Atlantic Monthly* (March 1982): 29–38; Walker, *A Critical History of Police Reform*, 39; Herman Goldstein, "Improving Policing: A Problem-Oriented Approach," *Crime and Delinquency* 25 (April 1979): 236–58; John E. Eck and William Spelman, *Problem-Solving: Problem-Oriented Policing in Newport News* (Washington, D.C.: Police Executive Research Forum, 1987).

36. Skolnick and Bayley, *The New Blue Line*, 13–49.

37. Skolnick and Bayley, *The New Blue Line*, 50–80.

38. Malcolm K. Sparrow, Mark H. Moore, and David M. Kennedy, *Beyond 911: A New Era for Policing* (New York: Basic Books, 1990), 60–67.

39. Skolnick and Bayley, *The New Blue Line*, 180–209.

40. Wadman and Olson, *Community Wellness*, 39–53.

41. James H. Robinson and Walter C. Farrell, Jr., "The Fire This Time: The Genesis of the Los Angeles Rebellion of 1992," in *Race, Poverty, and American Cities,* ed. John Charles Boger and Judith Welch Wagner (Chapel Hill: University of North Carolina Press, 1996), 166.

42. Charles J. Ogletree, Jr., Mary Prosser, Abbe Smith, and William Talley, Jr., *Beyond the Rodney King Story: An Investigation of Police Conduct in Minority Communities* (Boston: Northeastern University Press, 1995), 1–132.

43. David O. Sears, "Urban Rioting in Los Angeles: A Comparison of 1965 with 1992," in *The Lost Angeles Riots: Lessons for the Urban Future,* ed. Mark Baldassare (Boulder, Colo.: Westview Press, 1994), 237.

44. Christian Parenti, *Lockdown America: Police and Prisons in the Age of Crisis* (New York: Verso, 1999), 69–89.

45. William B. Berger, "Uniting Law Enforcement to Fight Terrorism," *The Police Chief* (December 2001): 6.

BIBLIOGRAPHY

Adams, Michael C.C. 1994. *The best war ever.* Baltimore: Johns Hopkins University Press.

Albanese, Jay S. 1999. *Criminal justice.* Boston: Allyn & Bacon.

Baldassare, Mark, ed. 1994. *The Lost Angeles riots: Lessons for the urban future.* Boulder, Colo.: Westview Press.

Ball, Larry D. 1992. *Desert lawmen: The high sheriffs of New Mexico and Arizona, 1846–1912.* Albuquerque, N.Mex.: University of New Mexico Press.

Bauer, Jack. 1974. *The Mexican War, 1846–1848.* New York: Macmillan.

Bellesiles, Michael A., ed. 1999. *Lethal imagination: Violence and brutality in American history.* New York: New York University Press.

Berg, Bruce L. 1992. *Law enforcement: An introduction to police in society.* Boston: Allyn & Bacon.

Berman, Jay Stuart. 1987. *Police administration and progressive reform: Theodore Roosevelt as police commissioner of New York.* New York: Greenwood Press.

Blumberg, Abraham S., and Elaine Niederhoffer, eds. 1985. *The Ambivalent force: Perspectives on the police.* 3d ed. New York: Holt, Rinehart & Winston.

Boger, John Charles, and Judith Welch Wagner, eds. 1996. *Race, poverty, and American cities.* Chapel Hill: University of North Carolina Press.

Branch, Taylor. 1998. *Pillar of fire: America in the King years, 1963–1965.* New York: Simon & Schuster.

Bridenbaugh, Carl. 1938. *Cities in the wilderness: The first century of urban life in America, 1625–1742.* New York: The Ronald Press Company.

———. 1955. *Cities in Revolt: Urban life in America, 1743–1776.* New York: Knopf.

Brown, Jennifer, and Frances Heidensohm. 2000. *Gender and policing: Comparative perspectives.* New York: St. Martin's Press.

Butterfield, Fox. *All God's Children: The Bosket family and the American tradition of violence.* 1996. New York: Avon Books.

Calhoun, Fredrick S. *The lawmen: U.S. marshals and their deputies, 1789–1989.* 1990. Washington, D.C.: Smithsonian Institution.

Carte, Gene E., and Elaine H. Carte. 1975. *Police reform in the United States: The era of August Vollmer, 1905–1932.* Berkeley: University of California Press.

Cei, Louis Bernard. 1975. "Law enforcement in Richmond: A history of police–community relations, 1737–1974." Ph.D. diss. Florida State University.

Christensen, Carol, and Thomas Christensen. 1998. *The U.S.–Mexican War*. San Francisco: Bay Books.

Chudacoff, Howard P., and Judith E. Smith. 2000. *The evolution of American urban society*. Upper Saddle River, N.J.: Prentice Hall.

Cocker, Andrew. 2001. *N.Y.P.D.: An illustrated history*. New York: James Brown House.

Conser, James A., and Gregory D. Russell. 2000. *Law enforcement in the United States*. Gaithersburg, Md.: Aspen Publishers.

Davis, Hugh, and Ted R. Gurr, eds. 1969. *Violence in America: Historical and comparative perspectives*. New York: Praeger.

Denhardt, Robert B. 1993. *Theories of public organization*. 2d ed. Belmont, Calif.: Wadsworth Publishing Company.

Dirosa, Andrew. 1991. "U.S. law enforcement during World War II." *Law Enforcement Bulletin* 60 (December): 1–6.

Doyle, William. 2001. *An American Insurrection: The Battle of Oxford, Mississippi, 1962*. New York: Doubleday.

Dray, Philip. 2002. *At the hands of persons unknown: Lynching in black America*. New York: Random House.

Eaton, Clement. 1966. *A history of the Old South*. 2d ed. New York: Macmillan.

Eck, John E., and William Spelman, 1987. *Problem-solving: Problem-oriented policing in Newport News*. Washington, D.C.: Police Executive Research Forum.

Ekrich, A. Roger. 1985. "Bound for America: A profile of British convicts transported to the colonies, 1718–1775." *William and Mary Quarterly* 3, no. 42: 184–200.

Ellis, John. 1986. *The social history of the machine gun*. Baltimore: Johns Hopkins University Press.

Fehrenbacher, Don E. 2001. *The Dred Scott Case: Its Significance in American Law and Politics*. New York: Oxford University Press.

Feller, Daniel. 1995. *The Jacksonian promise: America, 1815–1840*. Baltimore: Johns Hopkins University Press.

Fine, Sidney. 1989. *Violence in the Model City: The Cavanaugh administration, race relations, and the Detroit race riot of 1967*. Ann Arbor: University of Michigan Press.

Flaherty, David H. 1981. "Crime and social control in provincial Massachusetts." *Historical Journal* 24, no. 2: 339–60.

Flinn, John J., and John E. Wilkie. 1971. *History of the Chicago police*. Chicago: Police Book Fund, 1887. Reprint, New York: Arno Press and *The New York Times*.

Fogelson, Robert M. 1967. "White on Black: A critique of the McCone Commission Report on the Los Angeles riots." *Political Science Quarterly* 82, no. 3 (September): 337–67.

———. 1977. *Big city police*. Cambridge: Harvard University Press.

Foner, Eric. 1988. *Reconstruction: America's unfinished revolution, 1863–1877*. New York: Harper & Row.

Fosdick, Raymond B. 1969. *American Police Systems*. New York: Century Co., 1920. Reprint, Montclair, N.J.: Patterson Smith.

Franklin, John Hope. 1956. *The militant South, 1800–1861*. Cambridge: Harvard University Press.

———. 1994. *Reconstruction after the Civil War*. 2d ed. Chicago: University of Chicago Press.

Gale, Dennis E. 1996. *Understanding urban unrest: From Reverend King to Rodney King.* Thousand Oaks, Calif.: Sage.

Gammage, Allen Z., and Stanley L. Sachs. 1972. *Police unions.* Springfield, Ill.: Thomas.

Garmire, Bernard L. *Local government police management.* 1982. Washington, D.C.: International City Management Association.

Geller, William A., ed. 1991. *Local government police management.* Washington, D.C.: The International City Manager's Association.

Genovese, Eugene D. 1971. *In red and black: Marxian explorations in southern and Afro-American history.* New York: Pantheon Books.

———. 1976. *Roll, Jordan, roll: The world the slaves made.* New York: Vintage Books.

Gerard, Philip. 1994. *Cape Fear rising.* Winston-Salem: John F. Blair Publisher.

Gibbs, Jewell Taylor. 1996. *Race and justice: Rodney King and O. J. Simpson in a house divided.* San Francisco: Jossey-Bass.

Goldstein, Herman. 1975. *Police corruption: A perspective on its nature and control.* Washington, D.C.: Police Foundation.

———. 1977. *Policing a free society.* Cambridge: Ballinger.

———. 1979. "Improving policing: A problem-oriented approach." *Crime and Delinquency* 25 (April): 236–58.

Graper, Elmer D. 1969. *American police administration.* New York: Macmillan, 1934. Reprint, Montclair, N.J.: Patterson Smith.

Greenberg, Douglas. 1974. *Crime and law enforcement in the colony of New York, 1691–1776.* Ithaca: Cornell University Press.

Greenwood, Peter. 1975.*The criminal investigative process.* Santa Monica, Calif.: Rand.

Grimshaw, Allen D. 1969. *Racial violence in the United States.* Chicago: Aldine Publishing Group.

Gurr, Ted Robert, ed. 1989. *Violence in America.* 2 vols. London: Sage.

Hadden, Sally E. 2001. *Slave patrols: Law and violence in Virginia and the Carolinas.* Cambridge: Harvard University Press.

Hahn, Harlan, ed. 1971. *Police in urban society.* Beverly Hills: Sage.

Hale, George W. 1893. *Police and prison cyclopedia.* Boston: W. L. Richards Company.

Harris, Robert A. 1994. *Keeping the peace: Police reform in Montana, 1889–1918.* Helena: Montana Historical Society Press.

Harrison, Leonard V. 1971. *Police administration in Boston.* Cambridge: Harvard University Press, 1934. Reprint, New York: Arno Press and *The New York Times.*

Hawke, David Freeman. 1988. *Everyday life in early America.* New York: Harper & Row.

Heady, Ferrel. 1966. *Public administration: A comparative perspective.* Upper Saddle River, N.J.: Prentice Hall.

Hindus, Michael Stephen. 1980. *Prison and plantation: Crime, justice, and authority in Massachusetts and South Carolina, 1767–1878.* Chapel Hill: University of North Carolina Press.

Hoover, J. Edgar. 1936. "The confession and third degree methods." *Law Enforcement Bulletin* 5 (January): 11–13.

———. 1937. "Law enforcement as a profession." *Law Enforcement Bulletin* 6 (November): 3–4.

Horne, Peter. 1980. *Women in law enforcement.* 2d ed. Springfield, Ill.: Thomas.

Hurst, James Willard. 1950. *The growth of American law: The law makers.* Boston: Little Brown.

International Association of Chiefs of Police. *Police Yearbook.* Various years.

Isserman, Maurice, and Michael Kazin. 2000. *America divided: The civil war of the 1960s.* New York: Oxford University Press.

Jenkins, T. A. 1999. *Sir Robert Peel.* New York: St. Martin's Press.

Johnson, David R. 1979. *Policing the urban underworld: The impact of crime on the development of American police, 1800–1887.* Philadelphia: Temple University Press.

———. 1981. *American law enforcement: A history.* Wheeling, Ill.: Forum Press.

Kelling, George L. 1995. *Fixing "broken windows": Restoring order in American cities.* With a chapter by Catherine M. Coles and foreword by James Q. Wilson. Westport, Conn.: Praeger.

Kelling, George L., et al. 1974. *The Kansas City preventive patrol experiment: A summary report.* Washington, D.C.: The Police Foundation.

Kennedy, David M. 1999. *Freedom from fear: The American people in depression and war, 1929–1945.* New York: Oxford University Press.

Klockars, Carl B. 1985. *The idea of police.* Beverly Hills: Sage.

Konstantin, David N. 1984. "Homicides of American law enforcement officers." *Justice Quarterly* 1, no. 1 (March): 29.

Kruckenberg, Joanna, and Fred I. Klyman. 1978. "Police–community relations: An analysis," *Police Law Quarterly* (Winter): 3–21.

Kuhn, Thomas S. 1996. *The structure of scientific revolutions.* 3d ed. Chicago: University of Chicago Press.

Lader, Lawrence. 1973. *The bold Brahmins: New England's war against slavery: 1831–1865.* Westport, Conn.: Greenwood Press.

LaGrange, Randy L. 1993. *Policing American society.* Chicago: Nelson-Hall Publishers.

Lane, Roger. *Policing the city: Boston, 1822–1885.* 1967. Cambridge: Harvard University Press.

———. 1968. "Urbanization and criminal violence in the nineteenth century: Massachusetts as a test case." *Journal of Social History* 2, no. 2 (Winter): 156–63.

Lane, Roger, and John J. Turner. 1978. *Riot, rout, and tumult.* Westport, Conn.: Greenwood Press.

Law Enforcement Assistance Administration. 1976. *Two hundred years of American criminal justice.* Washington, D.C.: Government Printing Office.

Laythe, Joseph. 2002. "'Trouble on the outside, trouble on the inside': Growing pains, social change, and small town policing—The Eugene Police Department, 1862–1932." *Police Quarterly* 5, no. 1 (March): 96–112.

Lee, W. L. Melville. 1901. *A history of police in England.* London: Methuen.

Lemann, Nicholas. 1986. "The origins of the underclass." *Atlantic Monthly* (July): 54–68.

Leo, Richard A., and George C. Thomas, eds. 1998. *The Miranda Debate: Law, justice, and policing.* Boston: Northeastern University Press.

May, Samuel J. 1968. *Some recollections of our anti-slavery conflict.* New York: Arno Press and *The New York Times.*

McGrath, Roger. 1984. *Gunfighters, highwaymen, and vigilantes: Violence on the frontier.* Los Angeles: University of California Press.

McPherson, James M. 1988. *Battle cry of freedom: The Civil War era.* New York: Oxford University Press.

Meyers, Gloria E. 1995. *A municipal mother: Portland's Lola Greene Baldwin, America's first policewoman.* Corvallis, Ore.: Oregon State University Press.

Miller, Wilbur R. 1999. *Cops and bobbies: Police authority in New York and London, 1830–1870.* 2d ed. Columbus: Ohio State University Press.

Millett, Allan R., and Peter Maslowski. 1994. *For the common defense: A military history of the United States of America*. Revised and expanded edition. New York: Free Press.

Milner, Clyde A., II, Carol A. O'Connor, and Martha Sandweiss, eds. 1994. *The Oxford history of the American West*. New York: Oxford University Press.

Mitchell, Howard E., Jr. 1969. *Law enforcement in early Boston, 1660–1736: Controlling the social order in pre-industrial society*. Philadelphia: University of Pennsylvania Institute for Environmental Studies.

Mocho, Jill. 1997. *Murder and justice in frontier New Mexico, 1821–1846*. Albuquerque, N.Mex.: University of New Mexico Press.

Moenssens, Andre A. 1971. *Fingerprint techniques*. Philadelphia: Chilton Book Company.

Monkkonen, Eric H., ed. 1991. *Crime and justice in American history: Historical articles on the origins and evolution of American criminal justice: The frontier*. Westport, Conn.: Meckler.

———. ed. 1992. *Crime and justice in American history: The South*. Munich: K. G. Saur.

Mooney, Chase C. 1957. *Slavery in Tennessee*. Westport, Conn.: Negro Universities Press.

Mosse, George L., ed. 1975. *Police forces in history*. London: Sage.

Myer, Dillon S. 1971. *Uprooted Americans: The Japanese Americans and the War Relocation Authority during World War II*. Tucson: University of Arizona Press.

Nash, Gerald D. 1992. *The crucial era: The Great Depression and World War II, 1929–1945*. 2d ed. New York: St. Martin's Press.

Nash, Roderick. 1990. *The nervous generation: American thought, 1917–1920*. Chicago: Ivan R. Dee.

National Commission on Law Observance and Enforcement. 1969. *Lawlessness in law enforcement*. Washington, D.C.: Government Printing Office, 1931. Reprint, Zechariah Chafee, ed., *The Third Degree*. New York: Arno Press and *The New York Times*.

———. 1971. *Report on police*. Washington, D.C.: Government Printing Office, 1931. Reprint, New York: Arno Press and *The New York Times*.

National Institute of Justice. 1998. *The evolution and development of police technology: A technical report prepared for the National Committee on Criminal Justice Technology*. Washington, D.C.

Newman, Oscar. 1972. *Defensible Space*. New York: Macmillan.

Niederhoffer, Arthur, and Abraham S. Blumberg. 1970. *The ambivalent force: Perspectives on the police*. Waltham, Mass.: Ginn and Company.

Nishimoto, Richard S. 1995. *Inside an American concentration camp: Japanese American resistance at Poston, Arizona*, edited by Lane Ryo Hirabayashi. Tucson: University of Arizona Press.

Nolting, Orin F., ed. 1961. *Municipal police administration*. Chicago: International City Managers Association.

Oaks, Robert F. 1978. "'Things fearful to name': Sodomy and buggery in seventeenth-century New England." *Journal of Social History* 12: 275.

Ogletree, Charles J., Jr., Mary Prosser, Abbe Smith, and William Talley, Jr. 1995. *Beyond the Rodney King story: An investigation of police conduct in minority communities*. Boston: Northeastern University Press.

O'Hara, Ralph D. 2000. "Chronological listing of significant events and dates relating to law enforcement in the Willamette Valley and Portland, Oregon, 1841–2000." Portland Police Historical Society.

Omaha Police Department. 1909. *Annual report of the chief of police, Omaha, Nebraska*. Omaha: Rees Printing Company.

Owings, Chloe. 1969. *Women police: A study of the development and status of the women police movement*. Original published in 1925. Reprint, Montclair, N.J.: Patterson Smith.

Parenti, Christian. 1999. *Lockdown America: Police and prisons in the age of crisis*. New York: Verso.

Parker, William H. 1957. *Parker on police*, edited by O. W. Wilson. Springfield, Ill.: Thomas.

Parsons, Deborah, and Paul Jesilow. 2001. *In the same voice: Women and men in law enforcement.* Santa Ana, Calif.: Seven Locks Press.

Patterson, James T. 1996. *Grand expectations: The United States, 1945–1974.* New York: Oxford University Press.

Paxson, Frederic L. 1915. *The new nation.* Boston: Houghton Mifflin.

Perrigo, Lynn L. 1941. "Law and order in early Colorado mining camps." *Mississippi Valley Historical Review* 28 (June): 41–62.

The Police Foundation. 1981. *The Newark foot patrol experiment.* Washington, D.C.: The Police Foundation.

Pope, Jacqueline. *Bounty hunters, marshals, and sheriffs: Forward to the past.* 1998. Westport, Conn.: Praeger.

Prassell, Frank R. 1972. *The western peace officer: A legacy of law and order in the American West.* Norman: University of Oklahoma Press.

The President's Commission on Law Enforcement and Administration of Justice. 1967. *The challenge of crime in a free society.* Washington, D.C.: Government Printing Office.

Report of the National Advisory Commission on Civil Disorders. 1968. New York: Bantam Books.

Richardson, James F. 1970. *The New York police: Colonial times to 1901.* New York: Oxford University Press.

————. 1974. *Urban police in the United States.* Port Washington, New York: National University Press.

Riordon, William L., ed. 1995. *Plunkitt of Tammany Hall: Series of very plain talks on very practical politics.* New York: Signet Books.

Robinson, Charles M., II. 2000. *The men who wear the star: The story of the Texas Rangers.* New York: Random House.

Royster, Jacqueline Jones, ed. 1997. *Southern horrors and other writings: The anti-lynching campaign of Ida B. Wells, 1892–1900.* Boston: Bedford-St. Martin's.

Russell, Francis. 1975. *A City in terror: 1919, The Boston police strike.* New York: Viking Press.

Schmalleger, Frank. 1999. *Criminal justice today: An introductory text for the 21st century.* Upper Saddle River, N.J.: Prentice Hall.

Schneider, John C. 1980. *Detroit and the problem of order, 1830–1880: A geography of crime, riot, and policing.* Lincoln: University of Nebraska Press.

Senna, Joseph, and Larry Siegel, 1996. *Introduction to criminal justice.* 7th ed. minneapolis/ St. Paul: West Publishing Company.

Skolnick, Jerome H. 1975. *Justice without trial: Law enforcement in a democratic society.* 2d ed. New York: Wiley.

Skolnick, Jerome H., and David H. Bayley. 1986. *The new blue line: Police innovation in six American cities.* New York: The Free Press.

Smith, Abbot Emerson. 1934. "The transportation of convicts to the American colonies in the seventeenth century." *American Historical Review* 39, no. 2 (January): 233–34.

Smith, Bruce. 1949. *Police systems in the United States.* Rev. cd. New York: Harper Brothers.

Smith, David Paul. 1992. *Frontier defense in the Civil War: Texas' Rangers and rebels.* College Station: Texas A&M University Press.

Snead, Philip John, ed. 1977. *Pioneers in policing.* Montclair, N.J.: Patterson Smith.

Sparrow, Malcolm K., Mark H. Moore, and David M. Kennedy. 1990. *Beyond 911: A new era for policing.* New York: Basic Books.

Spero, Sterling. 1972. *Government as employer*. Carbondale, Ill.: Southern Illinois University Press.

Spindel, Donna J. 1981. "The administration of criminal justice in North Carolina, 1720–1740." *American Journal of Legal History* 25 (April): 141–62.

Spindel, Donna J., and Stuart W. Thomas, Jr. 1983. "Crime and society in North Carolina, 1663–1740." *Journal of Southern History* 49, no. 2. 223–44.

Sprogle, Howard O. 1971. *The Philadelphia police: Past and present*. New York: Arno Press and *The New York Times*.

Stampp, Kenneth M. 1989. *The peculiar institution: Slavery in the ante-bellum South*. New York: Vintage Books.

Stead, Philip John, ed. 1977. *Pioneers in policing*. Montclair, N.J.: Patterson Smith.

Teaford, Jon C. 1993. *The twentieth-century American city*. 2d ed. Baltimore: Johns Hopkins University Press.

The Boston Police Strike: Two reports. 1971. New York: Arno Press and *The New York Times*.

Tuttle, William M., Jr. 1970. *Race riot: Chicago in the red summer of 1919*. New York: Atheneum.

Tyler, S. Lyman. 1973. *A history of Indian policy*. Washington, D.C.: Bureau of Indian Affairs.

United States Commission on Civil Rights. 1966. *An analysis of the McCone Commission report*. Washington, D.C.: United States Commission on Civil Rights.

United States Department of Justice, Federal Bureau of Investigation. 2001. *Crime in the United States: 2000*. Washington, D.C.: Government Printing Office.

United States Senate. 1940. "Violations of free speech and rights of labor: Documents relating to intelligence bureau or red squad of Los Angeles police department." *Hearings before a Subcommittee of the Committee on Education and Labor, United States Senate, Seventy-Sixth Congress, Third Session*. Washington, D.C.: Government Printing Office.

Urban Coalition and Urban America. 1969. *One year later: An assessment of the nation's response to the crisis described by the National Advisory Commission on Civil Disorders*. New York: Praeger.

Urban police: Selected surveys. 1971. New York: Arno Press and *The New York Times*.

Vila, Bryan, and Cynthia Morris, eds. 1999. *The role of police in American society: A documentary history*. Westport, Conn.: Greenwood Press.

Vollmer, August. 1971. *Police and modern society*. Los Angeles: University of California Press, 1936. Reprint, Montclair, N.J.: Patterson Smith.

———. 1974. "Annual Report of the Los Angeles Police Department, 1924." Reprint, *Law enforcement in Los Angeles*. New York: Arno Press and *The New York Times*.

Wadman, Robert C., and Robert K. Olson. 1990. *Community wellness: A new theory of policing*. Washington, D.C.: Police Executive Research Forum.

Waldo, Dwight. 1948. *The administrative state: A study of the political theory of American public administration*. New York: Ronald Press Co.

Waldrep, Christopher. 1998. *Roots of disorder: Race and criminal justice in the American South*. Chicago: University of Illinois Press.

Walker, Samuel. 1977. *A critical history of police reform: The emergence of professionalization*. Lexington, Mass.: D.C. Heath.

———. 1992. *The police in America*. 2d ed. New York: McGraw-Hill.

———. 1999. *The police in America: An introduction*. 3d ed. Boston: McGraw-Hill.

Webb, Walter Prescott. 1996. *The Texas Rangers: A century of frontier defense*. 5th printing, 2d ed. Austin: University of Texas Press.

Weber, David J. 1992. *The Spanish frontier in North America*. New Haven: Yale University Press.

Weber, Max. 1958. *The city.* Translated and edited by Don Martindale and Gertrud Neuwirth. Glencoe, Ill.: Free Press.

Weibe, Robert H. 1967. *The search for order, 1877–1920.* New York: Hill and Wang.

Westley, William A. 1971. *Violence and the police: A sociological study of law, custom, and morality.* Cambridge: Massachusetts Institute of Technology Press.

Weston, Paul B., and Kenneth M. Wells. 1974. *Criminal investigation.* 2d ed. Upper Saddle River, N.J.: Prentice Hall.

White, Richard. 1991. *"It's your misfortune and none of my own": A new history of the American West.* Norman, Okla.: University of Oklahoma Press.

Wilson, James Q. 1973. *Varieties of police behavior.* Cambridge: Harvard University Press, 1968. Reprint, New York: Atheneum.

Wilson, James Q., and George L. Kelling. 1982. "Broken windows: The police and neighborhood public safety." *Atlantic Monthly* (March): 29–38.

Wilson, O. W. 1950. *Police administration.* New York: McGraw-Hill.

———. 1952. *Police planning.* Springfield, Ill.: Thomas.

Wilson, O. W., and Roy C. McLaren. 1972. *Police administration.* 3d ed. New York: McGraw-Hill.

Winslow, Robert W., ed. 1977. *Crime in a free society: Selections from the President's Commission on Law Enforcement and Administration of Justice, the National Advisory Commission on Civil Disorder, the National Commission on the Causes and Prevention of Violence, and the Commission on Obscenity and Pornography.* 3d ed. Belmont, Calif.: Dickenson Publishing Company.

Wintersmith, Robert F. 1974. *Police and the black community.* Lexington, Mass.: Lexington Books.

Woskow, Arthur. 1966. *From race riot to sit-in: 1919 and the 1960s.* New York: Doubleday.

Wyatt-Brown, Bertram. 1986. *Honor and violence in the Old South.* New York: Oxford University Press.

Zuckerman, Michael. 1968. "The social context of democracy in Massachusetts." *William and Mary Quarterly* 25: 538.

LIST OF ILLUSTRATIONS

INDEX

Transportation, modes of, 113–116, 131
Trespalcios, J. F., 57
Truancy task force, 156
Tumlinson, J., 57
Turkey, F., 32
Turner, N., 35
Tweed Ring of Tammany Hall. *See* Corruption
21st century policing. *See also* Criminal Justice
    Institute/ NAACP report
    computer technology in, 158
    growth of citizen involvement in, 155–158
    hate crimes in, 154
    paradigm shift in, 140
    zero tolerance policing in, 157–158
Tyler, J., 8–9

U

Uniforms
    badges with, 22–23
    first wearing of, 23
    noticeable presence from, 52
    origin of "coppers" in, 68
    with progressive reforms, 68–69
Union and labor, 85–89
    image damage from, 150
Union and labor radicalism
    Red Scare and Red Squad for, 87, 89
Urban growth
    migration and immigration with, 62, 63, 84–85
Urbanization
    boss machines with, 63
    crises of, 18, 61–64
    municipal police resulting from, 15–18
    police under boss system with, 64–67
    pre-Civil War police with, 14–26
U.S. Marshals
    African Americans as, 55
    in American West, 43, 46, 47
    authority and duties of, 55–56
    funding problems of, 56

V

Vigilantism
    in American West, 42, 43, 47–51
    as citizen response, 47–51, 117
    in early America, 16
    economics of, 48–49
    post-Civil War, 40
    public organization affected by, 24
Violent crime
    public organization resulting from, 24
Vollmer, A., 71, 129, 131, *132*
    case for patrol cars by, 114
    revolution in criminology by, 132–133
    survey of Los Angeles Police, 1924, by, 99

W

Wadman, R. C., 156
Waldo, D., 15
Walker, S., 64, 74, 80, 153
War and revolution
    crime resulting from, 9, 10, 12–13
    militia as community police, 10, 11
War Relocation Authority (WRA)
    self-government and police in, 104–105
Washington, G., 55
Watts, 1965 riots in, 144, 146, *147*
Weapons, 117–118. *See also* Guns
    early police without, 116
    use of high tech, 158
Webb, W. P., 59
Weber, M., 15
Wells, A. S., 70
Wells, H., of Wells Fargo Company, 56
Westley, W., 153
Whalen, G., 76
White, R., 44
White supremacy
    black police with, 39, 40
    Ku Klux Klan, 30, 39
    of vigilantes, 40
Wickersham, G. W., 99–100
Willet, T., 5
Williams, Captain A. "Clubber," 66
Williams, H., 27, 137–138, *138*, 151, 156, 157
Wilson, J. Q., 154
Wilson, O. W.
    Police Administration, 134
    Police Planning, 134
    as youngest chief of police, 130, 133–134
Wilson, W., 76
Women
    first, in Portland, Oregon, 52
    gender discrimination of, 71
Wood, J., 25
Woods, A., 79
World War I era, 83–89
    post-war crime wave of, 96
World War II era
    civil defense duties in, 103–104
    federal government/police in, 101–105
    Japanese internment camps in, 104–105
WRA. *See* War Relocation Authority
Wyatt-Brown, B., 30

Y

Young, C., 155–156

Z

Zero-tolerance policing, 157–158